Develo   Hu

2004

N 2004

2004

05

05

Developing Human Resources

Rosemary Thomson and Christopher Mabey

*Published in association with
the Institute of Management*

the Institute
of Management

FOUNDATION

BUTTERWORTH
HEINEMANN

Butterworth-Heinemann
Linacre House, Jordan Hill, Oxford OX2 8DP
225 Wildwood Avenue, Woburn, MA 01801-2041
A division of Reed Educational and Professional Publishing Ltd.

℞ A member of the Reed Elsevier plc group

OXFORD AUCKLAND BOSTON
JOHANNESBURG MELBOURNE NEW DELHI

First published 1994
Reprinted 1998

British Library Cataloguing in Publication Data
Thomson, Rosemary
    Developing Human Resources. – (Institute
of Management Diploma Series)
    I. Title   II. Mabey, Christopher
    III. Series
    658.301
ISBN 0 7506 1824 8

PLANT A TREE
British Trust for Conservation Volunteers

FOR EVERY TITLE THAT WE PUBLISH, BUTTERWORTH-HEINEMANN
WILL PAY FOR BTCV TO PLANT AND CARE FOR A TREE.

Composition by Genesis Typesetting, Rochester, Kent
Printed and bound in Great Britain

Contents

Series adviser's preface

This book is one of a series designed for people wanting to develop their capabilities as managers. You might think that there isn't anything very new in that. In one way you would be right. The fact that very many people want to learn to become better managers is not new, and for many years a wide range of approaches to such learning and development has been available. These have included courses leading to formal qualifications, organizationally based management development programmes and a whole variety of self-study materials. A copious literature, extending from academic textbooks to sometimes idiosyncratic prescriptions from successful managers and consultants, has existed to aid – or perhaps confuse – the potential seeker after managerial truth and enlightenment.

So what is new about this series? In fact, a great deal – marking in some ways a revolution in our thinking both about the art of managing and also the process of developing managers.

Where did it all begin? Like most revolutions, although there may be a single, identifiable act that precipitated the uprising, the roots of discontent are many and long established. The debate about the performance of British managers, the way managers are educated and trained, and the extent to which shortcomings in both these areas have contributed to our economic decline, has been running for several decades.

Until recently, this debate had been marked by periods of frenetic activity – stimulated by some report or enquiry and perhaps ending in some new initiatives or policy changes – followed by relatively long periods of comparative calm. But the underlying causes for concern persisted. Basically, the majority of managers in the UK appeared to have little or no training for their role, certainly far less than their counterparts in our major competitor nations. And there was concern about the nature, style and appropriateness of the management education and training that was available.

The catalyst for this latest revolution came in late 1986 and early 1987, when three major reports reopened the whole issue. The 1987 reports were *The Making of British Managers* by John Constable and Roger McCormick, carried out for the British Institute of Management and the CBI, and *The Making of Managers* by Charles Handy, carried out for the (then) Manpower Services Commission, National Economic Development Office and British Institute of Management. The 1986 report, which often receives less recognition than it deserves as a key contribution to the recent changes, was *Management Training: context and process* by Iain Mangham and Mick Silver, carried out for the

Economic and Social Research Council and the Department of Trade and Industry.

It is not the place to review in detail what the reports said. Indeed, they and their consequences are discussed in several places in this series of books. But essentially they confirmed that:

- British managers were undertrained by comparison with their counterparts internationally.
- The majority of employers invested far too little in training and developing their managers.
- Many employers found it difficult to specify with any degree of detail just what it was that they required successful managers to be able to do.

The Constable/McCormick and Handy reports advanced various recommendations for addressing these problems, involving an expansion of management education and development, a reformed structure of qualifications and a commitment from employers to a code of practice for management development. While this analysis was not new, and had echoes of much that had been said in earlier debates, this time a few leading individuals determined that the response should be both radical and permanent. The response was coordinated by the newly established Council for Management Education and Development (now the National Forum for Management Education and Development (NFMED)) under the energetic and visionary leadership of Bob (now Sir Bob) Reid of Shell UK (now chairman of the British Railways Board).

Under the umbrella of NFMED a series of employer-led working parties tackled the problem of defining what it was that managers should be able to do, and how this differed for people at different levels in their organizations; how this satisfactory ability to perform might be verified; and how an appropriate structure of management qualifications could be put in place. This work drew upon the methods used to specify vocational standards in industry and commerce, and led to the development and introduction of competence-based management standards and qualifications. In this context, competence is defined as the ability to perform the activities within an occupation or function to the standards expected in employment.

It is this competence-based approach that is new in our thinking about the manager's capabilities. It is also what is new about this series of books, in that they are designed to support both this new structure of management standards, and of development activities based on it. The series was originally commissioned to support the Institute of Management's Certificate and Diploma qualifications, which were one of the first to be based on the new standards. However, these books are equally appropriate to any university, college or indeed company course leading to a certificate in management or diploma in management studies.

The standards were specified through an extensive process of consultation with a large number of managers in organizations of many different types and sizes. They are therefore employment based and employer supported. And they fill the gap that Mangham and Silver identified – now we do have a language to describe what it is employers want their managers to be able to do – at least in part.

If you are engaged in any form of management development leading to a certificate or diploma qualification conforming to the national management standards, then you are probably already familiar with most of the key ideas on which the standards are based. To achieve their key purpose, which is defined as achieving the organization's objectives and continuously improving its performance, managers need to perform four key roles: managing operations, managing finance, managing people and managing information. Each of these key roles has a sub-structure of units and elements, each with associated performance and assessment criteria.

The reason for the qualification 'in part' is that organizations are different, and jobs within them are different. Thus the generic management standards probably do not cover all the management competences that you may need to possess in your job. There are almost certainly additional things, specific to your own situation in your own organization, that you need to be able to do. The standards are necessary, but almost certainly not sufficient. Only you, in discussion with your boss, will be able to decide what other capabilities you need to possess. But the standards are a place to start, a basis on which to build. Once you have demonstrated your proficiency against the standards, it will stand you in good stead as you progress through your organization, or change jobs.

So how do the new standards change the process by which you develop yourself as a manager? They change the process of development, or of gaining a management qualification, quite a lot. It is no longer a question of acquiring information and facts, perhaps by being 'taught' in some classroom environment, and then being tested to see what you can recall. It involves demonstrating, in a quite specific way, that you can do certain things to a particular standard of performance. And because of this, it puts a much greater onus on you to manage your own development, to decide how you can demonstrate any particular competence, what evidence you need to present, and how you can collect it. Of course, there will always be people to advise and guide you in this, if you need help.

But there is another dimension, and it is to this that this series of books is addressed. While the standards stress ability to perform, they do not ignore the traditional knowledge base that has been associated with 'management studies'. Rather, they set this in a different context. The standards are supported by 'underpinning knowledge and understanding' which has three components:

- Purpose and context, which is knowledge and understanding of the manager's objectives, and of the relevant organizational and environmental influences, opportunities and values.
- Principles and methods, which is knowledge and understanding of the theories, models, principles, methods and techniques that provide the basis of competent managerial performance.
- Data, which is knowledge and understanding of specific facts likely to be important to meeting the standards.

Possession of the relevant knowledge and understanding underpinning the standards is needed to support competent managerial performance as specified in the standards. It also has an important role in supporting the transferability of management capabilities. It helps to ensure that you have done more than learned 'the way we do things around here' in your own organization. It indicates a recognition of the wider things which underpin competence, and that you will be able to change jobs or organizations and still be able to perform effectively.

These books cover the knowledge and understanding underpinning the management standards, most specifically in the category of principles and methods. But their coverage is not limited to the minimum required by the standards, and extends in both depth and breadth in many areas. The authors have tried to approach these underlying principles and methods in a practical way. They use many short cases and examples which we hope will demonstrate how, in practice, the principles and methods, and knowledge of purpose and context plus data, support the ability to perform as required by the management standards. In particular we hope that this type of presentation will enable you to identify and learn from similar examples in your own managerial work.

You will already have noticed that one consequence of this new focus on the standards is that the traditional 'functional' packages of knowledge and theory do not appear. The standard textbook titles such as 'quantitative methods', 'production management', 'organizational behaviour', etc. disappear. Instead, principles and methods have been collected together in clusters that more closely match the key roles within the standards. You will also find a small degree of overlap in some of the volumes, because some principles and methods support several of the individual units within the standards. We hope you will find this useful reinforcement.

Having described the positive aspects of standards-based management development, it would be wrong to finish without a few cautionary remarks. The developments described above may seem simple, logical and uncontroversial. It did not always seem that way in the years of work which led up to the introduction of the standards. To revert to the revolution analogy, the process has been marked by ideological conflict and battles over sovereignty and territory. It has sometimes been unclear which side various parties are on – and indeed how many sides there are! The revolution, if well advanced, is not at an end. Guerrilla warfare continues in parts of the territory.

Perhaps the best way of describing this is to say that, while competence-based standards are widely recognized as at least a major part of the answer to improving managerial performance, they are not the whole answer. There is still some debate about the way competences are defined, and whether those in the standards are the most appropriate on which to base assessment of managerial performance. There are other models of management competences than those in the standards.

There is also a danger in separating management performance into a set of discrete components. The whole is, and needs to be, more than the sum of the parts. Just like bowling an off-break in cricket, practising a golf swing or forehand drive in tennis, you have to combine all the separate movements into a smooth, flowing action. How you combine the competences, and build on them, will mark your own individual style as a manager.

We should also be careful not to see the standards as set in stone. They determine what today's managers need to be able to do. As the arena in which managers operate changes, then so will the standards. The lesson for all of us as managers is that we need to go on learning and developing, acquiring new skills or refining existing ones. Obtaining your certificate or diploma is like passing a mile post, not crossing the finishing line.

All the changes and developments of recent years have brought management qualifications, and the processes by which they are gained, much closer to your job as a manager. We hope these books support this process by providing bridges between your own experience and the underlying principles and methods which will help you to demonstrate your competence. Already, there is a lot of evidence that managers enjoy the challenge of demonstrating competence, and find immediate benefits in their jobs from the programmes based on these new-style qualifications. We hope you do too. Good luck in your career development.

Paul Jervis

Acknowledgements

The authors would like to acknowledge the contribution of Jon Billsberry, author of Chapter 5.

1 Developing human resources for the twenty-first century

Introduction

Perhaps the single most important fact concerning the importance of human resources in the last decade of the twentieth century is that 80 per cent of the people who are likely to be in employment in the year 2000 are already in work. This doesn't mean of course that they will be doing the same work, or be employed in the same organizations or even in the same employment sectors; this relative stability in the labour force is not reflected in the changing environment in which it operates. Organizational change and development have become a part of working life. The removal of trade barriers and the inception of the European Single Market have brought about increasing imperatives for internationalization; the worldwide economic recession has seen organizations disappear, restructure and merge, changing their operations and their requirements; continuous improvements and break-throughs in new technology have revolutionized the industrial and financial sectors. The concept of having a lifelong career moving steadily upwards through a number of structured and foreseeable stages in a particular organization is out of date. For example, a study by the Organisation for Economic Co-operation and Development (OECD), reveals that the average number of years people in employ-ment are likely to remain with one employer is around thirteen years in America, with similar figures for Britain, Australia, Holland and Canada; the average in Japan, France and Germany is around twenty-two years. The trends in America and Britain suggest that this average length of time is likely to decrease sharply as fewer workers are offered permanent jobs. This trend is reflected in changing organizational structures in which a small 'core' of permanent, full-time staff, usually qualified professionals, technicians and managers, are supported by contracted-out specialists and a flexible workforce of part-time and temporary employees.

As organizations restructure, human resources tend to decrease in quantity but increase in quality and in their value to organizational effectiveness. Investing in the development of these valued resources makes sense. We invest in new technology, new machinery, new plant to increase productivity because better models have been developed but we need to develop our own 'better models' in the human resource area.

As you read through this book, you will encounter a number of 'self-development' activities that have been designed to make you think about your own situation as a manager and ways in which you might start or continue your own development as a manager. Not all will be appropriate to you or to your particular situation, but we hope that some of them, at least, will create a spark that may kindle a consideration of further development.

Box 1.1 Trends in employment in the last decade of the twentieth century

The occupational make-up of the workforce is changing rapidly and is likely to continue to do so. The decline in jobs in manual occupations seems set to continue while projected growth up to the year 2000 is likely to be concentrated in managerial, professional and associate-professional occupations, which will account for almost three-quarters of the new jobs created. There is also evidence of a clear trend among employers towards a greater use of all forms of flexible working in their drive for cost-effectiveness, enabling a much closer match between workforce provision and work requirements. In part, this trend shows how the labour market is adapting. Today (1993), less than half of employees have traditional 9 to 5, five days a week jobs. Many people want to work part-time. In 1991, part-timers made up 22 per cent of total employment. By the year 2000, this will rise to 25 per cent. The number of self-employed people is expected to rise by a tenth and by the end of the century this group will provide nearly 14 per cent of total employment. Specialist knowledge workers are likely to be increasingly needed by small or medium sized organizations who will not be able to take more responsibility for keeping their knowledge relevant and up to date.

The vision which emerges when the changes of the past decade are extrapolated is one of scaled down, 'leaner and fitter' organizations in both the private and the public sectors, new organizational structures made up of autonomous units, many more small businesses and a rise in self-employment, a shift of emphasis from collectivity to individualism, increasingly sophisticated information and communication systems and production technology and a business climate which is customer driven, quality focused and fiercely competitive . . . The old approaches of jobs for life, negotiations on every change, motivation through piece work and overtime to 'get the job done' are on the decline' (IPM, 1993).

The changing experience of work

Employees' expectations and aspirations have changed as a result of the organizational and environmental flux in which they work. There is evidence that the traditional career structures of bureaucratic organizations, with clearly defined pay and grading systems, are becoming increasingly unattractive to job hunters; central and local government, for example, are experiencing difficulty in recruiting professional specialists. Research has shown that, where the rates of pay are competitive, people choose a job first of all for its content and, secondly, on the basis of the kind of organization that is offering it – the kind of image it projects. Because there is no longer any real job security, other benefits become increasingly important; and, as the individual employee ages, his or her expectations and aspirations change – from the initial desire to make money to an increasing urge for power, autonomy and recognition at work.

The organizations in which people work are also changing in structure through delayering and downsizing, resulting in the 'leaner, fitter' organization, ready to meet the challenges of the next century. Snow, Miles and Coleman (1992) describe the increasing trend towards 'network' structures – clusters of business units, each of which performs certain activities related to the 'business' of the organization. So, for example, one unit might be dedicated to research and design, another to production and a third to sales and distribution. Networks may be 'internal', in that the parent organization owns most of them; each business unit, however, concentrates on a specialized function, interacting with other internal units and with external resources such as suppliers and customers. A second form of network, described as 'stable', has a small core organization (usually consisting of pro-fessional/mangerial staff) and the business operations are carried out by satellite companies outside its direct control but acting as its suppliers, producers and distributors. Finally, there is the 'dynamic' network, whereby the core organization acts as a broker for a number of independent suppliers, producers and distributors.

The implication of the shift towards network organizational struc-tures is that there are fewer layers of management (and fewer managers) but that the manager's role has changed. Instead of managing within one hierarchical organizational structure, he or she is likely to be managing in a matrix, operating across hierarchies and organizational boundaries.

The changing environment in which we work is reflected in the vocabularies we use to describe what we do, and Table 1.1 indicates the way in which the work-related terms we use now (in the 'information age') differ from those used previously in the 'industrial age'.

There are other initiatives and changes that are commonplace in the 'information age', most notably those relating to computer-mediated information and networking, and to the equality of opportunity for people in work. But one of the implications of the increase in

Table 1.1 Vocabularies of the ages

Industrial age	Information age
Capital-intensive	Information-intensive
Labourer	Knowledge worker
Capital expenditures	Education/training
Natural resources	Educated workforce
Inventory'	Data (information)
Production enhancements	Process enhancements
Management through control	Empowerment
Tangible rewards	Psychological rewards
Issuing orders	Communicating
Top-down planning	Commitment
Sales	Customer satisfaction
Inspection	Quality built in
Hiring and firing	Recruiting and redeploying
Hours of work	Flexitime
Manpower planning	Human resource management

(Adapted from Industry Week, 17 June, 1991)

information and the ease with which it can be accessed, is a radical change in the role of the middle manager.

In a survey of research into the role of middle managers, Dopson and Stewart found a generally negative picture of a dying breed, owing to the rise in the use of information technology and cited a particularly gloomy portrait of 'Whole layers of management who neither make decisions nor lead . . . instead their main, if only function, is to serve as relays, human boosters for the faint, unfocused signals that pass for communication in the traditional, pre-information organizations'. In their own study the authors, in contrast, found that, after restructuring, many middle managers indeed found that their jobs had changed and changed for the better; their responsibilities had increased and the range of tasks they undertook had become wider. Other changes included:

● an increasing span of control;
● responsibility for a wider mix of staff;
● increased accountability for their work;
● their performance as managers was more visible;
● they had better information on which to base decisions;
● they needed to be more flexible and adaptable.

Although middle managers had, in general, decreased in numbers, their jobs – and job satisfaction – appeared to have increased. As a result, their importance to the organization had increased and they were seen as having a pivotal role within it by senior management.

Self-development activity

Take a few minutes to reflect on your own experience of management and ways in which it has changed over the last five or ten years. These might include increasing use of electronic communication and information systems, changes in management style or working hours, organizational restructuring and, as Dopson and Stewart report, changes in role and responsibility. In what ways have these changes led to your continuing development as a manager?

One area in which the middle manager's role has changed significantly is in the way he or she manages human resources. The 'human resource manager' has entered the arena; not the personnel specialist – although many Heads of Personnel have changed their titles to 'Director of Human Resources' or similar – but the middle manager with line responsibilities for other managers and their staff, along with the recognition that human resources need more careful and sensitive management than ever before. Today's management literature abounds with terms and acronyms such as Human Resource Strategy (HRS), Human Resource Management (HRM), Human Resource Development (HRD) and in the UK we have initiatives such as Investors in People (IIP), Total Quality Management (TQM), Employee Assistance Programmes (EAPs), the Learning Organization, Opportunity 2000 and so on. By the time this book is published, new ones will have arisen. A new industry, one that deals with redundancy and unemployment, has sprung up, including numerous outplacement consultancies, employment action programmes, job review workshops and job clubs, the Job Interview Guarantee Scheme (JIG), enterprise allowance schemes and the launch of 'The Job Seeker's Charter'. New, and increasing, requirements from, among others, the European Community, the Equal Opportunities Commission, the Commission for Racial Equality, the Health and Safety Commission and the Employment Department need to be met in the employee's interests – and in the employer's, since failure to comply can result in legal action, heavy fines and even closure.

Human resource management and human resource development

In an effort to clarify some of the new terminology surrounding 'human resources', the following definitions will be adopted in this book. You may have, or find, different ones; indeed, many management books start off by giving a whole range of definitions, reflecting the confusion and complexity that currently exist in this area.

Human resources

These include all the individual employees who contribute to the operations of an organization, whether they are employed full-time, part-time, on a temporary or permanent basis, centrally, in separate business units or from home.

Human resource management

This approach to managing people embodies the following principles:

- people are the most important resources an organization has, and managing them effectively is the key to organizational success;
- human resource policies and procedures need to be closely linked with, and make a major contribution to, the achievement of organizational objectives and strategic plans;
- the culture of the organization needs to be one that values human resources and pervades the organization from top to bottom, so that all members of the organization work together with a shared purpose; all managers are, thus, responsible for human resource management (based on Armstrong, 1991).

Human resource management therefore depends on integrating the importance of human resources into the organization's strategic policy, and planning and ensuring that all line managers adopt its principles as part of their everyday work. If it is effective, not only will the organization achieve its objectives but its employees will be committed to its success. It depends on the match between employees and the human resource needs of the organization and the quality of working life. In their role as human resource managers line managers are likely to carry out activities such as:

- operating and allocating rewards;
- motivating and reinforcing their staff;
- giving positive feedback and support;
- managing conflict;
- appealing to higher authorities or third parties to resolve disputes;
- taking disciplinary action when necessary;
- developing job descriptions;
- recruiting, deploying and promoting people appropriately in line with organizational objectives and individual abilities and aspirations;
- ensuring their continuous training and development;
- coaching and counselling;
- preparing people for retirement or redundancy.

Many of these areas are covered in this book. For example, Chapter 3, 'Putting human resource strategies into practice' looks at ways in which organizational policies on human resource management can be implemented, depending on the type of organization and its level of human resource maturity. Chapter 5, 'Making fair selection decisions', is concerned with selecting the most appropriate people for appointment, redeployment and promotion and, in Chapter 7, 'Developing motivation and commitment', we look at different forms of motivation to work and individual perceptions of equity.

Human resource development

This is the main subject matter of this book and is concerned with the recruitment and retention of high quality people who are best fitted to fulfil the organization's objectives, defining and measuring levels of performance and providing continuous opportunities for training and development. Human resource development as part of human resource management calls for:

- recruiting and inducting high quality people and deploying them effectively;
- identifying and improving the skills and motivation of existing and longer serving employees;
- regularly analysing job content in relation to organizational objectives and individual skills;
- reviewing the use of technology and its use in replacing routine tasks;
- performance management and measurement through the identification of key tasks;
- focusing on people's skills and general intelligence rather than on educational attainment;
- identifying training needs;
- providing training to improve current performance and to enhance individual careers;
- providing opportunities for individual self-development and personal growth;
- helping employees to manage their own careers;
- encouraging employees to accept change as an organizational 'norm' and an opportunity.

Both human resource management and human resource development need to be fully embedded in the policy and strategy of the organization if they are going to be effective. Organizational policy, which sets out the broad direction of the organization and is often enshrined in its mission statement, needs to set human resource policy alongside more traditional areas such as financial and operational imperatives. Organizational strategies determine how policy is to be implemented through the achievement of organizational objectives, and form the basis for organizational planning – putting the strategies into action at the level of tactical and operational detail and providing ways of evaluating and measuring their success. While 'strategy' is usually considered to be the prerogative of senior managers, Pearson (1991) states that 'All managers can be capable of "strategic thinking" by being proactive in environmental scanning and recognising organisational threats and opportunities in advance; actively seeking reasons to change in the social and economic system and in the enterprise itself.' Strategies for human resource development are the subject of Chapter 2, 'Devising human resource development strategies'.

Other chapters take up important areas of human resource development that help to inform the human resource plan. Chapter 4, 'Auditing human resources', is concerned with ways in which we can make forecasts of human resource needs to fulfil organizational objectives. A knowledge of existing and potential skills will contribute significantly to planning requirements. In the same chapter we look at individual development and training needs. In Chapter 6 we consider career planning and management, and management succession planning as ways of helping individuals to manage their careers effectively even when the idea of a lifelong career has become unlikely. Teambuilding and the effective working of teams is the subject of Chapter 8 while Chapter 9 is devoted to performance management, measurement and appraisal. Finally, Chapter 10 aims to give a framework for managing organizational development and change which has human resource development as a central theme.

Human resource planning

As we pointed out earlier, human resource planning should follow from organizational/human resource policy and strategy formulation. It is during this planning stage that you can expect to identify mismatches between the stated organizational objectives and, from your experience as a manager, the expectations of the staff for whom you are responsible. Do you or your staff in fact *know* what the organization's objectives, policies and strategies are?

Self-development activity

If asked, would you be able to tell an outsider, perhaps a candidate for a job in your organization, what objectives, policies and strategies it pursues? Are these clearly communicated so that everyone can understand them?

Too often, organizational mission statements are vague, bland, out-of-date, composed of higher-order values and poorly communicated, if at all, to the great majority of staff. Given the environment in which we now operate, there is value in re-examining the mission statement regularly and, at least, translating it into a language that can be understood and 'owned' by everyone in the organization. Too often, that seems like a task that can be left on one side because no one has the time or energy to tackle it. At best, mission statements can (*a*) convey top management's vision about the future of the organization (presupposing that there is any vision at the top), (*b*) act as an agenda for organizational change and (*c*) be the focus for strategy formulation and planning. In some organizations the mission statement is incorporated into employees' job descriptions in such a way that jobholders can readily identify with it and recognize their own part in fulfilling its aims. Managers, in particular, need to behave in a way that is consistent with the mission statement in all their actions or it ceases to have value and credibility.

Let us assume you are familiar with your organization's stated policies and strategies, through its mission statement if one exists, and that human resources are an important part of these top management considerations. You are, like everyone else, struggling with the effects of the world economic recession and have probably already experienced structural changes, downsizing or streamlining as reasons for redundancy, if not in person then within parts of your organization. What should a human resource plan cover?

Any plan needs to consider all categories of staff for which you are, or will be, responsible, as shown in Table 1.2.

This is the framework in which more specific human resource plans can be developed in relation to all categories of staff, and the rest of

Table 1.2 Categories of staff and human resource planning areas

Category of staff	Planning areas
Existing employees	skills analysis performance measurement, review and appraisal deployment pay and rewards (motivation) training and career development succession planning promotion retirements and redundancy staff turnover
Potential employees	job/skill analysis job design recruitment job descriptions and further particulars methods of selection pay and benefits
New employees	terms of contract induction programmes training and development

this book is designed to provide you with some ideas of how such plans might be implemented. Armstrong has suggested that there are a number of interrelated plans which need to be constructed and brought together into the human resource plan

The **human resource development plan**, for example, needs to show:

- how many new staff are required and how they will be recruited and trained;
- training and development programmes for existing staff;
- management development and career development programmes;
- who will run training and development activities and how they will be evaluated;
- plans for employee assistance programmes and redundancy/ retirement counselling.

If you are a middle manager in a large organization with a commitment to training and development, your role should be that of adviser to whoever is responsible for training and development; you should know your own staffing requirements and be able to assess the skills and potential for promotion of your existing workforce. This information needs feeding into the organizational human resource planning process. In a smaller organization you may be wholly responsible for planning the training and development of your staff within a limited budget and your plans will need to reflect financial constraints. Not all human resource development needs to be costly; on-the-job training and coaching are two of the less expensive methods.

Box 1.2   Good practice at British Telecom

Line managers (at BT) were given training in career management and job skills development. They received a summary of the skills profiles of their staff from a two-day development centre workshop and used this information to prepare individual development planning meetings with their staff after they had returned from the development centres. Outputs from the workshops also fed into the design of a modular sales training programme, ensuring that skills training was targeted to meet the specific needs of each individual. The data was also used to design new sales training courses and has been fed back into the strategic planning process for UK sales operations (Beard, 1993).

The human resource recruitment and retention plan

Although recruitment is a vitally important part of human resource management, it is perhaps less problematic than tackling the issue of employee retention. The starting point for retention planning is an analysis of why employees leave the organization: reasons for this may include dissatisfaction with pay levels or job content, unclear performance standards, lack of training and career development, lack of commitment to the organization and its values, lack of group cohesion, dissatisfaction and conflict with managers and supervision, poor selection or promotion decisions or creating unrealistic expectations about career prospects (Armstrong, 1991). However, not all reasons will be clear-cut; the job climate is such that many people do not expect to stay with one organization and opportunistic employees will move on as a positive career strategy.

The human resource downsizing plan

You may reasonably argue that there is little point in making plans for staff retention when an organization is in the position of downsizing. But, as many organizations have found in recent years, streamlining their operations out of economic necessity has made them more efficient. It is the quality of the staff who are recruited and trained, not the quantity, which is the essential factor in downsizing. As we all know from experience, where there are programmes of voluntary redundancy, it is often the most skilled employees who go first because they are more marketable outside. Struggling on during the recession, without any clear plans for downsizing, has often resulted in widespread, unplanned workforce reductions with very little prior notice.

There is a legal requirement for organizations in most cases to offer employees their statutory or contractual period of notice, allow them paid time off to seek new employment, and make redundancy payments; otherwise redundancy can be termed 'unfair dismissal'. Good practice additionally requires some form of redundancy counselling provision either from within the organization or through external outplacement consultants. Plans for downsizing need to consider all these aspects as well as the method of communicating the need for downsizing, consultation with trade unions and staff associations where necessary and any arrangements for retraining and redeploying staff within the organization as an alternative to redundancy.

One area that has not been touched on in the discussion so far is that of employee assistance programmes (EAPs). Particularly as fears of redundancy grow and lifelong career expectations diminish, employees come under increased stress at work and at home. Often domestic or out-of-work stress, which may initially have been created by

---

Box 1.3 'When will they ever learn . . .?'

'The Head asked to see me and I had the impression that this was going to be an informal appraisal session. He asked me how classes were going and we talked a bit about the new curriculum. Then, out of the blue, he told me that he was having to make some staff redundant and that, because of my age, I would be one of them – I wouldn't be needed next term. I'd been teaching for 35 years . . .'

'All they told us was that you'd get a brown envelope with your pay packet if you were being laid off. I didn't get one the first week but you couldn't celebrate when your mates were standing there looking at these envelopes. It was a relief in a way when I got one the next week . . .'

'I just don't understand – none of us do. It's not because of the recession; the company survived that and we've got more orders coming through the door than we've had for years. No warning – nothing; just told the boss wanted to see me and he says my job's going, so I've got to go. Oh yes, there's a bit of money to keep me sweet, but it won't last for long. And it's not the money – it's pride and wanting to stay with the company and being treated right – treated like a human being and not just a pay packet.'

---

problems at work, starts to affect employee performance through symptoms such as increased absenteeism, poor timekeeping, loss of concentration and poor decision-making, erratic or low job perform-ance and so on. Recognition of this problem has resulted in EAPs which are designed to help the individual overcome stress-related problems that are not necessarily resulting directly from the work itself. There are, as you might expect, problems associated with the programmes. In-company assistance is often resisted, since the individual fears it will affect his or her career and promotion prospects and that colleagues and subordinates will find out about personal problems. Outside help is usually more welcome – unless you make the mistake that one organization did whereby the same consultants provided redundancy counselling and an employee assistance pro-gramme. This was hardly designed to reassure the stressed employee!

Managing human resources in the twenty-first century

The OECD survey quoted earlier found that formal training and development of human resources was more limited in countries with a higher labour turnover, confirming the belief that employers who believe workers are unlikely to stay with the organization for any length of time are more reluctant to expend money on training them. This is a common belief but creates a vicious circle. Employees are increasingly seeking jobs in which training and development are part of the job package; if these benefits don't exist, they are likely to move to another organization that does offer them. Traditionally, too, organizations relying on large numbers of temporary staff to match peak demand usually do not bother to provide anything but the minimum training for semi-skilled jobs.

Box 1.4   Whose idea was it anyway?

A recent study looked at a wide range of industries which had clearly defined training policies and a commitment to continuous employee development. These industries included organizations in engineering, chemicals, food processing, retail, construction, local government and hotel and catering. As might be expected, they found differences of interests between employers and employees as to the importance of training and development. Employers saw it as contributing to improved quality in goods and services and to increasing productivity and output. In general, they favoured organization-specific training since they saw this as increasing employee retention and making it more difficult for other organizations to 'poach' highly trained staff. Employees, however, were more interested in training and development which increased job security and helped them to progress in their careers; they favoured training opportunities which provided transferable skills, not necessarily in order that they could then leave the organization but so that they had more choice of career paths.

The organizations in the survey provided a range of training and development opportunities including those aimed at improving quality, changing corporate culture, restructuring, introducing flexible working practices and offering training and employment packages aimed at reducing staff turnover and improving retention levels. In most cases, however, the employees' interests were largely neglected at the expense of perceived organizational needs. It is likely, therefore, that employee turnover and retention targets would not be met (Rainbird and Maguire, 1993).

We hear a great deal about 'the flexible workforce' of the future where job stability and security are replaced with increasing temporary or part-time contracts at all levels of employment, including subcontracting and increasing use of consultants. Such an organizational climate does not breed commitment from its employees and there is a strong argument for 'the flexible organization' to counteract its effects. In our opinion the flexible organization is one that accepts and manages the reality of increasing staff turnover through strong human resource development policies and strategies. It is an organization that expects all its line managers to take responsibility for managing the development of its human resources.

The message should now be clear. Human resource development is seen as the key to economic success in the next century. As Sir Geoffrey Holland, permanent secretary at the Department for Education said at a recent seminar on lifelong learning, 'The only future for organizations and Britain as we go into the highly competitive twenty-first century is to have skills, knowledge, adaptability and flexibility coming out of our ears'.

The essential qualities needed to manage human resources effectively

In 1993 two management consultants published the results of an extensive five-year study of individuals in both public and private sector organizations who had been identified as models of excellence in the human resource field. From their study they derived a set of attributes and thought processes that they considered to be the source of human resource competency. The study was carried out on personnel managers and people wanting to enter the personnel profession and the researchers described their models of excellence as 'providing and striving to implement a philosophy rooted in a set of ethical principles and beliefs about people. They are based on trust and a desire to empower staff, linked to a recognition of the uniqueness of each individual and the need to fit the person and his or her talents to a role in which they can grow and be fulfilled' (Buckingham and Elliot, 1993, p. 29). This description would seem to us to have a broader application than limited to personnel professionals; it would seem appropriate to apply this description to any manager who takes responsibility for managing human resources in his or her line management role.

Box 1.5 lists the human resource attributes that Buckingham and Elliot identified in their models of excellence. As you read through them, you might like to reflect on the extent to which you agree with their findings and how far you feel that your own attributes and thought processes match them. The rest of this book is aimed at helping you to develop these kinds of attributes; and to improve your competency as a manager of human resources and in the development of the potential of those staff for whom you are responsible.

Box 1.5 Successful human resource attributes

Motivation (the mainspring and driving force for initiatives.

Attributes:

Dedication	the commitment which follows vision, empowers self and enables others
Credibility	defines self as a professional; takes pride in the quality of work accomplished
Achiever	the internal drive to be up and doing, to get things done, energetic, competitive and on the fast track
Growth orientation	selects for talent, focuses on people's strengths; derives excitement and purpose from conceptualizing how they might foster growth

Values and ethics (principles, ideals and standards of conduct)

Attributes:

People conscience	belief in the 'goodness' of people and drive to act on people-oriented values; an acute awareness of the central importance of the human resource
Responsibility	the capacity for taking psychological ownership of personal behaviour, especially work; an understanding of how to help others feel similar ownership for their work
Ethics	the capacity to live by a set of principles, choosing what is 'right'

Activation (presence and ability to have an impact)

Attributes:

Command	the ability to take charge and speak with authority; the propensity for adopting a proactive stance
Courage	the capacity to increase one's determination in the face of resistance

Implementation (strategic, organizing and prioritizing abilities)

Attributes:

Ideation	the ability to explain events; the possession of a conceptual framework for future goals; the capacity to act as a problem-solver and source of good ideas

Focus	the capacity to choose a direction and maintain it – goal-oriented; an attendant flair for identifying key priorities, for focusing attention appropriately and for targeting the attention and activities of others
Discipline	the need and ability to structure time and environment; a talent for getting systems in place which enhance efficiency

Relationships (interpersonal and coordinating strengths)

Attributes:

Developer	the desire to help others grow and develop as individuals; the capacity for taking satisfaction from each increment of growth of another person
Team	the capacity to get people to help each other use their strengths to achieve their goals
Arranger	the ability to coordinate people and resources for success; sophistication in understanding and working with 'organizational politics'

(Buckingham and Elliot, 1993)

Self-development activity

Finally, you might like to see how you rate on the following checklist. The questions are designed to set you thinking about managing human resources in largely financial terms and warrant further consideration if you are to argue the case for developing the human resources under your management.

Read through the checklist and see how many questions you can answer. If you can answer all of them, you are, or should be, a director of human resources already.

Checklist for human resource management

How much money was spent by your organization/department last year to recruit and select people?

Was this expenditure worth the cost?

_____

Does your organization/department have data on standard costs of recruitment, selection, and placement that are needed to prepare human resource budgets and to control human resource costs?

_____

Was the actual cost incurred last year less than, equal to, or greater than standard employee acquisition and placement costs?

_____

How much money was spent last year by your organization to train and develop its human resources?

_____

What was the return on your organization's investment in training and development?

_____

How does this return compare with alternative investment opportunities?

_____

How much human capital was lost to your organization/department last year as a result of turnover?

_____

How much does it cost to replace a key person in your organization/department?

_____

What is the opportunity cost of losing high potential managers or other key professionals?

_____

What is the total value of your organization's/department's human assets?

_____

Is it appreciating, remaining constant, or being depleted?

Does your organization really reward managers for increasing the value of their staff to the organization?

Do your organization's financial and other reward systems reflect an individual's present value?

Does your organization consider its investment in human resources when evaluating capital budgeting proposals requiring the allocation of staff?

Has your organization adopted human resource programmes such as Investors in People (IIP), Opportunity 2000 or BS5750.

What is the cost to the organization of these programmes?

(Adapted from Flamholtz, 1971)

Summary

We have tried to demonstrate in this chapter just how important human resources are to the success of the organizations in which they are employed. Today's environment is one of continuous, evolutionary change, and this situation is likely to continue into the foreseeable future. Many organizations have been forced to review their operations and restructure with concomitant changes and challenges to managers and the roles they now fill. No longer is 'human resource management' the sole province of the personnel specialist; it is a priority for every manager who has line responsibility for staff.

It is clear that, without integrated human resource policies and strategies, organizations are less likely to survive into the next century. The operationalization of these policies and strategies lies in the hands of line managers, in the development of a series of human resource plans, based on accurate and up-to-date information about all categories of their staff. These include plans and provision for human resource development, recruitment, retention and downsizing within a flexible framework designed to meet the challenges of the future.

References

Armstrong, M. (1991) *A Handbook of Personnel Management Practice* (4th edition). Kogan Page, London.

Beard, D. (1993) Learning to change organizations. *Personnel Management*, January.

Buckingham, G. and Elliot, G. (1993) Profile of a successful personnel manager. *Personnel Management*, August, pp. 26–29.

Dopson, S. and Stewart, R. (1990) What is happening to middle management? *British Journal of Management*, vol. 1, pp. 3–16.

Drucker, P. F. (1988) The coming of the new organization. *Harvard Business Review*, 45–53.

Flamholtz, E. (1971) Should your organization attempt to value its human resources? *California Management Review*

Handy, C. (1985) *Understanding Organizations* (3rd edition). Penguin Business Books.

Pearson, R. (1991) *The Human Resource: managing people and work in the 1990s*. McGraw-Hill Book Co, London

Pugh, D. S. and Hickson, D. J. (1989) *Writers on Organizations* (4th edition). Penguin Business Books.

Rainbird, H. and Maguire, M. (1993) When corporate need supersedes employee development. *Personnel Management*, February.

Snow, C. C., Miles, R. E. and Coleman, Jr, H. J. (1992) Managing 21st century organizations. *Organizational Dynamics*, Winter.

2 Devising human resource development strategies

Introduction

For many reasons senior managers in all sectors are paying an increasing amount of attention to the development of their organizations' human resources. In part this has been prompted by competitive pressure and the need to recruit and retain high calibre staff, as well as developing a more flexible and adaptable skills base to cope with volatile markets. Partly it is because the general terminology of human resource development (HRD) has gained wider currency with efforts by government and bodies like the Confederation of British Industry and the Department of Employment to raise the profile of training and development in the UK. Finally, as we saw in Chapter 1, it is partly associated with a somewhat belated recognition by employers that it is people – their competencies, expectations, technical knowledge, specialist skills, commercial awareness and general morale – that remain the key factor in delivering an organization's products and services in a profitable and customer-conscious manner. Hence there is a greater emphasis on the strategic nature of HRD via performance management and evaluation on the one hand and human resource and succession planning on the other. Incorporating all these elements, HRD could be defined as:

> The strategic management of training, development and of management/professional education interventions, so as to achieve the objectives of the organization while at the same time ensuring the full utilization of the knowledge in detail and skills of individual employees (Garavan, 1991 p. 17).

Sometimes HRD initiatives will be the spur that sets in motion a succession of wider personnel policies, while at other times training activities will form one small part of an organization's agenda for change, but either way they have strategic significance rather than being isolated tactical solutions. The definition implies that HRD is managed, but this doesn't necessarily translate into normal training programmes. Rather it means that organizations engage in deliberate and reflective learning activities, encompassing everything from on-the-job coaching, vocational education and training (VET) and skills training courses to mentoring and secondments for senior managers. Notice the definition also includes both the 'hard' and the 'soft' view of human resources. HRD is concerned with systematically co-ordinating the motivation, development and deployment of staff in order to achieve bottom-line objectives. But the very words human resource also suggest the notion of individuals possessing innate, creative potential the organization would do well to invest in and maximize. Of course even this more altruistic perspective has solid, economic consequences, because a company that invests in training its workforce is also likely to develop policies designed to retain and motivate them to use their skills to the utmost, thereby maximizing the return on investment (Keep, 1989).

Why the need for HRD?

How do organizations cope with the array of technological, legal, demographic, social and international changes in their operating environments, and what strategic approaches to management and HRD do they choose to, or are they forced to take? In 1988 a team from Warwick University's Centre for Corporate Strategy and Change set about answering this question for the Training Agency (then called the Training Commission). Drawing on evidence gathered from twenty case-study organizations covering a range of sectors, including two from the public sector (a water authority and a health authority) they identified a number of different strategic responses. These were:

- *Competitive restructuring* as a way of addressing new and often intensified patterns of competition.
- *Decentralization*, in order to gain competitive advantage via a closer customer relationship, devolved decision-making and improved response and service levels.
- *Internationalization*, as a way of responding to the globalization of their markets and the diminution of their UK customer base.
- *Acquisition and mergers* were often an important route for some organizations attempting to impose change on their business environment rather than to respond to it in a more reactive manner.
- *Quality improvement* was a way of meeting increased environmental pressures for enhanced quality of products and services that was coming from a variety of sources.
- *Technological change* was often the strategy adopted to cut costs, raise quality and reduce working capital by eliminating work in progress.
- Finally new concepts of *service provision* and distribution were important responses to change.

Whatever the source of pressure, the common feature of these triggers for strategic change is the highlighting of a skill performance gap. We look at ways in which a skill gap can be identified in Chapter 4. There are in fact a range of possible responses that a firm *can* make when a skill gap has been identified (see Figure 2.1). The research team

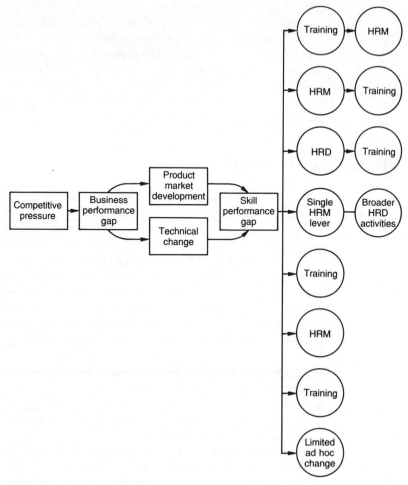

Figure 2.1 *The linkages between business performance and training (from Pettigrew et al., p. 41)*

discovered that 'the particular pathways towards a heightened training and development culture will vary from firm to firm. This departs from more simplistic views that training leads to improved business performance (and that firms can therefore be expected to train more), or that improved business performance leads to increased (and more effective) training simply because firms can fund it more easily'. (Pettigrew *et al.*, 1988 p. 41).

Getting investment in HRD

What does an organization do once it has diagnosed, discovered or been confronted by a 'skills performance gap'? We have already seen that there are a number of choices that can be made, most of which have training and development implications. The question is, what determines how an organization responds and – more crucially – how effective is their chosen strategy in sustaining training and wider HRD activity? Or to put it another way, how does a firm get training into its bloodstream?

Technological or product market changes are often the dominant driving forces for introducing a training strategy, unless the task skills identified only relate to a small number of simple, standardized products or services requiring short learning time. In this instance a dose of 'top up' training may suffice, and mitigate against a concerted strategy. The non-availability of required skills in the external labour market, and some degree of protection from economic pressures (now and anticipated) are also typical prerequisites to investment in training.

Organizations are more likely to invest in training when there is external support and leverage. This may well be in the form of well developed linkages with external training providers who are able to deliver appropriate and flexible modules; or where training is incorporated in the customer–supplier relation, so that, for instance, the cost could be incorporated within the necessary expense of buying in new machines, products and services; or where there is customer requirement for quality. 'External' support from corporate training functions is naturally another stimulus for training activity, as are external funds and grants, e.g. Department of Employment, Youth Training Scheme, EEC awards, although this influence tends to be more marginal.

On the other hand, there are many historical, political and cultural factors that threaten to blunt training provision by organizations in the UK, especially when compared with our other European partners. For example, the implications of the widespread adoption of the multi-divisional pattern of organization is likely to inhibit a strategic approach to HRM generally and training in particular – all the more so where investment decisions are dominated by the finance function (fairly typical in British boardrooms) and where short-term return on capital employed by institutional investors overrides longer term considerations of people development. Not unimportant however, is the role of government in either stimulating or stifling strategic investment by organizations in the future skills base of a given country (see Box 2.1).

Among the features of the internal labour market that promote training are moves toward multi-skilling of production and main-tenance staff, typically associated with reducing numbers of employ-ees and expanding the task/skills of those that remain. Also an organization may adopt a positive policy of training and development in order to attract a higher quality staff, particularly if it has had problems with attrition. Thirdly, when organizations have a tradition of high quality recruitment, retention and promotion, the training of higher level skills is a sensible option when preparing for and

Box 2.1 The need for action not exhortation

For policy-makers in government and governmental agencies, there is one overriding conclusion; exhortation is not going to be enough. Nor does it seem likely that simply continuing with the divulgation of 'best practice' will be anywhere near sufficient to engender a change in prevailing practices – especially if, as is so invariably so, the 'best-case' examples are drawn from business structures of the critical function type where the linkages between corporate plans and human resource plans are so much more self-evident than in the more mixed cases which frequently obtain. The time may well now be right for a more radical approach. Again this can be best illustrated using the crucial example of human resource *development*. A package of measures seems to be required which will encourage companies to work in the direction of policy objectives and to, in effect, penalize them if they do not. Examples of measures of this kind would be financial incentives to invest in training and development; a statutory requirement to publish details of investment in training and development committees based on the model of health and safety committees; enshrining individuals with the right to training and development opportunities perhaps using some form of 'credits' system.

At a broader level, public policy could move towards a clearer set of objectives and arrangements for the training of young people so that the present inchoate patchwork of vocational education and training is replaced with a simpler, more coherent and more effective system. The newly-proposed employer-led local training councils may or may not prove to be effectual, whatever institutional arrangements might eventually emerge; what matters is that budgets should be sufficient and that both employers and employees have appropriate incentives to make training a priority (from Storey, 1989, p. 175).

undergoing change because it represents an investment for the future. However, if the need is for specialist skills for a few and the lead time on training such skills in-house is long, organizations will often opt for external recruitment and/or use contract labour, thus removing the need for HRD investment.

A final set of factors instrumental in the triggering of training activity is the personalities and the political decision-making processes within the organization concerned. A positive culture toward the value of training will be assisted by the following driving forces: first, the presence of 'training champions', especially among senior management; second, adequate systems for the diagnosis and delivery of training activities; third, line managers 'buying in' to training and being relieved of the budgetary and time costs of releasing staff, and fourth, internal pressure for such things as health and safety training (from trade unions) or equal opportunity training (from EO groups).

However, no single factor is sufficient by itself. It tends to be the case that those organizations investing in training for their employees do so because they possess a wide spread of the driving forces described here, as well as being relatively unhindered by particular negative factors.

Organizational approaches to HRD

What approaches do organizations adopt when it comes to developing their human resources? Some organizations take a very expedient and instrumental view. For instance, their overriding interest in management development might be to secure senior management succession. Typified by top corporate control, their HRD initiatives might include highly selective graduate recruitment, followed by high-flier career planning, with prescribed moves and attendance at business school and in house seminars along the way. However, as can be seen from Box 2.2 few companies can now afford to have such an elitist and narrowly focused approach.

In other organizations HRD may be equally centralized in the form of standards set for analysing development needs and appraising performance, but employees at *all* levels participate in the development programmes and there is opportunity for individuals to move into the fast track at various stages of their careers. In this method a panel of senior managers usually meets on a fairly regular basis to review skill requirements and to audit current and future potential among all categories of staff. At United Biscuits, for example, the main process of the management appraisal process is to see whether the jobs people have match their apparent potential. Following this audit, a group level committee checks development plans, which may call for cross-divisional moves. In addition, a two-day workshop is held with the chief executive, managing directors and senior HR directors to review potential candidates for the top 100 staff. Subsequently a management development executive committee monitors the development of these identified individuals, relates it to rewards and generally keeps vacancies in the top zone under review. So, despite being a decentralized group, the company retains a fairly tight rein on its HRD activities.

In contrast, other corporations allow their subsidiary businesses to pursue any HRD approach they deem appropriate to support their profit performance, which is the overriding criteria of success. We might call this a delegated HRD approach in the case of organizations such as Rothmans and Nissan, where there is a strong ethos of participative teamworking and ongoing people development at the grass roots, or GEC, notable for controlling by financial results and

---

Box 2.2   Erosion of elitism at Marks & Spencer

Marks & Spencer used to see management development in the main as elitist, related to the top business succession. Development was almost entirely linked to promotion. The main activity had been placing people on business school programmes. The management development department had become almost a business school booking agency, as a current member of the department put it. Employees bumped into management development if they did well and only if they did well.

Now Marks & Spencer have recognized the need to change this approach, especially in the light of their extension into the international market and massive growth on all fronts. They need to identify potential at all levels and for all levels. It is essential that all employees feel valued and know that opportunities are there for all of them. Demographic concerns mean that there is no room for elitism. Plateaued middle managers need to be used effectively, which is less easy as layers of management have been reduced. But there is the problem of retaining staff and so it has become essential to use the full potential of everyone.

In achieving this, greater responsibility has been lodged with line management to develop their own staff. The small management development department acts as a coach of this process, especially for the 4000 staff at Headquarters, who are largely responsible for issues like buying and distribution. There has been a move away from paternalism to make everyone increasingly responsible for their own development, with company support.

Some people are still selected for accelerated progress, though the route is less exclusive and the boundaries between them and others less clearly marked. The company are also viewing development as a means of enriching the quality of work. They have a phrase 'planning for through-life training' . . . The only way of dealing with the demographic time bomb is to enable all employees to have a sense of a good career ahead with personal development and increasing responsibility. The company are recognizing that status counts for less and that structures are now looser and flatter. The job itself therefore has more than ever to give a sense of worth (Wille, 1990, p.11).

---

tending not to interfere outside that context with its subsidiaries (see Box 2.3).

In other cases, possibly too many, to describe the approach as delegated would be a charitable description because concerns for HRD in the subsidiary organization are largely absent: the development of

---

Box 2.3 The experience of two GEC subsidiaries

GEC Meters design electronic supply meters and the related software with a view not only to recording electricity used, but also using this record to gather a whole range of business and usage data. They have a wide range of training and development activities to cater for the more junior managers as well as for the high flyers. They have good training accommodation and pay attention to the educational needs of their staff. Learning off the job by special programmes blends with development through the job, linked with an open appraisal system. Real projects are used as learning media and total quality management is beginning to create learning needs and opportunities. Special seminars are held to prepare managers and supervisors for the forthcoming opportunities in Europe. Shopfloor people of potential are given the opportunity to undertake formal training outside the company to acquire business knowledge and cross the 'divide' into management.

GEC Alsthom are the leaders in power generation equipment in Europe and second in transmission and distribution equipment. There is an employee development programme which has wide application, comprising an appraisal system and related training programmes. Communication throughout the company, in particular the 'financial pack' on the basis of which the budget is regularly discussed, is a normal part of the work. In all this the HQ does not get involved, but when there was a bad set of figures one month Arnold Weinstock called in all the senior management, including the French partners, for discussions. That is the area of his central control; results – not process or methods (Wille, 1990, p.17).

---

staff is left to chance and opportunism, with little or no people strategy or training provision being offered from the parent.

Some organizations, irrespective of their operating relationship, have moved to the other end of the spectrum from the elitist, paternalistic HRD described earlier. Here all employees in the organization have a stake in HRD: there is a sense of responsibility engendered by being part of a team that sets targets and handles budgets; as a result, development is taken seriously for everybody, from team leader to newest member, and this in turn is supported by a culture that facilitates coaching, and mentoring at all levels, helping to diminish the 'them and us' mentality and encourage shared responsibility for quality and continuous improvement in everything they do. This perhaps sounds idealistic but there are examples of organizations which have radically altered their HRD stance, as Box 2.4 shows.

Elements of this approach to staff development – with its emphasis on learning on the job and coaching new members of staff – are characteristic of the way small businesses conduct their HRD. But it can be inappropriate to superimpose HRD systems relevant in large businesses on to the entrepreneurial value systems of small and medium sized businesses. As they grow, flexible, holistic processes of learning and the informal approach to staff development become inadequate; however, conventional HRD methods and values forged in larger company settings (critical and detached analysis, objective information for decisions, looking for 'correct' answers, formal learning, an emphasis on efficiency and long-term planning) may

---

Box 2.4 Turnaround at Isuzu

By 1987, after ten years of making losses, Bedford Commercial Vehicles, part of the Vauxhall operation at Luton, was facing closure. Poor labour relations and intense foreign competition had plagued the company such that it was then losing £500,000 a week. Drastic action was called for to avert massive redundancies in Luton. Such action came. In September 1987 General Motors entered a joint venture with Japan's Isuzu, who took a 40 per cent share in the business and appointed one of its Japanese executives as president of the new business.

One key plank in the newly formulated human resources strategy was the creation of twenty-nine teams of about twelve people who were formed across all parts of the operation. Each meets regularly, usually at the end of a shift to discuss matters of quality, time-keeping, housekeeping and the like. This was an essential part of devolving decision-making to the lowest possible level, replacing the existing hierarchial pyramid structure, where even minor problems would often be escalated to unit manager level for resolution. New skills and confidence were called for to enable team leaders to handle this more responsible role. Phil Steele, the Training Manager, lists the recruitment criteria as knowing the job requirements within the team (the applicants will probably have done each of the jobs themselves on a rotational basis), being a proven communicator, and having the ability to instruct team members. To develop these skills IBC uses a local college together with on-site training to practise the implementation of new work systems, As the chief executive Saki says, 'in this programme, team leaders appear to enjoy themselves and perform confidently in their monthly presentations to senior executives'.

badly mismatch what is required in a business-led environment (creative solutions, personal and intuitive insights, networking, an emphasis on effectiveness and short-term realism).

From the above discussion it can be gleaned that there is no single HRD blueprint for all organizations. It will depend in part on their operating relationships and their structure, in part on their degree of autonomy as a business unit, and in part on their culture and their size. For some it suits them to have a predictable, centrally controlled

Table 2.1 Life cycle stage, culture/strategy and implications for HRD activities

Life cycle stage	*Key culture/strategic features*	*Implications for strategic HRD*
1. Embryonic	High levels of cohesion	Owner may not perceive need for HRD
	Dominant role of founder	Limited management expertise and succession problems
	Outside help not valued	Changes may be unplanned/ad hoc
	Lack of procedures and planning systems	HRD may have to market its services aggressively
	Politics play an important role	
2. Growth	Large variety of culture changes	Initiation of career development activities
	Levels of cohesion decline	Inducting new recruits
	Emergence of middle management	Management development activities
	Tensions/conflict may arise in organizations	Development of high performing teams
	Need to get people to accept new ways of thinking	Involvement in the management of change
	Diversification of business activities	Reinforcement and maintenance of cultural values and briefs
	Line/staff differences	Dealing with ambiguity and uncertainty
3. Maturity	Institutionalization of values and beliefs	HRD function should be well established
	Evolutionary rather than revolutionary changes	Maintenance HRD activities may be more appropriate
	Inertia may emerge in organization	Lack of career opportunities may require novel HRD approaches
	Strategic logic may be rejected	
4. Decline	Culture may act as a defence against a hostile environment	Management of change
	Major decisions may have to be taken	Reassure employees that problems are being tackled
	Readjustment necessary	Organizing problem centred/project/task activities

Adapted from Schein, 1985

approach, for the limited purpose of top succession planning; for others human resource development is indivisible from business strategy – it is not something aimed at a few, select individual competencies or isolated functions but an essential part of everyone's role. Between these two extremes there are all shades of sophistication in HRD policy. Having said that, is one particular HRD approach better than another in certain circumstances? For Edgar Schein a key determining factor is the prevailing and desired culture of the organization concerned (see Table 2.1).

So, for instance, a rapidly growing medium sized company is inevitably going to lose its cultural cohesion and self-sufficiency in people development terms. As new levels of management and supervision emerge and as business activity diversifies, so a whole raft of imperatives compete for attention: the need to induct new staff more carefully, the need to set up management development that takes account of line and staff differences, the need to address team leadership skills, career planning activities and generally equip staff with the capability of managing business priorities that may shift from one month to the next. What Table 2.1 illustrates, then, is a likely agenda for HRD if it is to have a strategic contribution to organizational performance. But how is this agenda arrived at? How does an intuitive feel of what is needed by an organization (by way of knowledge, skills and general mindset) get translated into a well informed HRD plan?

Identifying training and development needs

A training needs analysis (TNA) is basically a process of collecting data that allows an organization to identify and compare its actual level with its desired level of performance. Performance here could be interpreted as meaning the skills, knowledge and attitudes necessary for staff to do the job effectively. Usually the process consists of collecting data on current levels of performance and comparing these with the current desired levels of performance and the desired level over the long term. The shortfall in these comparisons reveals both immediate and long-term training needs. In its crudest sense a TNA explores with each employee group what it is trying to achieve, the barriers to achieving this and the suitability of training as a means to remove or counteract these barriers (see Box 2.5).

While training needs analysis is frequently prompted by some kind of shortfall in current performance, like an upturn in labour turnover or customer complaints, it is an equally appropriate tool for determining how current competence could be *improved*, or for anticipating *future* staff knowledge/ skill requirements. The organization may be changing its corporate objectives, perhaps expanding into overseas markets, broadening its product mix, or introducing automated production processes. All such strategic shifts may require skills and

Box 2.5   Using TNA to enhance image

ABS is a small company of approximately eighty employees but with a high-prestige profile and impact both nationally and internationally. It maintains a visible presence in the financial markets in London, New York and Tokyo through its flagship system, a touchscreen-based system that handles both voice and data communications and is used extensively by financial traders. In order to maintain and develop its high profile in this changing and volatile market, ABS needs to enhance its image amongst its customer base by being perceived:

- to be professional in approach to all issues;
- to have quality staff and product;
- to have hi-tech product in a technology-based market;
- to be responsive to customer needs.

Being responsive to customer needs is a central vehicle for developing the ABS image. However, without a clear indication of what problems customers are experiencing, it is difficult to identify what action can be taken via training and development or enhanced marketing to improve the image and hence market position of the business. Hence the starting point for the training and skills audit is to identify the external and internal 'customers' – in other words, who needs to know about the products and the way the business operates. Then it is necessary to establish what staff need to know and which skills they require. Having defined the nature of the problems or skill deficiencies, the next step is to translate this information into training needs to which effective training solutions can be devised, using either direct training techniques or open and/or distance learning. In order to enhance ABS's image it is important to monitor the effects of this training and to obtain feedback on any further training requirements.

knowledge not present in the existing labour force. External constraints are less controllable by the enterprise but their impact may also require careful diagnosis to determine future training needs. An obvious example here is the changing educational and demographic profile of the labour market in the mid-1990s, with critical implications for training related to equal opportunities, women returners and ethnic minorities. Another example is the increasing need for managers in the public sector to be able to interpret a multiplicity of conflicting needs and demands, and to do this within newly devised performance criteria, but often without the benefit of bottom-line indicators.

How should genuine training needs, present or future, be diagnosed? There are a host of methods, each with their own advantages and disadvantages, e.g. observation, questionnaires, interviews, scanning available documentation, conducting works samples tests, consulting employee records and reports, and so on. Many of these are considered in Chapter 4. However, perhaps the most important factor is to ask the staff concerned to diagnose their needs. In so doing they are much more likely to become enthusiastic participants in any development activities that ensue. They are also likely to know – better than anyone else – what the problems, issues and future opportunities are for their jobs/roles and will probably have the best ideas on what training and development needs to take place.

A competence-based approach to HRD

The search for a generic set of competences in the context of management activity and development has been a long-term preoccupation of theorists in the field, and the reason for the attraction is not difficult to see. If a number of underlying characteristics can differentiate superior performance from mediocre performance, and if these competence clusters can then be applied universally to different levels of management, then all aspects of HRM from recruitment and selection, through appraisal and training, to reward, recognition and deselection strategies are made more straightforward. In the UK the Management Charter Initiative (MCI) has been in the forefront of attempts to define such universal competences, spearheaded by the National Forum for Management Education and Development (NFMED), and Training Agency. Competence standards have so far been produced for junior management (level 1) and middle management (level 2), with research currently being undertaken on standards for senior/strategic managers.

There has been a slow but impressive build-up of support among British organizations for the MCI and its mission, with a current membership of almost 1000 employers representing 25 per cent of the UK workforce. The benefits arising from this competence-based approach to HRD are numerous: it is based on real performance in the workplace (rather than classroom training, with all its ensuing transfer of learning problems); it prompts organizations to be clearer in identifying what they want their staff in various job functions to do, and to be more precise in their evaluation of subsequent training interventions; it facilitates an integrated approach toward HRM, whereby the same competences are used as criteria for selection, appraisal, and internal assessment, as well as informing the objectives of training and career development activities, such that staff can no longer complain of shifting goalposts ('I'm being appraised for one thing, trained for another and rewarded for something else again!'). It enables prior experience in the workplace (so called accreditation of prior learning or crediting competence) to be taken into account and for professional qualifications to be conferred on those who satisfy the required standards at various levels. Finally, it raises the public profile of management development, which has been badly neglected in the UK until recently, and causes much needed resource to be invested in a more systematic training of British managers.

Despite these undoubted benefits, the MCI movement and its advocacy of generic competences has not been without its sceptics. In particular, the approach has been criticized for undertaking or overlooking the fact that management:

- is a complex, holistic activity, which cannot be reduced to a toolkit of discrete managerial competences;
- encompasses moral and ethical responsibilities, as does any craft, and is not solely concerned with technical proficiency;
- is dynamic in that managers often have to create and define their own tasks; much activity defies predetermined performance criteria and methods of measurement;
- is a flexible craft that is adaptive to different circumstances and constraints, rather than being circumscribed by right ways of managing: so the more universally true any list is, the less use it is in specific, concrete situations;
- is very much dependent on individual differences: having a toolkit of competences gives no indication of how they are used, who is the person using them and how this person develops;
- is concerned with collective competence, yet for all sorts of organizational reasons, high levels of individual performance do not necessarily translate into group or organizational effectiveness;
- includes 'softer' personal qualities (like creativity, assertiveness and intuition), which, while important, are less amenable to direct observation and measurement.

An example of an MCI competence statement is given in Chapter 9 (Box 9.6), where some further difficulties with such formulations of competence are given. Partly in response to these perceived shortcomings, some organizations are taking the benefits of a competence approach but tailoring it to their own situation. So, rather than using a generic set of competences (as defined by the MCI) they are creating organizationally specific competencies (notice the different spelling), namely a core set of behaviours that denote effective performance at various management levels and couched in language that is meaningful and pertinent to the organization concerned. So what are the steps to devising an HRD strategy by means of this approach, and how does it differ from the standard TNA approach discussed earlier?

The launching point is the business imperatives of the organization. Whether these are documented or simply little more than a 'mental map' in the heads of the top team, a number of key human resource implications can be derived from them: perhaps the need for more line managers to increase their financial knowledge in preparation for devolved budgeting, or perhaps the requirement for team briefing skills before the introduction of new team-based structures, or possibly the need for greater customer awareness across all levels of staff. These priorities will inform the generation of competency requirements: the underpinning knowledge, practical skills and attitudes that people need to bring to a role in order to perform to the necessary level and help fulfil the business objectives. Although these competencies might be initially identified by a small group of HR practitioners using some kind of job analysis technique (possibly with external help if it is not something they have done before), it is crucial that wide consultation then takes place to ensure general understanding and acceptance of these behavioural repertoires. The language by which they are described needs to be relevant to a given organizational context – which is why off-the-shelf competency lists are so often inadequate – and they need to be capable of distinguishing excellent from average performance in the level of job or career stream targeted.

So far the process has been largely top down. However, as can be seen from Figure 2.2, it is important to complement this with the bottom-up process of auditing the knowledge, skills and latent talent available in the current workforce. This may uncover all sorts of potential contributions that are relevant to the future direction of the business but are as yet untapped.

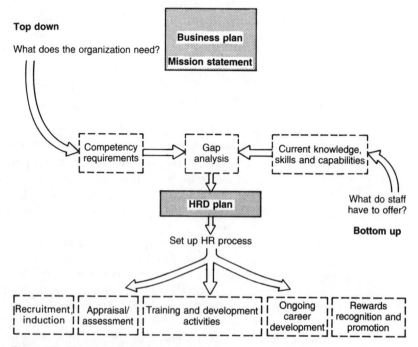

Figure 2.2 *The steps in competency-based HRD*

Box 2.6   Implementing competency-based HR strategy at BP

To answer the managers' concerns, BP chose to create a corporate-wide competency framework. It was appreciated that the process of decentralization and downsizing meant that implementation strategies would vary across businesses and countries. The performance criterion against which competencies were to be established, therefore, was the ability to enable change to happen (whatever that change might prove to be). A competency model was developed with consultants by comparing BP to other multi-nationals on their database and creating appropriate behavioural indicators that reinforced the culture and would enable Project 1990 to be implemented. It was essentially a desktop exercise and the labels chosen to group the sixty-seven identified essential behaviours were the same ones that had been used in relation to Project 1990, i.e. Open Thinking, Personal Impact, Empowering and Networking (OPEN).

Over a period of several months, the model was tested and validated internally and was then communicated throughout the business as awareness of the new competency model grew amongst senior managers. It then had to be developed across all the national businesses. The challenge was that the OPEN competencies (and the sixty-seven beheviours that evidenced them) had been designed to express BP's organizational culture, yet had to be adapted to suit a wide range of national cultures, the cross-cultural validity of the essential behaviours was challenged by non-British or non-American managers. They had been developed by a team of Anglo-Americans. Were they transferable to other countries?

BP ran a series of Focus Groups in France and Germany, in which it represented the intended objective of the behaviour contained within the competency and the intended meaning behind the English words. The Focus Groups each contained ten to twelve national employees who spoke English as a second language and were facilitated by consultants operating in the area of cross-cultural management and fluent in English, French and German. Each group was able to flex the behavioural indicators around each competency so that they were appropriate for their culture and organization. The feared barriers to cross-cultural implementation did not materialize.

Local business trainers and facilitators were then given instruction on how to present the OPEN competencies as part of change programmes being carried out in Europe and Asia-Pacific. It was found that it was better to instruct local trainers on the meaning and purpose behind the competencies and then let them fashion the actual training process used to introduce the competencies themselves (from Sparrow and Bognanno, pp. 54–5).

It is now that the two routes can be brought together. What does the organization need in terms of key competencies in order to achieve its short- and long-term strategic objectives, and is the current pool of skills, knowledge and potential capabilities among existing staff adequate. There might just be a gap between the two! And it is here that the HRD plan begins to take shape. Box 2.6 describes how BP went about a similar process in an international setting.

This account usefully summarizes the advantages of a competency-based approach to HRD: it relates key behaviours to the business plan, it customizes behavioural indicators for different parts of the organization (even across cultural boundaries), it focuses on outputs and performance rather than activities, it is future-orientated (rather than historical in focus) and, finally – perhaps most essentially – competencies encourage mutual behavioural reinforcement across a number of HRM policy areas and create multiple pressure points for change, e.g. behavioural ladders to facilitate rankings in performance appraisal, assessor observation guidelines for assessment exercises, checklists for training needs analysis and benchmarks for career planning processes.

Whether competency checklists are generic or specific when they are generated, there is always the danger that they will become inflexible and prescriptive. As we can glimpse from the BP case above, the original creation of competencies and the task of ensuring that they are contextually relevant and up-to-date is arduous and time-comsuming, although it must be said that the amount of work put into 'analysing the gap' pays great dividends later compared to more superficial attempts at training diagnosis, which tend to lead to only short-term and piecemeal solutions.

Becoming a learning organization

Partly in recognition of the difficulties and limitations associated with traditional approaches to HRD and the view that the MCI competence approach undervalues the creative nature of effective management, the concept of the 'learning company' has gained currency in recent years. In contrast to an organization that does a lot of training, the learning company is 'an organization which facilitates the learning of all its members and continuously transforms itself' according to Pedler *et al.* (1989). These authors offer a set of non-exclusive conditions against which organizations can test themselves:

1 Organizational policy and strategy formation, together with its implementation space, evaluation and improvement, are consciously structured as a learning process.
2 The debate over organizational policy and strategy is widely shared, participated in and identified with, among members of the organization. Debate implies recognition of differences, airing

disagreements, tolerating and working with conflicts to reach decisions.

3 Management control systems of accounting, budgeting and reporting are structured to assist learning from the consequences of managerial decisions.

4 Information systems, including the applications of information technology, are used to 'informate' as well as 'automate', enabling members to question current operating assumptions and seek information for individual and collective learning about organization norms, goals and processes.

5 Individuals, groupings, departments and divisions exchange information on expectations and feedback on satisfactions to assist learning (as in Total Quality programmes) as well as goods and services.

6 Members with outside contacts act as 'environmental scanners' for the organization (as well as delivering goods and services, etc.) and feed this information back to other organization members.

7 Organization members engage to share information and learn jointly with 'significant others' outside the organization, e.g. key customers and suppliers.

8 The culture and management style within the organization encourage experimentation, learning and development from successes and failures.

9 Resources and facilities for self-development are available for all.

Actual examples are hard to come by, but given the competitive pressures to survive and grow, the increasing need to improve quality of service and customer relations, the increasing pace of change and need to encourage active experimentation, together with the patent failure of superficial organizational restructuring, the learning company/organization does at least seem an appropriate metaphor if not a definitive model to work towards. At the very least, it highlights the value of promoting experimentation. Of course it is a contradiction in terms for an organization to issue an edict for its staff to be more innovative! But there are at least four things an organization can do to encourage the learning that results from creativity and risk taking: first, avoid too much homogeneity when recruiting managers; second, introduce flexibility into the structure of the organization so that change and the learning of new roles becomes a familiar experience; third, design reward systems such that they reinforce innovative behaviour and do not disadvantage the risk-takers; fourth, invest in information systems that focus on unusual variations (rather than smoothing them out), and on the bad news as well as the good (why orders are lost, as well as sales achieved). Indeed, how information is handled is a good index as to how seriously an organization takes its learning, both externally and internally (see Box 2.7).

Box 2.7   Learning from customers

With regard to *external* information the important point is to be assured of the quality of information received, rather than its quantity. The best way of doing this is to maintain direct contact with the environment. That is why the directors of Cadburys used to spend a few days every year on the road with a carload of samples, and why Robert Townsend, Chief Executive of Avis, used to insist that all systems people should spend at least a month every year hiring out cars. It is only through direct information like this that the company can be sure that it, and its employees, are adequately exposed to what is going on outside. Another example is provided by British Airways which has set up a department of marketplace performance which is totally independent of the main marketing department. The job of this department is to conduct surveys of customer and client relations which will not be in any way influenced by the existing interests of the marketing department (Easterby-Smith, 1988, pp. 26–7).

Self-development activity

Can you think of unproductive patterns of behaviour in your organization where learning opportunities are missed or stifled? Here is one example to get you started:

- senior managers are fed with the positive information that they want;
- this is used to confirm the views that they already hold;
- there is little open testing of ideas;
- staff become cynical and defensive, and less willing to provide accurate information;
- in the absence of bottom-up messages, senior managers try to get closer to the grass roots by asserting even more control over their subordinates and the production of information.

Becoming an Investor in People

Another term which is in the ascendancy alongside the learning organization is Investor in People (IIP). For an organization to be credited as an Investor in People it needs to satisfy four national standards in the view of an assessor appointed by a Training and Enterprise Council (TEC), or Local Enterprise Council (LEC) in

Scotland. In other words, this is an institutional attempt to encourage employers to become more like learning organizations where everybody is engaged in the development of themselves and others. The four standards are:

1 A public commitment from the top of the organization to develop all employees to achieve business objectives.
2 A method for regularly reviewing the training and development needs of all its employees.
3 Action taken to train and develop individuals on recruitment and throughout their employment.
4 Systems for evaluating the investment in training and development to assess achievement and improve future effectiveness.

Each of these standards is supported by a number of assessment indicators, which, if followed, translate these noble intentions into tangible and specific activities. The hub of the exercise is a written training and development plan, which is informed by the business plan, is regularly reviewed, and specifies targets linked to achieving external standards, e.g. National Vocational Qualifications, where appropriate. It is from this plan that HRD activities are generated for all categories of staff in the organizations, the emphasis being on employees identifying and meeting their job-related development needs, supported by their managers. To close the loop, senior managers should review the effectiveness of training at all levels against business goals and targets.

As with any attempt to establish uniform standards which are then externally assessed by a nationally recognized body, this approach is likely to entail its fair share of bureaucratic 'red-tape'. However the indicators are very much in the spirit of the competency-based approach to HRD outlined above (Figure 2.2) and enshrine many of the principles of good people development discussed in this book. Furthermore, they have been designed to be relevant to both small and large organizations in the public and private sectors, and to take into account the variations that there will inevitably be in organizations' approaches to HRD. To date, 542 organizations have successfully gained IIP accreditation, and it may well be that for no other reason than to satisfy their own customers, suppliers and staff that they take people development seriously, many more will follow suit.

Putting HRD on the corporate map

It is one thing to put together a carefully designed HRD plan, it is quite another to get it accepted and implemented in the way that the IIP approach looks for. We have already seen that the starting point for an HRD plan is the impact of competitive forces that expose some kind of business performance gap. In response the organization reassesses its product market or makes technical changes to its operation; this may call for new concepts of service provision, different channels of distribution, restructuring and/or decentralizing of business units, acquiring new businesses, and cost-reduction activities. Each constitutes a strategic shift and usually implies the need for new capabilities or skills amongst its staff. This much is common. It is how an organization then interprets the highlighted skills gap(s) and galvanizes the various driving forces for change that determine the effectiveness of its training strategy. This calls for individuals who have the capability of linking business and technical changes to HRD policies, who have a good grasp of the various training and development options appropriate to different organizational circumstances, and who have the necessary process skills to steer human resource initiatives through their internal decision-making channels. Cultivating a positive training ethos in a given organization will thus require:

- Linking training needs and predicted skill requirements to existing business planning processes. This ensures that HRD doesn't get overlooked at the strategic decision-making level, and that development needs are anticipated and integrated with other top team considerations.
- Articulating the need for HRD investment by using language that will be persuasive to non-HR specialists. This may mean assembling a financial/business case of lost opportunity, marketing edge, innovative capability or internal and external labour market gaps if training and development are *not* resourced adequately. Alternatively, it may mean pointing out the 'pay-off' in business terms of past investment in training based on evaluation studies perhaps with reference to competitor performance. Putting these arguments in the wider context of HRM, rather than as piecemeal training initiatives, is more likely to appeal to strategically minded colleagues.
- Targeting senior managers who are already sympathetic towards or convinced of the need for HRD to 'champion' the cause of training and development in their departments/functions and in the organization more widely.
- Gathering a database of external providers of training, assessing the calibre and credibility of consultancy and academic networks. This will also mean keeping in close touch with national training initiatives and funding opportunities.

A survey of ninety Irish high-technology companies (indigenous and multinational) contains some interesting revelations about how organizations operate their 'strategic HRD policy and planning processes' (Garavan, 1991). The results highlighted the following:

1 *HRD policy*: 95 per cent of companies had an established HRD function, 81 per cent had a written HRD policy statement. The most

important factors cited as shaping this statement were the organization's mission, goals and strategies, although prevailing culture, training needs, current state of technology, top management views and equality of opportunities were also mentioned.

2 *Policy formulation*: it was typically drawn up by the HRD specialist, approved by the personnel director and subsequently by other members of the management team. The recognized benefits of having a written policy statement (published as a policy manual or special brochure) were that it ensured consistency and equality of treatment, helping the managers to make more effective HRD decisions and facilitating the human resource planning process.

3 *Implementation*: three key issues were identified. Publicity for the policy statement (through briefing sessions, induction programmes, etc.) was necessary to ensure it was known, understood and accepted by those implementing it and affected by it. Simple, clear procedures e.g. yearly training plans, were seen as key mechanisims for driving policy through the organization. Monitoring was seen as a vital safeguard against drift from original intentions, and ensured continuous alignment with corporate strategy. In this respect, respondents saw HRD policies as flexible and open to modification, rather than static documents.

4 *Priorities*: the HRD plans of the indigenous high technology organizations tended to place considerable emphasis on technical training, management development, quality and the management of change. The multinationals gave more prominence to personal development and professional development activities. Garavan suggests this is because they were more likely to have their organization-centred HRD needs met, and could therefore focus more on personal/professional development activities.

5 *Diagnosis and support*: 85 per cent of respondents had a formalized system for the identification of HRD needs, e.g. questionnaires, performance reviews, discussions with managers and employees, task groups and corporate assessments by the management team, usually done on an annual basis and fed into the HRD plan for that year. As many as 95 per cent of responding organizations had training budgets to support their plan (54 per cent of these were centralized, 20 per cent departmental, the rest a mixture of both), and these budgets were up to 5 per cent of annual turnovers for 80 per cent of organizations.

6 *Roles*: The individual(s) identified as being responsible for implementing the HRD plan varied widely: 41 per cent of respondents saw it as the sole responsibility of the HRD specialist, 35 per cent indicated that it was the responsibility of the HRD specialist *and* the line manager, 8 per cent the line manager only, and 16 per cent the human resource specialist.

Perhaps most surprising is the last point, conflicting as it does with the notion of a strategically orientated human resource function, where the line manager – and indeed the individual employees themselves – play an active part in, and have a degree of responsibility for, the development of appropriate knowledge, skills and attitudes in the workplace. It could be argued that line managers are pivotal in the effective implementation of HRD. It is they who communicate the plans, demonstrate the commitment and linkage of training and development to strategic business goals; it is they who operate the procedures and monitor the performance; it is they who devote time and departmental resources to individual and team development; and it is they who, in many ways, influence the subculture of their department or business unit.

Managing the HRD strategy

Training and development is for the employee a journey, and it needs to be guided and prompted by the milestones of other HRM policies within an organization. It will instil confidence, for instance, if the criteria used for selection are the same competences looked for in performance reviews, as well as being reflected in the assessment dimensions of a development centre or internal promotion panel. As individuals or groups set out on a training programme or a set of development activities, they need to know how the anticipated learning will help them carry out their current, or future, responsibilities better. What will successful completion of the course or programme look like? What will be the organizational pay-off? How, if at all, will successful completion of the course or programme assist them in their own career development? What opportunities will there be to apply 'outputs' from the activities? How will effective implementation of the training be rewarded and recognized?

Deciding who undertakes training, when and for what purpose, is actually a joint responsibility shared between the individual, his or her line manager, the HR manager (and the human resource planning department, if there is one). The traditional approach where a central training function offers a 'menu' of internally or externally delivered training courses appears efficient, because the demand and provision of HRD activities can be regulated centrally to ensure a smooth and cost-effective throughput of trainees.

Self-development activity

What do you see as the likely pitfalls with such an approach to HRD provision?

Common problems associated with this HRD system are poor diagnosis of original training needs, inappropriate nominations, ill-prepared trainees, outdated training content and methods, little participation by line managers in the development process, over-dependence on the training department, hit and miss learning transfer, minimal impact on organizational goals and ultimate withdrawal of funding for what is seen by senior managers as ineffective HRD.

An alternative model is for the training specialists to provide more of a consultative HRD service to local line managers. The benefits of this approach are that line managers are likely to have more ownership of their staffs' development; training needs will be more accurately diagnosed and be linked to departmental and organizational perform-ance models/targets; trainees will arrive on programmes more motivated, ready to learn and apply knowledge and principles in their work situation, and the impact of HRD is likely to be greater, so attracting more more resources and funding in the future. The principal disadvantage is the more 'fuzzy' boundary issue between the HRM/HRD department(s) and local line management. The consult-ant–client relation is probably the most appropriate here, but may take a while to become smooth running, depending on the departmental personalities and the degree to which a learning culture exists more broadly within the organization.

Another key linkage here is the access of the HR specialist to the top management and his/her degree of input to strategic decision making. If this avenue is closed or hindered, the consultancy model may work well within itself, but HRD will remain reactive and one step behind events, and training activities will not secure the full confidence of organizational leaders.

Summary

Some organizations have impressive training plans that bear no resemblance to the way their staff 'experience' HRD on a day-to-day basis. Other organizations may have little in the way of written HRD objectives and policies, but development of staff can be observed at all levels. In this chapter we have sought to understand what it is that creates the difference. While, as we have emphasized, there is no single blueprint for successful HRD across all organizations, some key principles have been discussed. Whether it be a reactive response to competitors or a more pre-emptive recognition of future competencies, the stimulus for a fresh HRD approach is invariably prompted by some kind of skills performance gap. Once identified, the key task is to capitalize on internal forces for change – and to minimize the restraining forces – that come both from within and outside the organization. While the actual pattern of HRD 'delivery' will vary, we noted that the prevailing strategy and culture will be important factors in shaping training provision. Also important is some kind of diagnosis to determine what skills and competencies are, and will be, required at different levels in the organization. With this in mind, some of the virtues of a competency-based HRD strategy were argued, in that it can pave the way for a more coherent, consistent and enduring approach to recruiting, developing and assessing/appraising staff. Finally we looked at some of the key roles and skills required by those responsible for initiating and implementing HRD strategies within their organizations, recognizing the pivotal role of line managers themselves in this process. It is this translation of the HRD plan into practice that we consider more closely in the next chapter.

References

Easterby-Smith, M. (1988) Creating a learning organization. *Personnel Review,* 19. 5, pp. 24–28.

Garavan, T. N. (1991) Strategic human resource development. *Journal of European Industrial Training,* 15, 1, pp. 17–30.

Hendry, C., Pettigrew, A. and Sparrow, P. (1985) Changing patterns of human resource management. *Personnel Management.* November, pp. 11, 37, 41.

Keep, E. (1989) Corporate training strategies: the vital component? in Storey, J. (ed.) *New perspectives on human resource management.* Routledge, London.

Pedler, M., Boydell, T. and Burgoyne, J. (1989) Towards a learning company. *Management Education and Development* 2,3, pp. 19–41.

Pettigrew, A., Hendry, C. and Sparrow, P. (1988) The role of VET in employers' skill supply strategies. Training agency report in conjunction with Coopers and Lybrands Associates.

Pettigrew, A., Hendry, C. and Sparrow, P. (1988) The forces that trigger training. *Personnel management.* December, pp. 28–32.

Schein, E. (1985) *Organizational Culture and Leadership.* Jossey Bass, Boston.

Sparrow, P. and Bognanno, M. (1993) Competency requirements forecasting: issues for international selection and assessment. *International Journal of Selection and Assessment.* 1,1, pp. 50–8.

Sparrow, P., Pettigrew, A. and Hendry, C. (1988) Changing patterns of human resource management. *Personnel Management.* November, pp. 37–41.

Storey, J. (1989) (ed.) *New perspectives on human resource management.* Routledge, London.

Wille, E. (1990) People development and improved business performance, Ashridge Management Research Group Report for the Training Agency, August, Berkhamsted, Herts.

3 Putting human resource development strategies into practice

Introduction

We all know the feeling of arriving on a training course without really knowing why we are there. A host of distracting thoughts enter our heads as the tutor proceeds through the first session. 'Why did my boss send me on this programme – does he/she think I'm incompetent in this area?' 'How will I cope with my in-tray when I get back?' 'I've heard good reports about this course, but there's no way it's relevant to my department!' 'I'm moving jobs next month anyway . . . or at least that's what I've been told.' Such private thoughts are all part of the 'unfreezing' process at the start of a learning event. Often the training does prove to be relevant, timely and valuable. But too often it doesn't.

Having considered the process of devising HRD strategies in Chapter 2, we go on here to look at the same subject but from an individual perspective. No matter how elegant the design of an organization's HRD strategy, no matter how much is spent on internal and external training provision, if individual staff do not appreciate their part in the plan, and how the development activities can benefit their personal learning, their department's performance and the organization's effectiveness, they are unlikely to buy-in to the process.

In this chapter we assume that development needs at a workgroup and individual level have been diagnosed (more details on how to do this will be given in Chapter 4) and we move on to the assumptions and cultural 'givens' that prevail in an organization about the way people learn. An HRD plan which overlooks these beliefs – which are usually implicit, is liable to run into problems. The latter part of the chapter builds on these factors by examining a series of HRD initiatives and activities that can be provided for staff. Some are conducted away from the workplace and are heavily prescriptive, others are much more self-determined and can be carried out as part of everyday work experiences, the key feature being that the purpose of the training learning matches the methods and processes to deliver and facilitate it.

Models of HRD

A superficial observation of what development activities are taking place in an organization could be very misleading. Take a look at

Figure 3.1, which is based on an analysis of training and development activities in diverse organizations. The first 'intermittent' pattern represents a situation where there is little or no genuine commitment to HRD by most line managers, who are supposed to be the agents for ensuring that it happens, and this is reflected in a low level of activity. In this category you might expect to find small accountancy or legal practices where professional expertise accounts for everything, and managerial ability is traditionally undervalued; or perhaps a voluntary organization operating crisis management: not able to invest the time or money developing its staff.

The second pattern could be called institutionalized: it is where activity and apparent commitment peak, perhaps because there has been a push from above to record training activity, there is a need to use up development budgets, and/or the company compensation plan rewards active participation by line managers. This may be true of an organization with its own HRD function offering well established off-the-job programmes to the rest of the business on a 'menu' basis.

The activity level in pattern three appears to revert to that of the first level. But actually it depicts the more mature situation where HRD has become a natural and regular part of normal boss–subordinate relations: well internalized but less visible to the casual observer. This might represent a company where line managers are highly skilled in coaching and developing their staff, able to 'construct' everyday occurrences as learning opportunities for themselves and their staff, and where the prevailing ethos of people development militates against departmental talent hoarding. Ultimately more important than the number of training days per annum, or even the proportion of budget devoted to training and development each year is the degree to which line managers are committed to and participate in the development of themselves and staff for whom they are responsible.

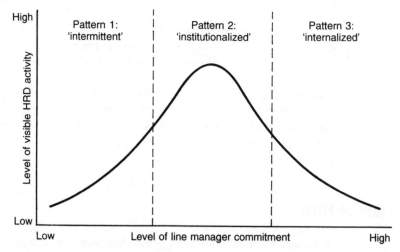

Figure 3.1 *Patterns of human resource development (adapted from Ashton et al., 1975)*

The way an organization's leaders approach HRD, and the 'model of HRD' that they unconsciously or consciously adopt, depends upon at least three factors: the type of organization and its conception of what managers do, the level of maturity of its human resource (particularly management development) processes, and its basic assumptions about how learning happens. Each of these will be considered more fully below.

Type of organization

Decisions concerning which competencies to pursue and how to develop them are closely tied to the nature of the organization. For instance, a mechanistic organization having well defined functions and roles with written job descriptions for each jobholder would probably favour a systems approach to HRD, based on competencies identified as relevant for each level of staff. If one such competency were 'thinking strategically', this would be confined to managers operating at a senior level; in a multi-layered organization it is unlikely that first line managers would be expected to, or be actually able to, contribute *significantly* to the strategic thinking of their organization. By contrast, if the organization is decentralized, characterized by autonomous business units, or is a much smaller entrepreneurial type of culture, then it is likely to have a single status philosophy and base its reward systems on performance. In this situation everyone would be expected to be thinking about strategy, new products, marketing initiatives and so on. Consequently training and development requirements would be defined according to some very different performance criteria. The difference of these two extremes, and every other shade of organization structure/culture in between demonstrate, by the way, why generic lists of competences are so inadequate. To put it another way, specific training initiatives can only be planned when it has been decided what staff generally, and management in particular, actually do and what roles they are expected to perform. Much of this thinking is taken for granted, but, as can be seen from Table 3.1, depending on what 'school' of managerial thought one adheres to the training implications are strikingly different.

Level of HRD maturity

Another important way of understanding an organization's approach to HRD is to look for the *connection* between its strategic business objectives and its people-development policies and practices. In reaction to your own organization, you might ask: 'To what extent are all levels of staff involved in knowledge and skills acquisition and self-development in a way that actually serves organizational purposes and growth as individuals?' The Centre for the Study of Management Learning at Lancaster University has an enviable reputation in this field, and, based on their pure and applied research over many years,

Table 3.1 Managerial thought and training implications

School of managerial thought	Themes	Training implications
Interpersonal behaviour	Human interaction at work is the focus. Motivation is seen as crucial	Skill development/people management important.
Group behaviour	Workshop attitudes and motivation to act important.	Leadership training. Group dynamics etc.
Co-operative social system	Cohesion encouraged; conflict 'ironed out'.	'Core value' systems and building up a unitary culture part of the brief for attitudinal change via training.
Socio-technical	Constant interaction between social (people) aspects of the organization and technology (equipment/work methods etc.).	Again people part of the equation, so groups/ individuals affected by interaction, e.g. new technology/machines etc., hence skill implications.
Decision theory	Organizations seen as a 'complex web of interlocking structures'. Analyse decision processes.	In many ways management comprises decision-making, shrewd training people 'switch into' the power structures to gain resources, etc.
Contingency	A horses for courses approach. No one solution, as it *depends* on the circumstances.	The uniqueness of the culture and organization must be understood and used by the trainer (staff or line).
Systems	The 'conversion' of external environmental inputs to outputs is the focus of this approach.	The changing environment is a useful focal point for needs analysis, and the systems approach may give a useful frame of reference to the trainer.
Classical/scientific management	'Scientific' selection and training of workers. Scientific analysis of time. Market division of labour (planners and workers). Differing responsibilities.	Training with its skill divisions seen to be a main premise of this school.
Behavioural	Groups and individuals important to counter the pure 'task' mentality. 'Contented cows give the best milk'	People to the fore, hence training and *development* important to this school.

Anderson, 1993, pp. 25–6

Professor John Burgoyne has devised a six-step model describing organizations in ascending degrees of 'maturity' on these dimensions (Table 3.2). Although the model refers primarily to managers, it can be applied usefully to a wider population and used to emphasize three features of effective HRD.

Table 3.2 Levels of maturity of organizational management development

No systematic management development (level 1)	Isolated tactical management development (level 2)	Integrated and co-ordinated structural and development test (level 3)	A management development strategy to implement corporate policy (level 4)	Management development strategy input to corporate policy formation (level 5)	Strategic development of the management of corporate policy (level 6)
No systematic or deliberate management development in structural or developmental sense, total reliance on natural *laissez-faire* uncontrolled processes of management development.	There are isolated and *ad hoc* tactical management development activities, of either structural or developmental kinds, or both in response to local problems, crises or sporadically identified general problems.	The specific management development tactics that impinge directly on the individual manager, and tactics of career structure management, and of assisting learning, are integrated and co-ordinated.	A management development strategy plays its part in implementing corporate policies through managerial human resource planning, and providing a strategic framework and direction for the tactics of career structure management and of learning education and training.	Management development processes feed information into corporate policy decision-making processes on the organization's managerial assets, strengths, weaknesses and potential, and contribute to the forecasting and analysis of the manageability of proposed projects, ventures, changes.	Management development processes enhance the nature and quality of corporate policy forming processes which they also inform and help implement.

Burgoyne, 1988, p 41

First, it has to be conscious and reflective. While a great deal of natural development takes place through the unplanned interpersonal and functional experiences encountered each day, and careers frequently unfold in an uncontrived manner, these cannot usually be classed as strategic processes, at least in organizational terms, until they are explicitly linked to the implementation of corporate policy. Second, the model infers incremental levels of maturity, such that an organization's approach to HRD is likely to grow gradually in sophistication rather than suddenly become level five or six. Of course it is not inconceivable that different aspects of HRD can vary in their connectedness to corporate policy within the same enterprise, and that HRD generally could slip downwards in maturity over time. The third, and perhaps the most important, point from Burgoyne's analysis is the linking of HRD with what he calls the 'hard systems' of HRM on the one hand and collaborative career planning on the other.

Self-development activity

Think about your personal experience of training and development in your current and other organizations. Select three examples of different levels if possible and locate them on Burgoyne's model, briefly stating why you have put them at that level.

In fact few organizations attempt to connect the systems that actually develop individuals to strategic objectives. Instead they rely on a continuing turnover of people to ensure that individuals match job requirements. In an organization that has little turnover skills quickly become outdated and the organization becomes less able to meet changing demands. Crash programmes of development are often seen as solutions, and often the training budget is too small to cope. This approach typifies levels 1 and 2 of Burgoyne's model, and he admits that the organizations operating consistently at levels 5 and 6 are exceptions rather than the rule.

Nature of learning

All of us have a preference for learning in different ways. Some of these preferences will be weak, some strong, and these will predispose us to certain kinds of learning activity. When there is a good match between our preferred style of learning and a given development activity, learning is likely to occur.

With a view to improving our capacity to learn in familiar or new situations, Peter Honey and Alan Mumford have developed the 'Learning Styles Questionnaire' from the work of David Kolb. It

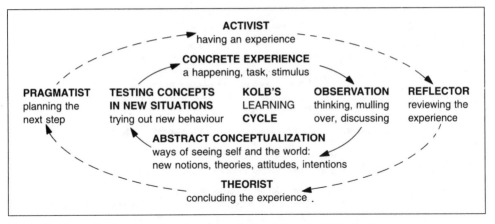

Figure 3.2 *Four-stage learning cycle (adapted from Kolb, and Honey and Mumford)*

reveals a person's preferred learning style(s) which correspond to Kolb's four-stage learning cycle, as can be seen in Figure 3.2.

For instance, an activist will relish new experiences, pursue ideas without constraint and gladly take up new challenges, but will shrivel in situations requiring a lot of data assimilation and solitary work. The reflector will stand back and observe, taking time to review or decide in his or her own time; he or she will be uncomfortable with cut and dried instructions and where instant reactions are required. The theorist revels in structure, and problems requiring analysis, and model-building, but is unhappy with emotional situations and incompatible techniques. Finally, the pragmatist is described as wanting to tackle real problems with ample opportunity for practice and experimentation; he or she will be less happy with arid instructions, especially if they have no particular relevance to the question in hand.

Like any descriptive list, this is interesting as far as it goes; the critical question is what is the nature of training and development in your organization? What assumptions prevail about the way people learn? Is there a reliance on formal training methods that begin with the tacit assumption that there is a body of knowledge or set of skills to be acquired? Or does development *start* with the real problems people face in their day-to-day work?

It has been demonstrated, for instance, that for senior executives, at least, formal management development processes do not figure very highly as learning experiences. Informal processes of management development are perceived to be equally insufficient and inefficient because individuals often lack the skills to make the most of them as learning opportunities. Based on these findings, Mumford devised a model of types of management development (see Figure 3.3).

Type 2, called 'integrated managerial opportunistic processes', combines the benefit of type 1 (learning is real and direct because it is

---

Type 1   Informal managerial – accidental processes

Characteristics	Occur within managerial activities
	Explicit intention is task performance
	No clear development objectives
	Unstructured in development terms
	Not planned in advance
	Owned by managers
Development consequences	Learning is real, direct, unconscious, insufficient

Type 2   Integrated managerial – opportunistic processes

Characteristics	Occur within managerial activities
	Explicit intention both task performance and development
	Clear development objectives
	Structured for development by boss and subordinate
	Planned beforehand or reviewed subsequently as learning experiences
	Owned by managers
Development consequences	Learning is real, direct, conscious, more substantial

Type 3   Formal management development – planned processes

Characteristics	Often away from normal managerial activities
	Explicit intention is development
	Clear development objectives
	Structured for development by developers
	Planned beforehand and reviewed subsequently as learning experiences
	Owned more by developers than managers
Development consequences	Learning may be real (through a job) or detached (through a course)
	Is more likely to be conscious, relatively infrequent

Figure 3.3   *Three of types of management development (from Mumford, 1993, p.35)*

related to the manager's immediate job performance) and type 3 (learning is conscious and more substantial because the process emphasizes the need for reflection and review before moving on to fresh planning and action). Mumford goes on to recommend some levers for success: in addition to clear and appropriate job activities, and effective selection for the job development, activities need to be driven by business opportunities, problems diagnosed and owned by the individual concerned as well as their managers, targeted at individual needs and based on managerial reality. Even better if various development processes are linked and some attempt is made to identify and review outputs.

Having made more explicit some of the assumptions and premises upon which approaches to HRD are based, we can now get down to the detail of training and development activities.

Choosing and designing HRD activities

Of the many approaches to learning and training, it is often difficult to decide which is best and who should design and deliver it. Sometimes an instrumental view is taken whereby mass attendance on training modules is advocated. In other situations development is seen in the more open-ended context of daily experience, which is structured, reviewed, and where learning is internalized. Both have a place of course, as do all the varying shades of training in between. The vital questions are what training and development methods are appropriate for the stated purpose of the HRD initiative, and how can the programme of activities be structured such that participants not only learn effectively but also apply this learning to their jobs in a way that benefits the organization?

To answer these questions we need to understand HRD from two perspectives: on the one hand, the organization – or the providers of HRD – will have a view about the best way to deliver training; on the other hand, those participating in HRD activities will have certain preferences and expectations about their degree of autonomy. We shall examine these two perspectives briefly below, before going on to give some examples of HRD.

Training delivery

Approaches to training can be placed on a continuum. At one extreme, as we've already seen, it is assumed that there is a body of knowledge to be taught: practice is deduced from theory and then applied with an emphasis on formal learning methods. In HRD terms this would result in fairly *instrumental* learning processes; subject matter will be covered in a predetermined syllabus where duration of study and quantity of learning are important outputs. Tutors are seen as teachers and experts, they will set and mark/give feedback on assignments and success/or completion of the training is often signified by formal qualifications or membership of an elite.

At the other extreme we have what might be called *experiential* learning contexts, which are based on the view that an individual's talent, ideas and views are to be drawn out, since knowledge evolves as we learn more about ourselves and the unbounded world we inhabit. This would lead an organization to arrange its training and development activities such that they are much more 'open-ended' and informal, with tutors acting as facilitators to help the learners discover their talents and realize their potential in order to achieve their own learning goals.

Learner autonomy

Those participating in HRD programmes and activities will also experience different degrees of freedom over both the content and the process of learning. In some situations this will be highly constrained, and in other cases the learning experience may be much more flexible and tailored to the needs of the individual. Learners will have a great deal of influence over what training and development activities they undertake, and also the timing, pace, sequence and depth of learning will be largely in their hands, within the parameters set by the organization.

These two dimensions – learner autonomy and training delivery – are naturally linked. Figure 3.4 depicts them on a graph, with the amount of autonomy given to the learner for determining the process (the way the training activities are organized) on the horizontal axis, and the amount of autonomy given to the learner for determining the content (the precepts, principles, skills covered) on the vertical axis. The 'training delivery' ranging from instrumental to experiential is represented as a diagonal axis. Such a representation is useful when evaluating the most appropriate training methods for the trainees and the subject matter in question.

Self-development activity

Below is a typical list of methods that organizations use to educate, train and develop their staff. Where would you place each method on Figure 3.4: role play, lecture, computer-based training (CBT), outward bound, secondment, case study, distance learning programme, encounter group, business game. Add others you have experienced if you wish.

In the bottom left corner we would place methods like lecture, programmed learning and case studies, which allow relatively little or no learner autonomy over both content or process. For example, the

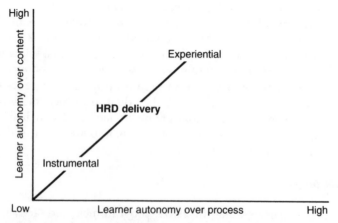

Figure 3.4 *Locating HRD delivery against learner autonomy*

learner arrives at the lecture, and the content is transmitted in the way the lecturer chooses, following a curriculum with set readings and so on. Even a case study, which may appear less constrained, usually conforms to a predetermined pattern of exploration, analysis and 'discovery'. One of the features of programmed learning techniques as harnessed by CBT, for instance, is the increased discretion it gives to the learner. But there are only a limited number of pathways through a given programme, so autonomy is greater than in a lecture but still prescribed.

Around the middle of the graph we would include such diverse activities as role plays, management simulations and business games, projects and small group work, which provide relatively more learner autonomy in terms of both content and process. For instance, during role play the learners have some choice in the way they portray the given role (content) but do so within a perspective normally set by the rules (process), usually modelled behaviour. However, it is possible to use experiential behaviour modelling, thus allowing the learner some autonomy over the process as well as the content.

Top right might contain such methods as encounter groups, counselling and unstructured process workshops, which traditionally have the highest levels of learner autonomy both in terms of content and process. At this level it is usual for the learner(s) to identify the content they wish to work on themselves. In addition, the process is facilitated by the tutor but in such a way as not to constrain the learner, which leads to the learners using and/or experimenting with processes that feel right for them at that particular time. An example here might be an assertiveness training course, where following tuition and tutor controlled role play, learners are given the freedom and space to experiment with different behaviours without inhibition. Even here of course environmental parameters are still imposed by the 'staff', although the learner always has the ultimate recourse of exercising autonomy by leaving the learning event by the nearest door or window!

Less easy to categorize are such things as outward bound and secondments. Possibly where the nature of the learning is relatively predictable, but *how* you take it on board is more idiosyncratic, they would be located top left. As the content of learning becomes more open-ended, however, so these approaches would move toward top right; whereas a distance learning course would move toward bottom right. The tutorials, assignments, residential schools and examination system are unalterable, but which modules you choose to cover and how rapidly is more self-determined.

Examples of HRD

In this section we look in more detail in some of the examples of HRD discussed above. First, we ask what it is that makes off-the-job training effective, and then we describe a number of training and development activities that can be successfully incorporated into the job without leaving the workplace. Further examples of development activities are discussed in other chapters. e.g. we devote a whole chapter to career development (Chapter 6) and in Chapter 8 we focus on training and development associated with team-building.

Off-the-job training

Learning by experience, or on-the-job, is an attractive HRD approach for a number of reasons: observing others and 'being shown how' by bosses, peers and subordinates are straightforward, cost-effective and not too time consuming. Some managerial competencies cannot be taught or explained and can *only* be learnt by imitating good role models. Especially where such learning is accompanied by action, feedback and error-correction (as in the learning cycle, Figure 3.2), an individual can rapidly build up an elaborate and discriminating repertoire of skills, ideas and practices. However, learning by experience has two important limitations. First, the sheer pace and complexity, and the fragmentary nature of our daily work, often inhibits reflection on practice; we may pick poor role models, learn the wrong lessons and blame others (overlooking inappropriate aspects of our own behaviour). Second, experience can be very restricting, particularly when we make a job or functional move: expertise and knowledge that served us very well in the past may be inappropriate and outmoded for our new responsibilities.

For these reasons organizations may choose off-the-job learning activities, such as training courses, off-site seminars and workshops and college programmes for particular development needs. Here there is an opportunity to pause, reflect and think through issues, to learn from other perspectives and a wider array of experience, to learn and practise new skills in a relatively safe environment, and to encounter new concepts and ideas (perhaps derived from the organizational theory or from social psychology) that help to make sense of everyday work experience. But learning transfer is not without its problems either.

Take the case of off-the-job training programmes. It is not unusual that before their arrival employees' previous learning experience was the latter stages of formal education or attendance on a less-than-satisfactory training event elsewhere; and this will probably conjure up unhelpful memories. Unlearning may need to take place, both emotionally and educationally, before new learning can begin; in other words, successful development may be as much about individuals' will as their learning style. This initial willingness to learn will also be influenced by the diagnosis and selection process leading up to the training event. Is the individual's boss knowledgeable about and supportive of the training activity? Have personal learning needs been identified? Do the aims of the training course match these? Is the

Box 3.1   Equal Opportunities in the Fire Brigade

During a course of series of seminars held with station officers within the London Fire Brigade, designed to identify and when necessary modify attitudes towards the introduction of non-white and non-male firefighters, a pattern of resistance was evident. The station officers were markedly unsympathetic to the message of the seminars. They frequently denied the truth of the explanation of the nature and purpose of Equal Opportunities legislation, and refused to accept the validity of the arguments presented in the seminar. A severe case of refusal to learn.

Initially, the temptation was to explain this resistance in terms of the conservatism, the possible racism/sexism of the officers. It looked like that. But reflection suggested that an explanation solely in terms of the existence of a strong white male organizational culture was inadequate, not least because of its circularity: station officers' refusal to accept the messages of the EO seminar was the result of their organizational culture. The racism of the organizational culture was seen to be revealed in officers' resistance to the EO programme.

A more plausible explanation for station officers' refusal to learn was that the programme represented a significant reduction in the traditional authority of fire station personnel to intervene in recruitment/selection, and to allocate advantage in these processes to applicants from among their own family and friends. The application of the EO procedures immediately eliminated this informal labour market and replaced it with a formalized, open system. It was this aspect of the change as much as the openness towards previously barred categories of applicant which accounted for much of the resistance.

Also relevant was the fracturing of the management structure: station officers were based with the watch at the fire station. They worked shifts, spent their days and nights with the firefighters. When a call came, the station officers went with the crew of the engine. Inevitably they developed close relations with members of the watch, and shared a world, composed of danger and boredom, a world of jokes, memories and myths. The next layer of management were spatially and temporally separated: they worked office hours, were based in regional offices and were seen to inhabit a different and more bureaucratic world far from the realities of actual firefighting. A marked 'them' and 'us' perspective developed and it was in this context of insiders and outsiders, that resistance flourished. For it was 'their' policies which were seen to be represented in the EO policy, and to conflict with the traditional 'rights' of the ordinary firemen (Salaman and Butler, 1990, p. 189).

programme timely and relevant to current and future personal/job demands? If not, expectations and motivations to learn are likely to be low.

Equally important is the reinforcement of new concepts, skills and attitudes in the workplace after the training event is over; again, the trainee's line manager plays a key role here in debriefing and overseeing the implementation plans. The less uncoupled the workplace and off-the-job training activities, the better – which is why on-the-job learning has many inherent advantages. Finally, at a wider level, unless the prevailing value system from which the course participant comes, and returns to, actively supports and rewards the new skills and behaviours being taught, little personal learning is likely to be sustained or consolidated. See, for example, Box 3.1.

In addition to these training process issues, the content of the programme, course or workshop has to be of a high standard to engage the participants in real learning; here the onus is on the quality of the material (its perceived relevance, depth and presentation), the tutors (their credibility and ability to create a conducive learning environment) and the methods (variety and suitability to the subject matter and trainees' aptitudes and background). It is easy for even experienced trainers to misjudge these factors. Take the conventional assumption that individuals, especially managers, owing to the nature of their work, learn best through working on topics with immediate practical application (akin to the activist and pragmatist styles), where certainty and prescription are valued and dry theory is eschewed. With management consultants and trainers largely dependent on course session appraisal of their 'performance' for their future tenure, it is not surprising that perhaps unwitting collusion occurs, with training sessions containing lots of variety, short input sessions, powerful professional presentations, with plentiful activities and exercises explicitly linked to the learners' own experience. Paradoxically, while superficially active, such an approach using pre-dissected cases and examples, can lead to learner passivity and little internalization of learning.

Action learning and self-development groups

Reg Revans is the originator of 'Action Learning', which is recognized as a powerful means of capitalizing upon learning experiences. Mumford (1993, p. 32) usefully summarizes the approach as follows:

- Learning for managers should mean learning to take effective action. Acquiring information and becoming more capable in diagnosis or analysis have been overvalued in management learning.
- Learning to take action necessarily calls for actually taking action, not recommending action or undertaking analysis of someone else's problem.

- The best form of action for learning is work on a defined project of reality and significance to managers themselves. The project should include implementation as well as analysis and recommendation.
- While managers should have responsibility for their own achievements on their own projects, the learning process is a social one: managers learn best with and from each other.
- The social process is achieved and managed through regular meetings of managers to discuss their individual projects; the group is usually called a 'set'. The managers are 'comrades in adversity'.

Box 3.2   Self-development groups at Merseyside Citizen's Advice Bureau (CAB)

Alison, the training officer at Merseyside CAB, has been experimenting with self-development groups for managers for some time. On the whole they have proved very helpful; people value taking time out to discuss problems, and the trust that can be built up in a group enables honest discussion and for members to challenge each other's actions and behaviour. In Alison's opinion:

'As CAB managers are responsible for a caring advisory service, they can be prone to "burn-out"; self-development groups can prevent this by encouraging self-awareness, the recognition of personal strengths and weaknesses, and by minimizing destructive competition between colleagues. Managers who take part say there are pay-offs in increased confidence, and in developing their interpersonal skills, required in other aspects of their work, such as conducting joint progress reviews (a form of appraisal interviewing)'.

Another of Alison's objectives for the groups has been for them to bridge the gap between training and actual performance. For instance, how can managers be supported so that they can transfer their learning and new skills to their workplace, without the pace, pressure and isolation of their jobs preventing them from making changes? Alison believes self-development groups have a part to play in this.

The downside of the groups is that they can take a long time to set up and need time to develop (CABs have been running for over two years): they are intensive, requiring time and energy for facilitators and members, and can lead to dependency – the decision of when to leave a group entirely on its own is a difficult one (from Paton and Hooker, 1990, p. 47).

- The role of people providing help for members of the set is essentially and crucially different from that of the normal management teacher. Their role is not to teach (whether through lecture, case or simulation) but to help managers learn from exposure to problems and to each other. As Revans says, action learning attacks 'the inveterate hankering of the teacher to be the centre of the attention'.

From this 'pure' form of action learning the term has come to have a more popular usage, incorporating all kinds of self-development and self managed learning in organizations. The key features of such groups are that they are responsible for managing their own process (often with the help of a facilitator, at least in the early stages), they usually have their own agenda (perhaps to address specific problems brought by individuals for analysis or to support members using other learning methods to pursue particular goals), and they do not necessarily rely on organizational support – indeed they are often formed precisely because the organization is not formally supporting personal development. As can be seen from Box 3.2, there are pitfalls with such groups, but when they work well, they can be extremely effective in designing problem-solving and group working skills, building bridges between departments and achieving practical outcomes – the original essence of action learning.

Mentors

A mentor is someone who guides another individual through important career and life events, encouraging and supporting them, usually because, as mentors, they possess greater experience, knowledge and skill. Mentors are valued specifically for their achievements, but even more crucially because they have already trodden the path ahead, thus making them invaluable as guides or role models to provide advice and support and generally to share their own management experience. However, a mentor is *not* there to give formal instruction, to try to influence a person's career path unnecessarily, to drag them into company politics or to delegate any of their work to those they are mentoring.

What might be looked for in a mentor? Successful mentors are usually about seven to ten years older (or more) than the person they are mentoring. This age gap helps because a mentor will have had sufficient time to develop his or her experience and reflect on it for others' benefit. They should be able to show interest in the development of others and be good communicators. They should not have too much to do with the work of those they are mentoring: bosses are not usually mentors. It is also crucial that they have some time available to invest in the relationship and preferably have undertaken management development themselves. They should be of a higher status, but not so remote that it is difficult to gain access to them. It does not matter if they are generalists or specialists by training, as long as they feel confident in referring on to one of their colleagues on the occasions when they themselves cannot help.

What does a mentor gain from the relationship? People who act as mentors often find that it sharpens their own thinking, increases their status in the eyes of their peers and generally satisfies their desire to share their knowledge and experience. These factors themselves can be very rewarding.

When and how does mentoring take place? This will be negotiated between the two individuals concerned, but about one to one and a half hours once a month is not untypical. These occasions can be very informal, such as a discussion over lunch, and may only consist of generalities for a while, until both parties grow used to one another. The mentors' role is to give feedback and to keep those they are mentoring informed of relevant developments in the organization. In general:

- meeting with a mentor will encourage individuals to collect their thoughts and talk them through with someone else, which in turn helps to give structure and support to their learning;
- mentors will not necessarily have all the answers, but by questioning and challenging they can help to clarify the thinking of those they are mentoring;
- therefore, being able to listen well and to probe is an important skill for mentors;
- mentors are not necessarily there to advise, although this may happen on occasions.

Mentoring does raise some equal-opportunity issues. For instance, the relationship should not be used as a meal ticket to which others do not have access. However, used positively and fairly, it can enhance opportunities for people who may be at a disadvantage. For a woman in a predominantly male environment or individuals who feel isolated because they are from another minority group (disabled, ethnic, etc.) finding a suitable mentor may be useful in overcoming problems. However, for a woman choosing a male mentor (or *vice versa*) there are dangers in attracting gossip and innuendo. It might be wise to make the relationship common knowledge, and, as a precaution, to meet in public places. We return to the issue of mentoring in Chapter 6.

Computer-mediated training

One final type of training deserving special mention is that delivered or mediated by computer. Advances in this field are progressing rapidly and it is important for organizations to be aware of the educational merits and ramifications of various training media to avoid being driven by technological solutions alone. Furthermore, whether a company develops its own in-house capability in this area or commissions external providers, the decision to purchase course-ware and/or hardware is a strategic one, bound up not only with the philosophy of the training department concerned but also organiza-tion-wide computing policy and longer-term corporate intentions.

Different educational media imply different degrees of learner autonomy and different teaching strategies. So, for instance, pro-grammed learning, CBT, expert systems and interactive video course-ware all use a strategy whereby the knowledge to be learned is held within the computer and should be taught to the learner – entirely appropriate where the purpose is to instruct in basic data and information but less suited to the training of something like appraisal skills, which are situation specific; here second generation interactive video, simulations and intelligent knowledge based tutoring systems come into their own (Topham, 1992).

Educational courseware is only as effective for the job in hand as the teaching strategy it employs, *whether this be technologically driven or not.* Consider technical engineers, who are required to perform quick, accurate fault diagnosis on sophisticated equipment. A text-based programme is going to help with recognition and recall of important components and rules but fall far short of giving them hands-on confidence. The opportunity to problem-solve by the use of actual equipment in a simulated environment would be ideal, but extremely expensive to set up and/or limited to a central location. A middle way may be to use computer-based training (CBT) to provide student-centred learning at the pace, level and location appropriate to each individual.

This is a solution that British Telecom adopted some time ago at their technical training college. It was found that CBT reduced the length of many engineering courses (e.g. diesel engine appreciation, system X) by about one-half and was both an effective and acceptable means of delivery in the eyes of students. Based on a 32-terminal system costing £190,000 it was also calculated that a saving of £515,000 was made over a five-year period compared with conventional tuition. A subsequent evaluation of CBT courses delivered locally (rather than centrally at the college) demonstrated similar time savings and even greater cost savings.

Given some of the attractions of computer-mediated training, how does an organization go about choosing which technologies and which programmes to use? A number of different factors should be considered:

- *Pace.* The vast storage capacity of computers gives CBT and interactive video the opportunity to diagnose the students' level of mastery before they start (and when they finish!) and the capability of providing varying learning sequences through branching. This potential for individualizing instruction may be particularly bene-ficial when the trainer/designer anticipates a wide range of ability and prior knowledge among his or her student population.

- *Multi-audience.* A further feature of interactive video, which is not afforded by other media, is the capacity to author a training programme in such a way that several different user audiences can take a pathway through the learning package that is pertinent to their needs, while the core video material on the last disc remains common. Thus, for instance, new product information on video disk could accompany courseware on the floppy disk programmed for sales managers (overview), field salesforce (more detail on features, market segment, etc.), maintenance and sales support officers (deeper technical knowledge) and customers (basic product information).
- *Learning styles.* As we discussed earlier, students differ in the way in which they learn. Some are relatively independent in their learning and can therefore be given considerable scope to explore resources on their own, whereas others need the reassurance of a highly structured learning environment. Some learn best by doing rather than reflecting on what they have discovered, others by watching an expert and then having a go themselves. Care needs to be taken in selecting not only the material, but also the environment which is most conducive to learning for individuals.

A final factor in media selection, and whether to use external or develop in-house capability is that of organizational resources to support the training programme. Two of the key issues are:

1 *Skills.* Training design for distance learning courseware requires some of the same skills employed on conventional course design but also some new ones, such as authoring, programming, scripting, video shooting, on-line editing, disk pressing and so on. Even if some of these are 'bought in', the crucial skills of commercial negotiation, contract setting and licensing come to the fore. Whether the design and production team are in-house or provided by external consultants, or a mixture of the two, strong project management abilities are also essential. Thus the hiring or developing of these types of skills enter the judgement equation.

2 *Cost.* It is easier to identify the factors that enter the equation than it is to calculate the precise cost of distance learning production and delivery. Start-up costs include both people (the range of skills mentioned above) and initial investment in delivery hardware. Ongoing costs include course production, delivery and updating. These, in turn, depend on the anticipated shelf life of the programme, the degree to which existing material is used, the number of sub-audiences targeted for training, the volatility of course materials and so on, and not least the ratio of academic work hours per student hour of work generated. While it is estimated that it takes between two and ten working hours to generate one hour of conventional lecture material, the equivalent figure for broadcast television is 100 hours, CBT 200 hours and interactive video a conservative 300 hours.

Summary

While Chapter 2 dealt with the formulation and planning of HRD strategies from an organizational perspective, in this chapter we have considered the design and delivery of HRD from an individual and workgroup point of view. We have emphasized the importance of thinking about an organization's cultural 'models' of HRD together with any assumptions about what constitutes effective learning. This led us to a discussion about learner autonomy and how questions concerning both the content and process of training delivery can lead to a more informed choice of development activity. Finally we highlighted a number of off-the-job HRD approaches. Whichever is chosen, the following design principles apply.

- Be clear about what *outcomes* are expected from the training, at what level, for which groups, and over what timespan.
- Be sure the *content* is informed by appropriate techniques for discovering training needs.
- Be sure the *methods* and approaches to learning adopted suit the organization's norms about what constitutes good management and effective learning.
- Do not assume all trainees *learn* in the same way, at the same pace, or that they will respond uniformly to different types of learning event.
- Ensure, as far as it is possible, that there is a *readiness* to learn among trainees and a *willingness* to support the learning transfer by their line managers.
- Avoid being locked into one particular delivery medium, perhaps missing the benefits of other approaches and combinations of media.

In the next chapter we look at ways in which we can assess our current and future human resource needs and how this assessment links with training and development.

References

Anderson, A. H. (1993) *Successful training practice*. Blackwell Publishers, Oxford.

Ashton, D. Easterby-Smith, M. and Irvine, C. (1975) *Management development: theory and practice*. MCB, Bradford.

Burgoyne, J. (1988) Management development for the individual and the organization. *Personnel Management*, June, pp. 40–4.

Honey, P. and Mumford, A. *Manual of learning styles* (3rd edition). Honey, Maidenhead.

Kolb, D. (1984) *Experiential Learning*. Prentice Hall, Englewood Cliffs, NJ.

Mumford, A. (1993) *Management development, strategies for action*. (2nd edition). IPM, London.

Paton, R. and Hooker, C. (1990) *Developing managers in voluntary organizations, a Handbook*. Open University and Employment Department, Sheffield.

Salaman, G. and Butler, J. (1990) Why managers won't learn. *Management Education and Development*, 21,3, pp. 183–91.

Topham, P. (1992) A review of computer mediated development B884 Human Resource Strategies, Supplementary Readings No.2, pp. 64–8, Open University.

4 Auditing human resources

Introduction

In the earlier chapters in this book we were concerned with the development of a strategy for managing human resources. In this, and other, chapters we shall be discussing ways in which you as a line manager can implement human resource plans in particular areas of your job. The first of these is in analysing the skills and abilities of your existing and potential staff in relation to the jobs currently being performed and future organizational requirements.

Skill audits are commonly carried out as part of job analysis, but this only provides information on which essential skills are required to perform a particular task or set of activities. It fails to provide information on additional skills that the jobholder may possess and may be of use to the organization in other jobs or in relation to changes in work practice; and, unless skill audits are regularly used as part of performance review, additional skills that may be gained through work experience, training or personal development will be unrecognized and individual potential will not be achieved.

The analytical and diagnostic techniques reviewed in this chapter should be part of the line manager's inventory, so that they can be combined to produce a picture of existing skills and experience against which to measure forecast skill requirements. This information can be used for selection, redeployment and promotion decisions as well as for the identification of training and development needs as part of performance management.

Auditing existing resources

We have emphasized the need to increase human resource retention rates and to improve the quality of human resource development. Unless we have accurate knowledge about the skills and potential of existing staff, we cannot devise effective human resource plans that reflect these skills.

Auditing the skills of existing staff takes time and calls for a number of simple research techniques which are designed to elicit the required information. Ideally all the necessary information should already be contained in personnel records but these are often inadequate and out-of-date; usually they refer to details gleaned in the selection and appointment process, so they are only as good as the selection interview and accompanying paperwork. They may carry information about jobs held in the organization but not about the skills needed to perform those jobs. Not all your staff may be easily accessible or even well known to you; they may work on different sites or be taking a career break or secondment. There is also the problem of the nature of the data you require since it needs to relate to future developments and not just to present organizational requirements. The starting point for any audit therefore has to be the human resource plan in relation to organizational policy and strategy.

Some simple data should already be available such as the gender, age and length of service in the organization of individual employees. An analysis of staff by age is useful in identifying, for example, a large number of people approaching retirement, which will create promotion and appointment opportunities, or too many staff in the middle-age range, creating a block to promotion prospects for younger staff. Analysis by gender will probably demonstrate that there is an imbalance between women and men in senior positions, which is important in the consideration of equal opportunity policies in practice. Personnel records should also contain details of existing educational or vocational qualifications – although these are not always kept up-to-date and frequently omit any reference to any personal development and training that individuals may have undertaken at their own expense and in their own time. It is naive to rely on outdated qualifications as a measure of current ability and skill or on qualifications which rely solely on attendance at courses rather than on any assessment. Even traditional assessment is dubious; the ability to pass an unseen, written examination, for example, can be argued as demonstrating the individual's capacity for memorizing data and presenting them in an acceptable manner within a constrained timespan rather than as evidence of ability in the topic area. 'Experience', too, should not be relied upon; too many job rotation schemes only provide a taste of other operations in the organization rather than true experience. A golden rule of the human resource audit is never to accept data at face value.

The kinds of information that you will need on your staff include current data on:

● relevant training and development already undertaken or in progress;
● occupational experience;
● associated skills and abilities.

This sort of information can be collected through a questionnaire initially but will require one-to-one interviews with every member of your staff and/or the use of an assessment centre in order to ensure the data are accurate. Assessment centre techniques are costly, unless you are using them for a large number of people in one particular category, such as managerial staff, and require professional administration; interviews, while time-consuming, can be combined with annual appraisals. The questionnaire can be designed in such a way that it will guide the interview and reduce the amount of time required; where feasible, as much information as possible should be gathered in a way that enables it to be computerized, otherwise analysis and presentation of data will extend the timescale even further. One way of doing this is to list relevant skills and abilities so that individuals only have to indicate which of these they feel they possess to a high, medium or low extent, and to verify these with each person or their supervisor or line manager.

Core skills

We often describe jobs and their content by the skills required to perform tasks adequately; at the selection and appointment point we match candidates against this job-specific range of skills, usually ignoring other skills the person may possess. There are a range of definitions and lists of core skills that are deemed to underpin competent performance at different levels.

Box 4.1   Core skills

The conscious acquisition of core skills by individuals will enhance their occupational competence and normally have immediate benefits for performance in employment. Moreover, it will provide a stronger foundation for transfer and progression, and the potential to cope with future changes in technology and work practices (Jessup, 1991).

The main core skills common to most lists are:

- communication;
- problem-solving;
- interpersonal skills;
- personal skills;
- numeracy.

Other lists include information technology and a modern foreign language, both of which are likely to increase in importance in the twenty-first century. Both the National Council for Vocational Qualifications (NCVQ) and its Scottish equivalent, SCOTVEC, have broken down these core skills into elements at the different levels of competence, which, in NCVQ terms, are:

Level 1:   routine, predictable or foundation activities.
Level 2:   more   demanding   activities   with   more   individual responsibility.

Level 3: skilled activities in complex and non-routine situations, and perhaps supervising others.

Level 4: competence in a broad range of complex, technical or professional work performed in a wide variety of contexts and with a substantial degree of personal responsibility and autonomy. Responsibility for the work of others and the allocation of resources is often present.

Level 5: competence in the application of a significant range of fundamental principles and complex techniques across a wide and often unpredictable variety of contexts. Very substantial personal autonomy and often significant responsibility for the work of others and for the allocation of substantial resources feature strongly, as do personal accountabilities for analysis and diagnosis, design, planning, execution and evaluation.

These levels identified by NCVQ are not intended to be rigid but to provide a framework within which jobs can be categorized rather than by job title or grading systems. Generally speaking, you would expect a supervisor to be at Level 3, a first line manager at Level 4 and a middle to senior manager at Level 5. Levels 1 and 2 are intended to relate to manual and semi-skilled workers respectively.

The full specifications of core skills at each level are available from NCVQ. They are not intended to replace job-specific skills but to complement them, so that you have some idea of the all-round competence of individuals and can provide training and development activities to help them acquire the necessary core skills as well as help them to achieve their potential.

Self-development activity

How useful do you find the idea of 'core skills'? Could you describe your own job in terms of the common core skills and where would you place your job in relation to the Levels 1–5 specified by NCVQ?

The concept of core skills on its own is not enough. It is a useful starting point from which to determine the more precise *level* of skill that would be required in a particular job. For example, there are many different ways of using the skill of 'communication'; in person face-to-face, in writing, by electronic mail or satellite, in large presentations, visually or verbally and so on. Some jobs will require a high level of communication that is used a great deal; others will require different levels and frequency rates.

Categorizing human resources

There are difficulties with placing people in simplistic occupational categories when auditing existing human resources. The most common form of categorization is by job title, but we know the title itself is rarely descriptive of the requirements for the job; and, as a human resource manager, you are concerned with people's potential use rather than with their current position. Broader categories are preferable to narrow ones, and may be related to the organization's operations in terms such as 'marketing', 'finance', 'primary health care', 'auditing' and so on. Using these broad categories and an assessment of job-related experience (both past and present), you can begin to build up a profile of current and available experience as shown in Figure 4.1. Similar profiles can be built up to indicate individuals' job-related and core skills – skills inventories.

Figure 4.1 shows the amount of experience acquired by staff in a fictional company. Not all that experience is currently being used, but the chart gives an indication of how much experience would be available if the company refocused its activities. There would be no problem if this refocusing was used to increase the amount of engineering work being carried out, although those people not currently using this experience would have to be drawn from other areas which might leave such areas depleted. On the other hand, if the company decided to increase its computing activities, it is obvious that

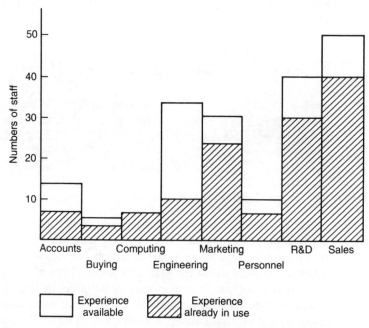

Figure 4.1 *Experience of staff by occupational category (from Pearson, 1991)*

there are no existing staff with this experience; this would call for retraining or recruitment.

It is important when categorizing staff to realize that this should not be a 'once-and-for-all' statement. Experience, training and personal development should all be taking place on a continuing basis, and charts such as that shown in Figure 4.1 could look quite different in eighteen months' time.

Planning for the future

Analysing your existing human resources is the basis for future planning. There are a number of ways in which you can estimate future resource needs in terms of people and skills but none of them is foolproof! Completing an audit of current resources, however, means that you have already moved some way towards one of these methods – supply forecasting.

Supply forecasting

Your audit should not only cover existing staff, skills and an assessment of potential but should also identify potential losses through wastage, turnover, retirement and internal movements due to promotion. Supply forecasting relies not only on the accuracy of this information but also on an evaluation of the effect of any planned (or unplanned but likely) changes in work practices due, for example, to downsizing, new technology or increased organizational flexibility in working hours. Other factors might include changes in policy towards overtime-working and/or retirement age, shift-working and increases in the length of holidays.

This form of forecasting is based on the *supply* of human resources available, both internally and externally, to fill posts that become vacant through wastage, staff turnover, promotion or retirement. Internal candidates might include people identified as high flyers or with potential for promotion, and they should already have been identified at the audit stage. Obviously, unless the organization is in the process of downsizing, their movement will leave gaps lower down, and, with changing organizational demands, there may not be enough existing staff suitable for promotion, despite training and development opportunities. There is a need therefore to analyse the labour market at all levels – local, national and international.

The current labour market at the local level will depend on a number of factors, such as any changes in local competition in your organization's sector, changes in training and educational provision or changes in house prices or interest rates. For example, with the change to university status and funding, providers of higher and further education are becoming more customer-oriented in the courses they offer; this may work in your favour or against it, depending on your particular skill needs.

At the national and international levels you need to be aware of national training schemes, which may or may not produce potential employees, and changes in the legal regulations concerning employment of foreign nationals or immigrants or those that govern health and safety, sex or race discrimination and pay. In particular, changes in employment law as a result of European Union directives are increasing substantially.

Demand forecasting

Another form of forecasting is based on the operations of the organization and the future quantity and quality of the human resources it will require to carry these out. Expected changes in these operations should be detailed in the organization's strategy. Armstrong describes four basic methods of demand forecasting:

- managerial judgement;
- ratio–trend analysis;
- work-study techniques;
- human resource modelling.

We outline these methods below, but you should explore them in more depth if you are considering carrying out any of the more complex techniques.

Managerial judgement

This method relies on all the managers in the organization understanding that they are responsible for human resource management and being able to contribute knowledgeably to forecasting their long-term departmental needs accurately, so that, at an organizational level, proposals from line managers can be considered by senior management. Senior management may provide guidelines that indicate broad assumptions about future work practices and operational activities. The information required by senior management would include information from the human resource audit on forecast staff turnover and internal movement, and an estimate of when replacement staff would be required. Naturally this assumes that there are budget constraints, and it may be necessary to offer some creative ideas for overcoming a shortfall in human resource requirements.

Ratio-trend analysis

Such analysis looks at the relations between employees and whatever activities the organization carries out, with a view to improving performance in the future. So, for example, if an organization currently employs 100 people to produce 10,000 items or to provide a service to 10,000 clients in 1993, and this figure rises to 11,000 in 1994 and 12,000 in 1995, a clear (if crude) upward trend can be seen in the ratio of employees to productivity. It is unlikely that an upward trend can continue indefinitely, and there may well be intervening factors which create it, such as improved technology or job design. A reverse trend would of course be a cause for concern and, again, a reason should be sought; it may be due to changes in trade union agreements or working hours rather than a drop in individual productivity levels.

Work-study techniques

These techniques are related to the length of time it takes an average employee to carry out a particular activity or set of activities, and is more suited to operations where it is possible to calculate the length of time the operation will take and the amount of labour required. In a manufacturing context it is relatively easy to calculate fairly accurately the cost of hours of labour in relation to one unit of production, and to compute from this the total planned hours for a period of, for example

---

Box 4.2   Line managers as end-users

Many line managers distrust computerized personnel information systems because they are unaware, or unsure, of what data these contain or what use could be made of the data. In one company where line managers had a poor opinion of such a system an annual human resource report was sent to them all. It included analyses of employees by grade, length of service, age, etc. It reported on career paths and issues of available skills; in fact it was a comprehensive summary of the major human resource data items held by the computerized personnel information system. The managers made little use, if any, of the information contained in the report.

In fact the company had recently restructured, making the former personnel department into a devolved profit centre providing a service to line managers. Unfortunately, the department had not considered asking line managers what information and support they wanted in order to manage their human resources more effectively; instead, it had asked what use managers could make of the existing computerized system. The existing system held an adequate record of personal details about individuals but this was not organized in such a way that it could readily provide information for line management activities such as recruitment, appraisal, absence control, discipline, training and development, promotions and transfers and so on.

one month or one year. In this calculation, however, allowance needs to be made for time off for sickness, annual leave and for overtime.

Human resource modelling

Such modelling creates a representation – a model – of a real-life situation, usually on a computer, since this makes the movement of data simpler. Computerized personnel information systems can be transformed into human resource models, since computers (should) contain up-to-date, comprehensive data on every employee. Their application for human resource modelling, however, depends on the way in which the system has been designed.

Job analysis

Job analysis doesn't just happen, it has to be planned, and if you are unfamiliar with the technique or your organization is not in the habit of carrying out such analyses, the planning stage is likely to be extended. You may have to submit a plan for job analysis to senior management and discuss your ideas with jobholders, line managers and supervisors in order to get their co-operation. If you have not undertaken any form of job analysis before, it is wise to test out whichever methods you intend to use on a small sample.

The purpose of job analysis is to determine why a particular job exists and the skills and abilities the jobholder should possess in order to perform the job to a specific standard. It can provide a basis for job evaluation if there is a need to compare different jobs for the purpose of differential payment schemes, and for job descriptions and employee specifications as part of the recruitment and selection process.

Dawson (1992) has provided a useful framework for analysing a job in terms of its basic requirements. It offers a basis from which to analyse any job and compare it with others. She identifies the following basic elements of any job as follows:

- *Task*: the objective(s) of activity(ies) – what is the jobholder expected to *do* in the performance of the job?
- *Method*: how is the jobholder expected to carry out the job – what is the nature of the activities required?
- *Technology*: what plant, machinery or equipment is the jobholder expected to operate in the performance of the job?
- *Variety*: how many distinctly different activities are there in the job?
- *Sequencing*: in what order is the jobholder expected to carry out these activities, and does he or she have any freedom in determining the sequence?
- *Timing*: what is the optimum time in which the jobholder should be able to complete the sequence of activities?

- *Pace*: to what extent is the pace of work predetermined?
- *Quality*: are quality standards specified or not?
- *Specialization*: to what degree is the job specialized?
- *Interdependence*: to what extent is the job related to the jobs of others?
- *Partialness*: to what extent is the job related to completion of a product or service?
- *Performance*: how is performance of the job measured?
- *Monitoring*: who decides on action in the light of information about job performance?
- *Accountability*: what happens as a result of poor/good performance?

Table 4.1 gives examples of these basic job elements in three jobs – an accounts clerk, a maintenance engineer and a software engineer.

Table 4.1 Examples of basic job elements in three jobs

Requirement	Accounts clerk	Maintenance engineer	Software engineer
Task	Record financial transactions	Maintain electrical equipment in good order	Write programmes for in-house users
Method	Writing, reading and filing	Diagnosing and rectifying faults	Thinking and writing
Technology	Typewriter and computer	Craft tools	Computer
Variety	Very little	Moderate	Moderate
Sequence	Predetermined	Some leeway	Great leeway
Timing	Five minutes	5–200 minutes	Open
Pace	Set by input	Self-determined but output monitored	Self-determined but output monitored
Quality	Specified	Specified	Open
Specialization	Medium	Medium	Low
Interdependence	High	Medium	Low
Partialness	Very small part	Whole part	Whole part
Performance	Number of records made; accuracy of records	Supervisor's/user's assessment	Long-term success of programmes
Monitoring	Supervisor	Supervisor	Self/manager
Accountability	Supervisor intervenes	Supervisor intervenes	Self/manager intervenes

Dawson 1992, p. 18

Self-development activity

Try out this framework for yourself. When using it initially, it is easier to analyse a relatively simple job and work up to more complex ones such as your own. Comparing different jobs via the same framework can enable you to pinpoint differences that may affect individual job satisfaction and intrinsic motivation.

You might like to add to this framework developmental and environmental factors related to the job. For example, what opportunities does it provide for individual promotion and career development and the opportunity to acquire new skills? In the environmental sense are there any factors related to working conditions, health and safety regulations or unsociable hours that may affect performance of the job?

Collecting data for job analysis

Analysing any job means asking the right questions, which can be done in a variety of ways. No single method is foolproof and you should aim to use a combination of techniques to verify your information. Your analysis should include an evaluation of the skills required to perform the job. Some of the methods used to collect data include the following.

Interviews

You may conduct interviews with jobholders and their supervisors; you may also like to interview other jobholders whose jobs are closely related. This method is time-consuming and, unless you are well organized, the data can be confusing and difficult to categorize. The answers you receive will be largely determined by the questions you choose to ask and these should reflect the framework you are using. For example, in relation to Dawson's framework in Table 4.1, you would expect to ask questions such as:

● what is the objective of the job you do?
● how do you carry out the activities which make up your job?
● what kind of equipment do you use in your job?
● can you break down your job into a series of activities or tasks?

The interview with the jobholder in particular will provide you with a rich source of data, but this needs to be checked with other people, such as the jobholder's supervisor. This may be the way the jobholder performs the task but is it the way in which it is intended to be performed? A mismatch between the jobholder's perception and that of the supervisor is likely to raise some interesting issues.

Questionnaires

Questionnaires – answered by the jobholder and verified by the person's supervisor. These can be designed to relate to your job analysis framework and save time in interviewing if a large number of jobs are being analysed. Verification should highlight issues you might like to follow up, perhaps with an interview at a later stage. Questionnaires benefit greatly from piloting on a small sample first since it is very easy to ask ambiguous or leading questions. They can also be designed as checklists, which cut down the time people need to spend in filling them in.

Observation

Observation – studying the jobholder actually performing the job. This method is limited in that it is usually only appropriate for relatively simple manual tasks that can be easily observed and it is less suitable for jobs that incorporate a number of interrelated tasks or jobs requiring mental activity.

Self-report job diaries

Such job diaries are records kept by jobholders about the activities and tasks they perform over a given period such as a day, a week or longer, depending on the variety of tasks they do. This method is suitable for complex jobs, such as managerial ones where there is a wide variety of activities, but of course it is highly subjective. No jobholder is likely to admit to unproductive activities in such a report, for example, and may even invent tasks to make the job look more demanding than it really is.

More complex and technical methods of collecting data for job analysis include critical incident technique, use of the repertory grid and hierarchical task analysis. All these are effective but they require some training in their operation.

Benefits and pitfalls of job analysis

Jobholders rarely appreciate the benefits of job analysis and see it as a convenience for managers, but it has advantages for both. For jobholders there is the benefit of having a clear idea of the responsibilities of the job – not always clarified in other ways. Job analysis can provide the basis for an argument for job redesign, improved working conditions or pay increases, and can provide information for use at appraisal or in individual objective-setting. For managers it provides data for job descriptions and employee specifications when recruiting new staff; it is a basis for performance

---

Box 4.3   The job analyst's job

The job analyst (or personnel analyst): collects, analyses and prepares occupational information to facilitate personnel, administration and management functions of the organization; consults with management to determine data and compiles distribution reports, organization and flow charts, and other background information required for the study. Observes jobs and interviews workers and supervisory personnel to determine job and worker requirements. Analyses occupational data, such as physical, mental and training requirements of jobs and workers and develops written summaries, such as job descriptions, job specifications and lines of career movement. Utilizes developed occupational data to evaluate or improve methods and techniques for recruiting, selecting, promoting, evaluating and training workers, and administration of related personnel programmes. May specialize in classifying positions according to regulated guidelines to meet job classification requirements of civil service system and be known as Position Classifier (*Dictionary of Occupational Titles*, p. 111).

---

assessment and appraisal and for job evaluation; and it can highlight training and development needs.

The jobholder's perception, however, emphasizes one of the major pitfalls of job analysis – employee resistance and suspicion. This is a natural reaction where no attempt has been made to explain the purpose of the analysis to the people whose jobs are being examined, and may be avoided by explaining why it is being carried out and seeking co-operation. The choice of the analyst is also important; he or she has to have some knowledge of the organization and the types of job as well as interpersonal skills in interviewing and establishing rapport with jobholders. An external analyst has the advantage of relevant objectivity, but, in the eyes of the jobholders, he or she can be seen as being brought in to achieve economies and even job losses. Box 4.3 outlines the responsibilities of a job analyst.

As you can see, analysing jobs is not something you take on during a wet Friday afternoon!

Skill analysis

Traditional job analysis is no longer adequate for human resource managers; they need to know how people will develop in their jobs and, where necessary, incorporate development activities into job design. By analysing the skills required in each job, managers have a basis for devising appropriate training and development programmes. Armstrong (1991) suggests the following techniques for skill analysis:

- *Job breakdown* – analysing the job into discrete operations, processes or tasks that can be broken down into manageable parts for training purposes.
- *Manual skill analysis* – developed from work study and used for jobs with a high degree of manual dexterity, such as assembly-line work, this technique observes and records the hand, finger and other body movements of experienced manual workers. The analysis is used as a basis for training new operators.
- *Task analysis* – particularly relevant to clerical jobs, this technique analyses the individual tasks in the job, the relevant levels of significance of each task to performance of the whole job and the level of skill or knowledge each task requires. This data is used to determine training techniques required for performance of the job.
- *Job learning analysis* – focuses on the inputs and process of the job rather than its content by analysing skills that contribute to its satisfactory performance. These skills include physical skills, complex sequences of activity, non-verbal information, memorizing, prioritizing, looking ahead, diagnosing, interpreting and adapting.
- *Faults analysis* – concentrates on the common faults made by jobholders in performance of the job, resulting in a fault specification that is used to train new jobholders by making them aware of faults that can occur, how to deal with them and how to prevent them.
- *Competence analysis* – related to the concept of competence as defined by the UK Management Charter Initiative and NCVQ, this technique for analysing managerial jobs focuses on what managers do, what situations they face and what distinguishes people at different levels of competence in terms of their behaviours. The National Standards for Managers at NCVQ Levels 4 and 5 provide very detailed analyses of competence at each level, broken down into units of competence, elements and performance criteria. An example of this is given in Chapter 9 (Box 9.6).

Defining team and organizational requirements

If you are able to undertake some kind of job and skill analysis of existing employees and relate this to the developing needs of the organization, you are likely to discover a considerable gap between current and expected skill requirements. You may also become rather discouraged at the prospect of all the analyses you have to undertake to reach this point, especially if you are working in a small or medium-sized enterprise where there are no resources for carrying out such investigations. Many small businesses contract out such work to specialist consultants, which is one option; it may be an expensive outlay, but can you afford *not* to do it? There are considerable advantages in working in the smaller organization in that you have much more control over what you do and are less constrained by bureaucratic hierarchies; you also have less jobs to analyse and probably know your staff better than managers in larger companies.

In Chapter 8 we discuss effective teambuilding and teamworking, and this is an area you need to consider when you are looking at the gaps in your organization's skill needs. If the organization is already committed to teamworking, there is less of a problem, since you are probably already aware of the kinds of skill that are necessary in this context. Organizations that rarely use teams are likely to experience difficulty in moving to this type of structure, because it calls for a culture change. In organizations relying on specialists, having little interdependence on others and valuing individual creativity highly, teamworking is likely to lead to resistance and perceived loss of autonomy.

Box 4.4   Creating a team that breaks apart

An insurance company decided to restructure its traditionally anarchistic and individualistic culture into a hierarchical series of self-managed teams. Each team contained a number of accounts, the more prestigious being handled by the Senior Team, the medium accounts by the Junior Team and the Small Accounts Team handling the remainder. Each team had appropriate administrative support and was self-governing with an elected head.

The restructuring was aimed at creating a cohesive team effort in preference to individualism and competition; it was hoped that the new structure would provide opportunities for promotion and facilitate mentoring. After several months, coordination within the organization had improved as had the uniformity of procedures; people were clearer about their responsibilities and customer service was more consistent. However, there were constant intra-group conflicts over priorities and morale was low; people felt they had lost control over their work and individual performance was suffering (Keating, 1993).

Using job analysis for recruitment, selection and promotion decisions

In the next chapter you will be looking at selection methods that can help you to make the best choice of staff in a competitive situation. Detailed job analysis can inform the recruitment and selection process for new staff and the promotion of existing staff by outlining the skill and aptitude requirements of the job. It is the basis for any job description and employee specification – as important in promotion as in recruitment.

The job description should 'describe' the job in terms of its content, relation to other jobs, accountability, environment and conditions of employment. Its purpose is threefold; it describes the job to potential recruits or candidates for promotion; it is a guide to new jobholders about what they are supposed to do in the job; and it provides comparison between what jobholders are supposed to do and what they actually do.

The employee specification, derived from the job description, should contain the minimum acceptable skill and educational requirements that someone must possess to perform the job successfully; it should be closely scrutinized to ensure it does not exclude minority groups, such as the physically disabled or ethnic minorities. A biased employee specification can create serious problems if candidates claim that they were discriminated against in selection.

It is often too easy to treat promotion as a right rather than as another form of selection unless there are a number of candidates of equal worth in the running. Length of experience in an existing job, or series of jobs, should not alone determine promotion; it is the quality rather than the quantity of experience that matters, and the extent to which an individual has assimilated that experience and is ready to take on extra or different responsibilities. Matching candidates for promotion against the job description and employee specification for a promoted post should be normal practice.

Candidates for promotion may often lack essential skills which are necessary in the promoted post and this is where your human resource development plan should identify training and development needs.

Diagnosing individual training and development needs

Skill analysis as part of job analysis should not be confused with the diagnostic process of *skill assessment*, which is used for assessing an employee's competence in certain skill areas for the purpose of general self-development.

Formal techniques

An example of how one company uses skill assessment for its first-level managers is given below. It is based on three premises: first, that the appropriate management skills *can* be developed, and that they are not necessarily hereditary; second, that the most effective development takes place on the job , with regular practice and feedback from the line managers; and, third, that the salient skills are those used by successful first-level operations managers already in post. One of the nine skill dimensions identified by the company as important for its managers is *leadership*, as defined below:

- directs and coordinates the activities of others;
- delegates authority and responsibility to others and holds them accountable;
- sets examples for others; provides feedback to others on their performance.

Using this dimension as an example, we can follow the process of skill assessment step by step:

Step 1 *Observation.* We must generate a list of job situations that are likely to yield observable behaviour in the skill areas desired (see Table 4.2). In this case the focus is on situations where leadership skills could potentially be displayed.

Step 2 *Rating by manager.* Each skill dimension is broken down into a number of associated job behaviours that can be observed as employees perform their jobs. Each is rated according to how much development is needed (rather than as a subjective assessment of the jobholder's current job performance, as is the case in skills analysis), as exemplified in Table 4.3.

Step 3 *Self-rating.* Employees complete the same skills assessment form about themselves. The individual will only feel free to be honest if assured that this is not part of a performance appraisal or management selection process.

Step 4 *Skills diagnosis discussion.* At this point the manager and the staff member discuss the respective assessments, seek agreement on and prioritize training needs, and start to plan a skill development programme.

Step 5 *Development projects.* On-the-job assignments may be suggested, to provide the opportunity to practise and receive feedback on identified skill areas. These target-specific skills are short term. Other developmental projects may be longer in duration (two to three months) and address several of the nine skills. Table 4.4 is an example of a developmental project for leadership skills.

Step 6 *Monitor and evaluate.* Throughout the development plan, the individual should schedule progress meetings with his or her manager to discuss problems and possible corrective actions. The final evaluation will focus on how well the individuals implemented the plan, what skills they demonstrated and what continuing development is required.

The particular sales and marketing company identified nine skills, deriving them from extensive interviews across the organization; these are similar to the skills assessed in the company's succession planning and other management validation processes. This approach is similar

Table 4.2 Sales manager skills assessment: observation opportunities

Skill areas:

Situations	Communication (oral and written)	Control and follow-up	Decisiveness	Flexibility	Interpersonal	Judgement	Leadership	Organizing and planning	Perception and analysis
Staff/team meeting	×			×	×		×	×	
Plan and review	×	×	×	×					
Customer/user interaction	×			×	×	×			
Assignment/project/workload management		×	×				×	×	
Monthly planner		×	×	×				×	
New employee training	×	×			×		×	×	
Special assignments	×	×	×				×	×	
Peer interaction	×			×	×	×			×
Cross-functional interaction	×		×	×	×	×			×
Presentations	×			×		×		×	×
Month end close		×	×	×				×	

Table 4.3 Rating leadership, using job behaviours

Job behaviours	Major development needed	Considerable development needed	Some development needed	Minor/no development needed	More observation required
1 Solicits and encourages the development and recognition of others' ideas					
2 Provides guidance and direction to others in the application of policies and procedures					
3 Projects a strong role model for other employees to follow; is sought out for advice and counsel					
4 Demonstrates the ability to influence others in a positive manner					
5 Encourages others to develop their skills in order to improve their performance					
6 Provides direction and assistance to others in accomplishing tasks					
7 Establishes a climate of openness and trust with others					
8 Encourages cooperation and teamwork from others					
Summary responses					
Overall rating					

Definitions of rating categories

Major development needed	Employee rarely displays the behaviour
Considerable development needed	Employee occasionally displays the behaviour
Some development needed	Employee frequently displays the behaviour
Minor/no development needed	Employee consistently displays the behaviour
More observation required	Employee requires more close observation

Table 4.4 Developmental project to enhance leadership skills

Skill	Short-term projects	Long-term projects
Leadership	Conduct a monthly staff/team meeting	Analyse the department's workload distribution and make recommendations in report form
	Provide orientation for a new employee	Run a cross-functional project team to develop, implement and monitor a support plan for a customer/user group
	Implement a staff/team activity requiring direction of others	Monitor a support plan for a customer/user group

to the competency-based approach discussed in Chapter 3, in that it ensures a consistent approach to skill assessment and development, decreasing subjective judgements about skill level, providing a common 'skill language' for all managers and employees, and, finally, tying in the skill dimensions to the business objectives of the company.

It is tempting for managers to lift skill dimensions 'off the shelf', but it is necessary for each organization to generate its own unique set of key skill dimensions, since these depend on a whole host of internal and external factors. Even though there are generic managerial and supervisory skills and competences, the way they manifest themselves as behaviour – which can be observed and assessed – will inevitably vary from one organizational context to another. There is no short cut to diagnosing the skills and behaviours that are important for the effective implementation of *your* organization's *strategic* goals and objectives. It is also important that you and other employees are clear about the purposes of skill assessment and the way in which the results will be used.

Box 4.5 Assessing people out of the organization

A skill assessment carried out by independent consultants on a London council has resulted in nineteen finance staff facing redeployment or redundancy. These staff failed the assessment process, which included ability tests, interviews and individual skill assessment as well as a personality test. No training or development opportunities were offered to the unsuccessful candidates; only redeployment in jobs that did not require the agreed level of skill or voluntary redundancy.

Development centres

Another means of diagnosing individual training needs and determining personal development plans is the development centre. This uses a similar approach to that of an assessment centre – a series of exercises observed by trained assessors and rated against predetermined criteria, or 'dimensions'. Whereas the assessment centre was originally designed to provide a more objective means of making selection and internal promotion decisions, the development centre is more collaborative and focuses on training needs. The intention is to heighten an individual's self-awareness of strengths and weaknesses, particularly pertaining to the skill requirements of some future, targeted job, and to construct an individualized plan of learning that builds on existing potential.

Research has shown that participants in development centres will only be motivated to pursue training plans and apply new learning to their jobs if they perceive the assessment process to be accurate and credible. In particular, assessors must be perceived to possess appropriate skills in observation, giving feedback and the facilitation of development recommendations and action plans. Also important is the provision of adequate information before participation, explanation of the role of the centre in the organization's career development system and the actual follow-up of development plans. Centres where there is an incremental sharing of feedback with participants during the event, leading to a jointly agreed diagnosis and development plan at its conclusion, are more likely to be successful. Not unnaturally, if participants suspect that data from the 'development centre' will also be used for assessment purposes to feed present or future promotional decisions, the openness and trust of a collaborative approach will be significantly undermined. We address the issues of confusing performance appraisal with employee and career development further in Chapters 6 and 9.

Business simulations

A variant of the development centre is the use of an extended behavioural simulation, long and realistic enough to allow the observation of everyday group processes and interpersonal behaviour, so overcoming the limitations of conventional role play. This is usually followed by debriefing sessions during which participants share their observations of each other and receive feedback from one of a team of trained observers.

The diagnostic value of such simulations is that participants tend to 'unfreeze', and become interested in their roles, and proceed to carry them out as best they can, often recreating their own back-at-work social environment. Seeing these same behaviour and decision making patterns evolve with minimal task requirements imposed by the simulation itself causes individuals to ask why they enacted the type of organization they did, and why they didn't build a very different type of organization, one in which they would have preferred to work and which would also have worked more effectively. The result of this guided reflection is immense personal learning about influence and leadership styles, energy levels and communication patterns, helpful and dysfunctional behaviours, untested assumptions and self-imposed constraints.

Such programmes can be expensive, owing to the high tutor/ student ratio and the sophistication of the case material and equipment required. Because the intention is diagnostic rather than skill-acquisitive, primary learning benefits are not always tangible and immediate. However, the intensive and multi-sourced feedback is a learning opportunity that the everyday work experience rarely allows, and it tends to be a powerful watershed of self-awareness that results in long-term personal and organizational pay-off.

Informal techniques

The approaches to diagnosing training needs so far discussed, as well as those described in Chapter 3, tend to assume well defined roles, requiring specific skills and techniques that can be reliably cultivated among people willing to acquire them. However, especially in voluntary and smaller organizations, it is often less straightforward because job roles are unstructured, less specialized and more fluid and key skills and abilities may not be obvious from lists of the activities required and possibly not readily 'trainable'. Indeed, in some cases, the organization may do better to fit the role around what a person can offer.

For these reasons, a less formal training needs analysis may be more fruitful, one that could include the following.

Critical incident technique

This can be used to analyse the strengths, weaknesses and development needs of individuals or small groups by identifying how individuals have influenced performance in the past and how they might do so in the future (see Box 4.6)

This is an inexpensive method with potential for building workgroup identity as well as specifying actual skills and abilities required in the future. Sometimes a facilitator may help to prevent an unhealthy negative construction of past events leading to recrimination and the opening up of old wounds.

Box 4.6   Analysing critical incidents

In a group of between five and fifteen people, think of twelve critical incidents in the recent history of the organization. Most group members must agree that these incidents were 'critical'. They can have had either positive or negative outcomes. Then ask the following questions:

● What was it that made them critical?
● How well or how badly were the incidents handled; would this happen the same way again?

Next ask:

● Do any patterns recur?
● Would the group prefer to prevent, continue or improve these patterns?

Then determine:

● In the light of events how does current practice need to be improved?
● What knowledge, skills or abilities were needed; which of these was not available?
● What development needs does this point to?

(Paton and Hooker, 1990)

Peer group diagnosis

The use of peer perceptions to stimulate self-awareness and support self-development in a group context is described below. Unlike traditional appraisal schemes, the approach has the advantage of not necessarily involving hierarchical relationships, not relying on a rational definition of tasks and roles and being intrinsically developmental in that it provides resources for meeting training needs (see Box 4.7)

For structural and cultural reasons many organizations are moving away from traditional bureaucracies towards more fluid networks and project-based ways of working. In such an environment line managers are no longer well placed to appraise and assess the development of staff. Fellow project team members and peers are far more likely to be familiar with the strengths and weaknesses of their colleagues, and it is here that a method like SAPA comes into its own. Nevertheless, such an approach does presuppose a high-trust climate, where there is mutual respect between the different levels and functions of the organization.

Box 4.7 Self and peer assessment (SAPA)

This is an approach to improving performance through individuals assessing their own strengths and weaknesses with the help of colleagues doing the same or similar work, and drawing up and implementing action plans to improve areas of weakness. This process is job and work related and has been successfully applied in education, the NHS and in industry. It is a group process which provides a structure for identifying key performance areas, generating appropriate criteria and standards for measuring performance, receiving feedback from a group of peers and working on ways of improving job-related behaviour and skills. Although a group process, SAPA may be something of a misnomer since experience confirms a strong individual focus with peer involvement aiding self-assessment.

SAPA consists of a number of stages. The process is managed by the SAPA group and all stages except No 8 take place in group meetings. The support of the group does, however, provide a continuing resource during implementation. The stages are listed below:

1 The group identifies an area of performance it wishes to examine.
2 The group defines criteria of performance within this area which individuals can use to assess their performance.
3 Individuals choose criteria from the agreed list and, privately, assess their own performance against their chosen criteria. (It is possible that individuals will choose different criteria.)
4 The individuals then, if they wish, share their personal assessment with the group, i.e. tell other members.
5 Following this sharing, the individuals can choose if they wish to receive feedback from other members of the group. There are a number of options which can be chosen, including questioning, negative feedback and positive feedback.
6 Individuals go through stages 4 and 5 in turn and then may each re-appraise their personal assessments.
7 Individuals then construct a personal action plan which can be done with or without help from the group.
8 The final stage is implementation of action plans. Progress achieved will be the first item of business at the next meeting when, if agreed, the process can start again.

(Stewart, pp. 3.17–3.18)

Self-diagnosis

Psychometric tests are best known for recruitment and assessment purposes; the ideal ones will combine reliability and validity for the people or jobs in question as well as ensuring objective, standardized scores and, once enough have been conducted, appropriate norms (see Chapter 5 for a discussion of psychometric tests in the context of selection). These benefits can also be reaped in the development context, where the results can yield more significant information about an individual's job and career development needs than an interview alone. Although self-administered, such tests are best interpreted by trained occupational psychologists, who have a good knowledge of their various purposes and properties.

Observing role models

This approach to self-diagnosis, which most of us probably share unconsciously, is to observe the personal characteristics and career paths of successful role models. In fact there is a fine line between those who become successful top managers and those who 'derail' just ahead of arrival!

Self-development activity

Research into factors that contribute towards executive stress has shown that certain characteristics are crucial in differentiating between those who achieve top management positions and those that 'derail'. Look at the eleven characteristics listed below and see if you can select the five crucial ones.

1 Very bright, technically or as a problem solver.
2 Identified as a high flyer early in career.
3 Outstanding track record.
4 Has a few flaws.
5 Ambitious.
6 Willing to make sacrifices.
7 Diverse track record.
8 Maintains composure under stress.
9 Handles mistakes with poise.
10 Focuses on problems and solves them.
11 Outspoken but not offensive.

According to McCall and Lombard's (1983) close analysis of twenty US executives, the last five factors were the key differentiators. The subjects had typically been successful in a diverse range of functions and had built up, over twenty to thirty years, a depth and breadth of perspective. Both those who had made it to the top, and those who had not, obviously experienced stressful situations, but while the latter eroded trust and cooperation by their volatile reactions, the former were predictable in their calmness and confidence. They did not deny mistakes but handled them with poise and moved on to something else rather than blaming others or getting defensive. They were single-minded in their problem-solving, developing many contacts along the way. Finally, their style was described as direct and diplomatic, as opposed to 'charming but political', on the one hand, or 'direct but tactless', on the other. Admittedly the sample is small and based on North American rather than European managers, but it does serve to show why a lot of bright, ambitious high flyers plateau early.

Perhaps another limitation of these findings is that it is not everyone's ambition to become a senior executive. In addition, the traditional succession strategy is appropriate for mature multinational organizations that inhabit a relatively stable marketplace, who need continuity amongst their top cadre of managers and who employ individuals who have developed international and general management experience through corporately planned rotating placements. For many organizations, however, a flatter, project-based or business unit structure calls for more individually focused, flexible career development. Even in large, diversified organizations, comprising a variety of business units, the hierarchical succession model based on long-term loyalty and simple product knowledge is equally untenable and outmoded.

However, these comments do highlight two important issues. First, we should include not just an assessment of skills and preferences but also take account of values, both personal and organizational. Second, it is more fruitful to conduct self-diagnosis in the context of the opportunities and career strategies afforded by the organization and sector in which we work.

Self-development activity

Consider the formal and informal skill assessment techniques we outline in this chapter. Which of them might you find useful in your organization – and why?

Table 4.5 gives a comprehensive survey of the advantages and disadvantages of most of the forms of skill assessment we have discussed in this chapter. Aspects of assessment will recur throughout this book, in relation to selection, to career development and to performance measurement and appraisal. Although Table 4.5 has been prepared in relation to skill and need assessment, it is equally applicable to the use of these forms of assessment for most other purposes.

Table 4.5 Training and development needs analysis methods: the pros and cons

Method	Advantages	Disadvantages
Observation		
• technical (time and motion studies) • unstructured (walk through the factory or office) • normative (distinguish between effective and ineffective behaviours, structures and/or process)	• minimizes interruption of routine work flow or group activity • generates *in situ* data highly relevant to the situation where response to identified training needs/interests will impact • provides for important comparison between inferences of observer and respondent	• requires a highly skilled observer with both process and content knowledge (unlike an interviewer who needs, for the most part, only process skill) • data can only be within the work setting (the other side of the first 'advantage') • respondents may perceive observation activity as 'spying'
Questionnaires		
• surveys or polls (random or stratified sample or entire 'population') • question formats can be open-ended, forced choice, priority ranking • can be self-administered (by mail) or controlled (presence of an interpreter)	• reach a large number of people in a short time • are relatively inexpensive • give opportunity for self-expression without fear of embarrassment • yield data that are easily summarized and reported	• make little provision for free expression of unanticipated responses • require substantial time and technical skills, (especially in survey model) for development of effective instruments • are of limited utility in getting at causes of problems or possible solutions • suffer low return rates (mailed), grudging responses or unintended and/or inappropriate responses
Key consultations		
• information from key persons (who are in a good position to know what the training needs are)	• are relatively simple and inexpensive to conduct • permit input and interaction of a number of individuals, each with his/her own perspective on the needs of the area, discipline, group, etc. • establish and strengthen lines of communication between participants in the process	• carry a built-in bias, since they are based on views of those who tend to see training needs from their own individual or organizational perspective

Print media

- Professional journals, legislative news/notes, industry rags, trade magazines, in-house publications

  - are an excellent source of information for uncovering and clarifying normative needs
  - provide information that is current if not forward-looking
  - are readily available and likely to have already been reviewed by client groups
  - less useful when it comes to data analysis and synthesis into a usable form (use of clipping service or key consultants can make this type of data more readily usable)
  - some will contain an element of 'hype'

Interviews

- formal or casual, structured or unstructured
- with a sample (board, staff committee, diagonal slice) or everyone concerned in person, by phone, at work or off site

  - are adept at revealing feelings, causes of and possible solutions to problems the client faces (or anticipates)
  - provide maximum opportunity for client to represent him/herself spontaneously on own terms (especially when conducted in open-ended, non-directive manner)
  - are usually time-consuming
  - can be difficult to analyse and quantify results (especially from unstructured formats)
  - rely for success on skilful interviewer who can generate data without making client(s) feel self-conscious, suspicious, etc.

Group discussion

- structured or unstructured, focused on job (role) analysis, group problem analysis, group goal-setting (brainstorming, force field, consensus rankings, organizational mirroring, simulation and sculpting)

  - permits on-the-spot synthesis of different viewpoints
  - builds support for the particular response that is ultimately decided on
  - decreases client's 'dependence response' toward the service provider, since data analysis is (or can be) a shared function
  - helps participants to become better problem analysts, better listeners, etc.
  - is time-consuming (therefore initially expensive) both for consultant and agency
  - can produce data that are difficult to synthesize and quantify (more a problem with the less structured techniques)

Tests

- hybridized forms of questionnaire
- functionally oriented (like observations)
- sampling learned ideas and facts, administered with or without an assistant

  - can be especially helpful in determining whether cause of recognized problem is a deficiency in knowledge or skill or, by elimination, attitude
  - results are easily quantifiable and comparable
  - the availability of a relatively small number of tests that are validated for a specific situation
  - do not indicate if measured knowledge and skills are actually being used in work place

Table 4.5 continued

Method	Advantages	Disadvantages
Records, reports		
• organizational charts, planning documents, policy manuals, audits and budget records • employee records (grievance, turnover, accidents, etc.) • minutes of meetings, service records, programme evaluation studies	• provide excellent clues to trouble spots • provide objective evidence of the results of problems within organization or group	• causes of problems or possible solutions often do not show up • carry perspective that generally reflects the past situation rather than the current one (or recent changes) • need a skilled data analyst if clear patterns and trends are to emerge from technical and diffuse raw data
Work samples		
• products generated in the course of the organisation's work, e.g. programme proposals, market analyses, letters, training designs • written responses to a hypothetical but relevant case	• carry most of the advantages of records and reports data • are the organization's data (its own output)	• case study method will take time away from actual work of organization • need specialized content analysis • assessment of strengths/weaknesses disclosed by samples can be challenged as 'too subjective'

Adapted from Olivas, 1988, pp. 19–41.

Summary

The issue of assessment is central to human resource planning, management and development, since it is through assessment that information about current skills and training and development needs can be acquired. The starting point is the skill audit, carried out on existing staff, which can be used to inform human resource planning and improve human resource development.

Personnel records, if available, should be a basis for a skill audit, but the information they contain may not be appropriate or adequate. Data are required on an individual's portfolio of skills and abilities, the amount of work experience and the relevant training and development undertaken or in progress. There is a need to consider what skills are relevant to the performance of a particular job and at what level these skills require to be; we introduced the concept of 'core skills' that are believed to be common to most work situations. Finally, in an audit of existing skills there is a need to consider how the human resources under your management can be categorized so that relevant information can readily be obtained; this might include categorizing by occupational experience, age, gender etc.

The skill audit is part of future planning in that it should highlight areas in which existing skills to meet future requirements are in short supply or absent altogether. There are a number of ways in which human resource planning for the future can be undertaken, including supply forecasting and demand forecasting.

There is also a need to consider the job in relation to the skills required to perform it adequately. Job analysis is necessary for the provision of information from which a job description and employee specification can be drawn up and for its use in making selection decisions. However, there is a danger in relying too strongly on the current jobholder's perceptions of the skills required to perform the job since these will be highly subjective. Instead we suggest a skill analysis should be used to identify the basic job elements in skill terms.

Finally, we considered assessment in relation to individual training and development needs, including a review of some of the common assessment methods, formal and informal, and their relative advantages and disadvantages.

References

Armstrong, M. (1991) *A Handbook of Personnel Management Practice* (4th edition). Kogan Page.

Cole, G. A. (1991) *Personnel Management: Theory and Practice* (2nd edition). DP Publications Ltd, London.

Dawson, S. (1992) *Analysing Organizations* (2nd edition). The Macmillan Press Ltd.

De Cenzo, D. A. and Robbins, S. P. (1994) *Human Resource Management: Concepts and Practices* (4th edition). John Wiley and Sons, Inc, New York and Canada.

Jessup, G. (1991) *Outcomes: NVQs and the Emerging Model of Education and Training.* Falmer Press, Brighton.

Keating, D. (1993) Restructuring an Independent Property and Casualty Insurance Corporation. Paper given at American Academy of Management, Atlanta, Georgia, August.

McCall, M. and Lombard, M. (1983) Off the track – why and how successful executives get derailed. Technical Report, Greenboro Centre for Creative Leadership, N. Carolina.

Olivas, L. (1988) Designing and conducting training needs analysis: putting the cart before the horse. *Journal of Management Development*, Vol. 2, No 3. pp. 19–41.

Paton, R. and Hooker, C. (1990) *Developing Managers in Voluntary Organizations: a Handbook*. Open University and Employment Department, Sheffield.

Pearn, M. and Kandola, R. (1986) *Job Analysis*. Institute of Personnel Management, London.

Pearson, R. (1991) *The Human Resource: managing people and work in the 1990s*. McGraw-Hill Book Co., London.

Salaman, G. (1994) *Managing Development and Change*. The Open Business School Diploma Course.

Stewart, J. (1989) Self and peer assessment: a development tool. *Training and Development Methods*. MCB Press, Bradford, pp. 3.17–3.18.

US Department of Labor (1991) *Dictionary of Occupational Titles* (4th edition). Government Printing Office, Washington DC.

5 Making fair selection decisions*

Introduction

For many reasons the selection of staff, whether for recruitment, promotion or redundancy, is central to human resource development. HRD is primarily concerned with the systematic coordination, motivation, development and deployment of staff. Organizations can only do this if they are able to identify the skills and abilities that they need and a well designed selection system helps organizations do this. In this chapter we shall look at the strengths and weaknesses of the main selection techniques so that you can develop a selection system to suit your own circumstances.

We begin this chapter by considering the equal opportunity issues in selection. These are at the heart of good selection procedures and, as we shall see, are not to be feared by organizations or managers. Indeed, by adopting a fair selection system you are likely to increase the likelihood of choosing staff better suited to your needs. In practice this means basing all selection decisions on selection criteria derived from a thorough job analysis. This is a theme that we shall return to time and again in this chapter.

The main body of the chapter is devoted to the lessons that can be learnt from research on selection techniques. The key points that we make are that there is no perfect selection technique, and that the key to good selection is identifying the skills and abilities that you want to recruit and then designing a selection policy that identifies them in each of the applicants.

At the end of the chapter we consider selection as a social process, i.e. selection is a two-sided process in which both sides, organization and applicants, make choices at every stage. Furthermore, we assert that selection is more than the gate through which applicants must pass before they can relate to the organization. Instead selection is part of the relation between organization and employee.

We end the chapter by drawing the strands together and we suggest a method of selection process design that takes account of the latest research and the practical considerations of managers. The suggested model takes account of both the need to retain the highest possible predictive validity and social process arguments. It is a model that recognizes the crucial role of the unstructured interview.

In addition to recruitment, all the selection techniques described in this chapter could be used for promotion and redundancy. Indeed

---

* This chapter was written by Jon Billsberry.

research has shown that the choice of whom to make redundant when downsizing is necessary is commonly done very poorly. In these situations it is vitally important that organizations identify the skills and abilities that they will need in the future and use appropriate selection techniques to identify which of their staff possess these skills and where skill shortage exists. However, to make our discussion easier to follow, we shall concentrate on the use of selection techniques for identifying skills and abilities when recruiting new staff. Although we concentrate on the recruitment of new staff much of the discussion is equally applicable when choosing staff for redundancy. But, there is research demonstrating that the choice of selection technique for promotion is much less important, probably because organizations have employees' past performance to help them make decisions. We shall discuss this in greater detail when we consider analogous tests.

Fair selection

Selection is, by its very nature, a discriminatory process. The purpose of the process is to discriminate in favour of the people who will perform well in the vacant job and to reject those who will perform poorly. It is therefore a process in which people have to make judgements on other people, often with only scant information to help them. Individuals' judgements are inevitably influenced by their own prejudices, stereotyping, unconscious assumptions and social and cultural beliefs and behaviour. These can surface in all sorts of very subtle ways: 'she's not very assertive' (sexual discrimination), 'he did well to get a degree' (racial discrimination), 'she's done well not to let her disability affect her career' (discrimination against people with disabilities), or 'I think he'll make a very good leader' (bias in favour of white men).

There are important economic reasons why equal opportunity policies are important, as you will see from Box 5.1. But we stress equal opportunities for another reason: you can only make good selection decisions if you are aware of the factors influencing your choices.

So how do you design a fair system of selection? Primarily this means taking subjective judgement out of the selection decision and replacing it with decision-making based on job-related criteria. These job-related criteria form the backbone of any good and fair selection system.

There are two practical reasons why you should only discriminate on job-related issues: first, selection that is not based on job-related issues will disadvantage the organization and will be unlikely to select the most suitable people available, but it has been shown that the use of poorer selection techniques, i.e. ones that are generally poorer at selecting the better candidates, work out in the long run to be very expensive for the organization; and, second, you are likely to be breaking the law in areas covered by the Sex Discrimination Act 1975,

---

Box 5.1   Equal opportunities

Coussey and Jackson (1991) give the following five economic benefits for adopting equal opportunity policies:

- the most flexible and effective use of staff gives an employer a competitive edge in the labour market;
- a sound equal opportunity programme for ethnic minorities gives advantages to companies bidding for local authority contracts;
- a diverse workforce reflecting your market can result in a better informed, more adaptable organization, which is closer to customers, giving a market edge over your less responsive competitors; if the market is changing there is no sense in having white males making all the decisions;
- a thriving local community brings economic advantages to all businesses;
- managing change through effective equal opportunity programmes costs less than any changes that may be imposed.

---

the Race Relations Act 1976 or the increasing number of EU laws and directives. In essence, these laws prevent organizations making selection decisions that are not based on job-related criteria. Organizations, and their managers, should not fear this, because selecting people on job-related criteria results in a choice of the most suitable staff available.

Job-related criteria usually evolve from the following process. First, a thorough *job analysis* is carried out. We covered job analysis in Chapter 4, and in relation to selection we would only make one further observation. There are many techniques that you can choose from to help you analyse jobs but they boil down to three lines of investigation: they are worker-oriented, task-oriented or ability-oriented. This is important because it affects the way in which you develop your *selection criteria*. Generally it is much safer, and possibly fairer, to investigate the tasks or skills and abilities needed to do the job. If one investigates the way the worker does his or her job one is likely to be biased by the present incumbent and this may not be the only way, or indeed the best way, to do the job. For example, 'Bert always acted tough with the suppliers, kicking butt and bullying them into reducing their prices. Therefore, we need someone equally aggressive and ruthless'. These qualities can easily be misinterpreted as masculine and can make it difficult for people to realize that the job can be done equally effectively (or probably *more* effectively) in other ways and by women.

The analysis is normally written up as a *job description*. At this stage it is important to compare the job description with a model of job design such as that proposed by Hackman and Oldham (1976) (see Chapter 7).

Once you have a job description, you need to specify the sort of person required. As with job analysis, there are two slightly different ways to do this. The first is to use the job description to produce a *person specification* – a detailed description of the person required. Again, although this is based on a job analysis, there is a slight danger that it might be biased by the characteristics of the current or previous jobholders. Instead it is usually better to produce a *job specification*, which is a detailed list of the skills, experience, qualifications, etc. that are required if the job is to be performed well. It is wise to state these qualities in two lists: essential and desirable. These normally act as the *selection criteria* – the standards by which you judge the applicants.

By following this route you ensure that you select the person most likely to perform the job well. However, it can be very difficult to set criteria for selection. The criteria for an unskilled worker might be fairly easy to set: physical fitness, reliability, dexterity, availability, etc. The criteria for a copy typist might be error-free typing at sixty words per minute and fluency in two languages. The criteria for an accountant might be an appropriate qualification plus a year's post-qualification experience and knowledge of the industry. But what are the criteria for more general appointments, such as managers and supervisors? This is one of the reasons why selection is not an exact science.

Self-development activity

Often without realizing it many organizations have been operating unfair recruitment and selection procedures for many years. This might reveal itself in an analysis of the current workforce. Before reading the rest of this chapter, briefly consider the following questions and for each one think what you can do to eliminate the unfair discrimination that might have been previously practised in your organization against each of the groups:

- Do you have any women on your board of directors?
- Do you have many black managers in your organization?
- Are there any disabled people in your organization?

Many organizations have realized that they have been unfair in their selection procedures in the past and are now trying to rectify the balance. To do so, many jobs are advertised in media likely to be seen by members of the minority they want to attract. This suggests that the choice of recruitment method is an important factor in determining the fairness of the selection procedure, and especially important when one

---

Box 5.2   Headhunters

Many headhunters use very idiosyncratic selection techniques: we know of one headhunter who would never shortlist anyone with a beard and another headhunter who swears by the use of graphology (the analysis of handwriting) to select candidates. But despite this, there are some very good headhunters around. These idiosyncratic selection methods mask the headhunters' most valuable selection technique: their research, which should lead to multiple recommendations or peer assessments from knowledgeable, independent and impartial sources. Good research should produce a list of people who have the skills to do the job well. The headhunters' task is to assess whether each candidate would be able to adapt and thrive in the recruiting organization's culture. It is essential therefore that headhunters are properly briefed on the job-related criteria before they begin the assignment.

---

realizes that many senior appointments are advertised in the 'hidden' market.

The 'hidden' market comprises agencies and executive search consultants (aka headhunters). Are these unfair ways to recruit staff? Agencies are open to anyone with the skills or experience that the agent deals with. Normally the agent bombards the organization with details of all suitable candidates on its database in the hope that one will be chosen, thereby giving everyone on the database an equal chance.

Headhunters are asked to help with recruitment when skills that are believed to be in short supply are needed, or when it is believed that qualified people will not apply. Headhunters should carry out a job analysis and should use the same selection criteria that any responsible selector would use. The only difference with traditional recruitment techniques is the fact that headhunters go looking for suitable applicants rather than waiting for them to arrive. However, although the system may be fair, the headhunters themselves may not be. It is a profession that is seeking legitimacy because of the large number of 'cowboys' trying to make a 'fast buck'.

What does one need to keep in mind to ensure fair selection? The following checklist comes from Coussey and Jackson (1991):

● base selection on analysis of the essential tasks of the job and essential skills needed to carry these out;
● base decisions on assessment methods that use evidence of ability to carry out tasks similar to the tasks of the job;

- check all assessments to ensure that they relate to job performance and are not overemphasizing qualities or skills that are not needed;
- monitor results by ethnic group, sex and disability to check for bias;
- make sure all staff carrying out selection are trained and use a systematic process for their decisions;
- where you have an adverse impact, consider the scope for training in the skills lacked by the group concerned.

Selection techniques

So far we have looked at equal opportunities and the need to design a fair selection system. Now it is time to look at the main selection methods so that you can begin to design a practical selection system that is appropriate to your circumstances. If you have read any other texts on selection, you are likely to have come across a table listing the predictive validities of the main selection techniques. In broad terms, the predictive validity coefficient is a measure of how good each selection technique is at choosing the best person for the job from those considered.

Table 5.1 shows the range of predictive validity of each of the main selection techniques. This table shows a range because academic research cannot give definitive validities to each technique, as the validity of any particular test is dependent on the situation in which it is used. Unless you are very good with statistics, these figures probably mean very little to you. So, what do these numbers really mean?

Table 5.1 Comparative validity coefficients for commonly used selection techniques

Selection technique	Range of predictive validities
Unstructured interviews	0.31–0.36
Structured interviews	0.45–0.62
References	0.17–0.26
Biodata	0.24–0.38
Mental ability tests	0.25–0.53
Aptitude tests	0.27–0.28
Personality tests	0.00–0.24
Assessment centres	0.37–0.43
Analogous tests (work samples)	0.38–0.54
Graphology	0
Astrology	0

Table 5.1 shows the comparative validity coefficients for the most commonly used selection techniques (Wiesner and Cronshaw, 1988; McDaniel *et al.*, 1987; Reilly and Chao, 1982; Hunter and Hunter, 1984; Vineberg and Joyner, 1982; Schmitt *et al.*, 1984; Blinkhorn and Johnson, 1990; Tett *et al.*, 1991; Gaugler *et al.*, 1979. All figures have been corrected for range restriction, etc.).

The numbers are correlations, which means that they show the relation between selection test scores and employees' future job performance. A score of zero correlation indicates chance prediction, i.e. there is no relation between the selection test and job performance, whereas a score of one would indicate a perfect relation between the selection test and job performance, which would mean that the test always selected the best person for the job. But a high validity score of 0.5 does **not** mean that 50 per cent of the time the test selects the best person for the job. It is simply a measure of correlation.

Perhaps the best way to interpret these numbers is to think of them in terms of the amount of job-related factors the test examines. If the validity coefficients are squared, one arrives at something called the coefficient of determination, normally referred to as R^2. Don't be afraid of the term, it is unimportant, but what it measures is not. It reveals the percentage of factors affecting job performance measured by the test. So, if we take analogous tests that have a predictive validity range of 0.38–0.54, the coefficient of determination would be 14 per cent to 29 per cent. Therefore analogous tests measure between 14 per cent and 29 per cent of the factors important for future success at work. The remaining 71–86 per cent is unaccounted for.

Perhaps this is not surprising. If a selection test perfectly predicted success at work, then all the factors that affect an individual's performance after they are selected would be insignificant. These factors include the organization's culture, how the job is designed, how the employee gets on with others in the new organization, how well the job matches the individual's expectations, how factors outside work affect the individual's motivation to do well and so on. Given all of the possible factors that can influence how well an individual performs in a new organization, a selection test that measures about 25 per cent of these factors seems a very useful tool. Table 5.2 shows the percentage of factors that each of the most commonly used selection techniques measures.

Table 5.2 Factors relating to job performance that are measured by each selection technique

Selection technique	Coefficient of determination (%)
Unstructured interviews	10–13
Structured interviews	20–38
References	3–7
Biodata	6–14
Mental ability tests	6–28
Aptitude tests	7–8
Personality tests	0–6
Assessment centres	14–19
Analogous tests (work samples)	14–29
Graphology	0
Astrology	0

But this analysis still has not told us how good each candidate might be. It does not tell us how good each technique is at differentiating between individuals. This is critical, because the principal concern of selection is to differentiate between candidates. Instead all we can say is something like 'Janice scored 1 per cent higher than Jim and Jan, and 3 per cent higher than John, in a test that measured 20 per cent of the factors affecting job performance'. Furthermore, when looking at the range of predictive validities and coefficients of determination, it is important to realize that they are specific to the research study and that generalizing from them might be misleading. It is essential to check that the selection techniques you choose are both suitable and appropriate. This is best done by analysing the job specification and seeing which features of the job can be tested. If you do not test for suitability and appropriateness and you use unsuitable and inappropriate tests, the test results will be virtually meaningless and might lead you to make very poor and unfair decisions.

One interesting idea raised by this discussion is the concept of *incremental validity*. As we know what percentage of job performance factors each test measures, it would logically follow that if tests measure different factors, then using more than one test will result in higher validity. However, the concept of incremental validity has not been proved by research. There are problems combining the results of different tests, especially if they are contradictory, and in assessing exactly what each type of test is measuring.

How can we summarize this somewhat critical review of selection? First, while selection techniques measure less than half of the factors, the differences between them are significant. So, if you use the tests with higher predictive validities when they are suitable and appropriate, you will increase the likelihood of selecting candidates who will perform well in the job. This is particularly so if you are regularly having to select staff. Second, we can divide the selection techniques into four bands, based on their predictive validity and coefficient of determination when they are used suitably and appropriately. Remember, though, that these four bands are comparative. The grouping is my own subjective one based on my interpretation of the predictive validities and coefficients of determination. You should be able to draw your own conclusions and decide for yourself what constitutes a good selection test for choosing new recruits and when each might be apposite.

Selection techniques range from good to unproven, as follows:

- *Good selection techniques*
    Analogous tests
    Assessment centres
    Mental ability tests
    Structured interviews

- *Moderately good selection techniques*
  Biodata
  Unstructured interviews
- *Poor selection techniques*
  Aptitude tests
  Personality tests
  References
- *Unproven selection techniques*
  Astrology
  Graphology

One might expect that organizations would use the good selection techniques with the higher predictive validities. But all research into organizations' choice of selection techniques has shown a predominance of techniques with lower validities, notably unstructured interviews and references. There are a great many reasons for this: perceived cheapness, availability of resources, preservation of existing practices and so on. However, the trend from several surveys suggests that there is an increasing use of the higher validity tests. The graph in Figure 5.1 illustrates the findings of a survey by Industrial Relations Services in the UK in 1991. The findings hold true for all manner of organizations: public, private, non-profit, UK- and foreign-owned (no matter where they are located in the UK, nor in which industry they operate). It is the traditional tests that dominate – interviews, application forms, references and *curriculum vitae* *(CV)* – but about 50 per cent of organizations now use tests – personality, mental ability or work tests – on a regular basis.

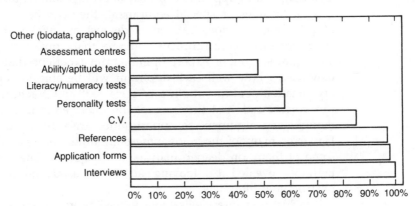

Figure 5.1 *Frequency of use of selection techniques by organizations (Industrial Relations Services, 1991)*

In the rest of this section we shall look critically at each of the selection techniques that are available to you as a manager. We shall outline the strengths and weaknesses of each technique and discuss when each technique might be suitable.

Interviews

Interviews are used by virtually all organizations for virtually all jobs. Often they are combined with other selection methods, but much of the time interviewers make selection decisions that contradict or override the results from the other selection methods they use. This dominance of selection by interviews has attracted researchers throughout the twentieth century. Until the late 1980s almost all this research demonstrated that the interview was an extremely poor selection tool. Indeed many surveys suggested that the interview had less predictive validity than references – an amazing finding given the interview's 'face' validity and that referees are usually chosen by candidates to be their 'champions'.

Meta-analysis is a statistical technique used to combine research studies to provide a more authoritative and more significant picture. It was developed in the late 1970s and is still being refined. The findings of several meta-analysis surveys has repositioned the interview among selection techniques. A study by Wiesner and Cronshaw (1988) suggests that the unstructured interview has a validity of 0.31, while the structured interview has a validity of 0.62. This makes the unstructured interview a moderately good selection technique and the structured interview one of the highest rated selection techniques around. A *structured interview* is a face to face interview whose questions have been derived following a job analysis, and then the same set of job-related questions are presented to every candidate and applicants' responses are judged on a predetermined scale.

On the surface unstructured interviews appear to have many advantages: they appear cheap, easy to arrange and require little in the way of facilities or special equipment; they can be organized very quickly, and decisions can be made just as quickly; they are the expected form of recruitment and one that applicants prefer; they allow for the input of 'expert' opinion from experienced line managers; they assess how well each applicant will be able to cope with the organization's culture; applicants' social skill and practical intelligence can be assessed; and they permit the interviewer to follow lines of thought and argument as opportunities arise during the interview. However, many of these advantages are little more than illusion, and some of them, on deeper analysis, are major weaknesses. These are perhaps revealed by looking at the research findings into the unstructured interview.

Unstructured interviews have indeed been shown to be good at assessing intelligence (particularly practical intelligence), social interaction, career motivation, motivation (although interviewers do not normally do this correctly), and, perhaps most importantly for this discussion, organizational fit. Rynes and Gerhart (1990) reported that interviewers from the same organization agreed about organization-specific requirements. This suggests that it might be possible to use interviews to assess how well individuals fit the culture of an organization.

But other studies have shown that all the following often occur in unstructured interviews:

- first impressions are very important; two surveys have shown that interviewers make decisions very quickly, after only 4 minutes or 9 minutes;
- candidates are asked different questions;
- when one calculates the cost of managers' time, interviews can be expensive;
- attractiveness helps candidates get selected;
- 'halo and horns' effects, where a particularly good or bad comment from the interviewee is transferred to their other comments;
- interviewers tend to look for reasons to reject candidates rather than for reasons to select them;
- as much as half the factual content of the interview is forgotten by interviewers;
- poor questioning techniques, such as leading or multiple questions, are used;
- interviewers spend too much time talking and not enough time listening.

These are problems of bad practice or inexperience, which trained and/or experienced interviewers should be aware of and able to combat or limit. However, there are a range of problems that are more difficult to eradicate from the process. These are of a more theoretical nature.

How does an interviewer come to a decision? Unlike most other selection methods, there are normally no clear acceptance criteria. The interviewer has to balance the candidates' comments with information gleaned from the application form and/or CV and from any references that might have been taken up. Candidates are then compared without any ground rules. The situation is made worse when different interviewers are used for different candidates. Without a frame of reference how can results be combined and how can the process be fair to all those interviewed? Interestingly though, research suggests that unstructured interviews are not themselves an unfair or biased way to select people. However, the interviewers might not be so unbiased, and if someone wanted to discriminate, the unstructured interview would certainly be the selection method he or she would choose.

For these reasons researchers have tried to find ways to improve the unstructured interview. Perhaps the greatest problem with the unstructured interview is, not surprisingly, its very lack of structure. With greater structure it is likely that candidates will be treated similarly and poorer interviewers will be helped by removing much of the uncertainty and the need to make subjective decisions. The structured interview addresses these problems and, in particular, reduces the influence of non job-related and interpersonal factors, such as attractiveness, first impressions, halo effects, etc., affecting the selection decision.

In a structured interview the interviewer derives a number of questions and a marking guide to judge applicants' replies from a job analysis. The degree of structure varies from a set of topics that must be examined through to a scripted series of questions from which the interviewer cannot stray. The purpose of this type of interview is to ensure that each candidate is treated similarly and judged on job-related criteria. Structured interviews have been shown to be one of the most valid and reliable selection tests around, and they are appropriate in many situations.

Analogous tests, the situational interview and work samples

Perhaps the most logical and sensible way to select people is to ask them to replicate the work for which they are being selected. In an ideal world, we would ask each of the applicants to do the job for a period of time so that we could assess how good they were at the work and how they responded to the organization's culture. However, in the real world this is rarely possible, so tests have been developed that try to simulate the work that the successful applicants will be doing.

There are several very well known examples of analogous tests, such as the typing test for secretaries and VDU operatives, and there are other tests for computer hardware engineers, bricklayers, chefs and waiters. These jobs, or some of the most vital skills in these jobs, are fairly easily converted into a manageable test that can be applied to a shortlist of candidates. Research has shown these tests to be one of the most effective forms of selection for skilled, non-managerial work. Moreover, it is usually a very fair way to select people.

Unfortunately there are difficulties in transferring this selection technique to other levels and occupations. In particular, it is very difficult to design analogous tests for supervisory or managerial work, although there have been attempts to do so: the in-tray tests, presentations and group problem-solving exercises are examples. But these simulate only one or several aspects of managerial work. It would be very difficult to do more, as we know from Mintzberg that managerial work is very complex and fragmented and usually more concerned with the process than the tasks. This highlights the greatest problem of analogous testing; its limited applicability.

Self-development activity

Consider your own team for a moment. For how many of the jobs could you use an analogous test to select applicants?

The high validity and apparent fairness of *analogous tests* has encouraged researchers to try, despite the difficulties, to extend such testing to other jobs and occupations. Perhaps the most interesting advances in recent years has been the development of situational interviews, which have been shown to be one of the most valid selection techniques.

The *situational interview* is a further development to the structured interview. It uses a technique called critical incident analysis to analyse the vacant job and to produce about twenty situations typical to the job. These situations are written up and current employees are asked what would be a good, average and poor response to the situation. These responses become the marking guide, which is used to rate applicants' answers.

In addition to high validity, the situational interview has other advantages: it forces interviewers to pose the same questions to all applicants and to rate applicant's answers on the same predetermined marking scale; candidates are judged on job-related criteria; and because a face-to-face interview is being used, part of the session can be used to answer applicants' questions or to 'sell' the job and to assess each applicant's interpersonal skills. However, there are considerable difficulties with the situational interview: it is highly specific and every time one opts to use a situational interview, one must go through a lengthy process of critical incident analysis and situation compilation; owing to the time-consuming process of compilation it is a relatively expensive and slow selection technique; the predetermined marking scale might penalize radical and/or imaginative answers, thereby risking the likelihood that the organization only selects clones of its current workforce; and, finally, applicants' answers may not correspond to how they would perform in practice. Because of this last weakness, the situational interview is not a true analogous test.

Analogous tests are important when one is judging people for promotion or redundancy; an employees' track record of work is, in effect, an analogous test. However, past success does not necessarily ensure future success, although it is usually as accurate a guide as one can find, and so one must be a little cautious extrapolating future performance. Moreover, when looking at track records one needs to examine how much of the success or failure can be attributed to the jobholder and how much was out of his or her control. Finally, a good track record in one job does not mean that the person will be as successful in a different, more senior job. Peters and Hull (1970) analysed hundreds of cases of incompetence, leading to their formulation of the 'Peter Principle' whereby, in a hierarchy, an employee tends to rise to his/her level of incompetency.

One survey looked at the effectiveness of different selection tests for both recruitment and promotion. The researchers found that while the choice of selection test for recruitment was very important, as different selection methods widely varied in their predictive validities, the choice of selection technique for promotion was much less critical. Although work sampling, or analogous tests, were the best indicator of future success, they rated only marginally ahead of other techniques: ability tests, experience ratings, job knowledge and assessment centres all received very similar ratings. The reason for this is that these tests are not the sole selection technique used: organizations also have employees' track records and superior, peer and subordinate ratings to help them choose.

Tests of aptitude, mental ability, literacy and numeracy

There are a whole range of tests that managers can deploy on unsuspecting applicants. The range includes tests of physical ability, health, dexterity, suppleness, intelligence (in its many forms), literacy and numeracy. These tests can have quite high validities when used appropriately. In this context 'appropriately' means when the tests are used to measure job-related criteria. For example, tests of physical ability can be very useful for selecting unskilled manual workers and numeracy tests are a sensible way to screen school-leavers entering financial service organizations. Indeed, literacy and numeracy tests are mainly used for screening purposes. They add some validity to a normally haphazard task.

But let us concentrate on intelligence tests, as these have the highest validity of these tests and appear to be a very useful selection technique. Intuitively, recruiting candidates with higher levels of intelligence seems very sensible. Usually one would expect a more intelligent employee to require less training and pick up skills more quickly. Indeed, in a dynamic environment where change seems ever present, employees with above average intelligence should help organizations better respond to change. Academic research has produced results that appear to confirm this, and it has been known for many years that intelligence correlates very well with job performance. The predictive validities obtained for intelligence tests range from moderate to good, often on a par with structured interviews and analogous tests. Squaring the correlation reveals that intelligence, as measured by these tests, contributes to about 25 per cent of employees' performance. Consequently, if it is not possible to use analogous tests, intelligence tests would appear to be the next best technique. In addition, intelligence tests are relatively cheap, widely available, easy to use and judge candidates on the same criteria. In short, intelligence tests seem an excellent selection technique. So why are they not more widely used?

First, there are many intelligence tests around and they vary enormously in quality and validity, not only in their format, but also what they test. Consequently, it can be very difficult matching a job analysis to the type of intelligence test that will discover the most suitable candidates. Similarly, while it seems sensible to judge people on their intelligence, how does one incorporate experience or relevant skills? One would expect managers to value these qualities above straightforward intelligence for many jobs. In addition, many jobs cannot, unfortunately, offer high degrees of mental stimulation, so the use of intelligence tests may be inappropriate in many situations. But where one has many applicants for non-skill-specific jobs, such as school-leavers, or graduate entry, they are perhaps the most useful and valid screening technique available.

In the USA in recent years concerns have been raised about the fairness of using intelligence tests for selection, and these concerns may, or should, extend to Europe. The argument runs like this: 'People's intelligence is influenced by their education background. We know that many minorities receive a below-average standard of education. Therefore selection procedures that measure intelligence are selecting people on their educational and social background thereby disadvantaging many. Furthermore, you are selecting people without reference to a job analysis; how do you know that intelligence is job-related?' These points are difficult to dispute and the scientific nature of intelligence tests makes investigation of bias in organizations a relatively straightforward task. However, the concerns raised about intelligence tests discriminating unfairly on educational background could be applied just as strongly to many other selection techniques, perhaps even more so to unstructured interviews.

Personality tests

Personality tests have been around for about a century and are surprisingly popular; over half of UK organizations regularly use them for selection. I said 'surprisingly popular' because they are one of the poorest methods of predicting success at work. In fact a paper published in *Nature* in 1990 suggested that there is no evidence demonstrating that personality tests make informed decisions.

Personality tests come in all shapes and sizes. Perhaps the best known is the Rorschach inkblot test, in which applicants describe what they see in inkblots to psychologists. But these types of test are seen as too subjective and unprofessional to be used in a commercial environment. Instead psychologists have developed tests in the form

---

Box 5.3 The insignificance of personality tests

We are not suggesting that personality tests have no uses, or that there are no stable underlying aspects of temperament which are important in the determination of behaviour. Indeed, for counselling purposes, or in other situations where self perception is as important as the truth, they may be invaluable. But we see precious little evidence that even the best personality tests predict job performance, and a good deal of evidence of poorly understood statistical methods being pressed into service to buttress shaky claims. If this is so for the most reputable tests in the hands of specialists, one may imagine what travesties are committed further down market (Blinkhorn and Johnson, 1990).

of questionnaires to reveal candidates' personality traits. Commonly they are described on a series of linear scales such as introvert–extrovert, self-assured–self-doubting, expedient–conscientious, practical–imaginative, undisciplined–self-disciplined, etc. These somewhat limited dimensions are not always job-related and often they are not true opposites. For example, is imaginative the opposite of practical?

For these reasons and others, such as discrimination, personality tests are viewed somewhat sceptically by most researchers. However, the advocates of personality tests would counter this by claiming that they provide additional information, e.g. how the individual will fit into the team, and that they will also help reveal whether the applicant is suited to the type of work and/or the organization's culture. Hence, they tend to be used as part of a battery of tests for school-leavers or graduate entry programmes to help identify possible career directions for people new to commercial organizations. Very few would advocate the use of personality tests in isolation, and most would always try to find other ways to assess the candidates' suitability.

Assessment centres

In practice, selection techniques are often combined in the belief that this will yield more information about the candidates and thereby make the selection decision fairer and more informed. One might think that this would make assessment centres the best selection technique available. Unfortunately this is not the case. In fact several surveys have shown that the validity of assessment centres is actually lower than many of the techniques they employ. Why is this?

Perhaps the greatest problem with the assessment centre is the selection criterion. How do selectors use all the data that they have to hand? For example, how does one integrate the results from an intelligence test with the results from role plays and presentations with interviews? Decisions are often made by the subjective judgement of the managers present, and this allows for bias and discrimination to enter the process – though there is little research evidence to suggest that assessment centres are unfair. In fact they have a high 'face validity' as they utilize many exercises that appear relevant to managerial work: in-tray exercises, presentations, chairing meetings, and problem-solving, for example. However, assessment centres are not always based on a thorough job analysis and they generally use tests that purport to measure qualities that are not necessarily job-related, e.g. intelligence and personality tests.

Assessment centres, being very expensive, tend to be used for managerial appointments or graduate recruitment, thereby adding weight to Cook's Law: 'the more important the selection decision, the more time must be taken, or must be *seen to be taken*, to reach it'. You can find more on assessment centres in Chapter 9.

Application forms, CV and biodata

Most job advertisements ask those interested in the job to send in their CV or to request an application form. Agencies, headhunters and executive selection consultants usually initially introduce candidates to organizations through a CV. Application form and CV sifting is virtually universal, and it is the time in the selection process when the organization is in greatest control, as it may be selecting only a small percentage of candidates to take to the next stage.

The selection of applicants at this stage is very important. If you make good filtering decisions, it should increase the validity of the rest of the process. Unfortunately, the sifting of application forms and CVs is generally one of the most unscientific and least valid of all selection techniques. What do you do with a pile of thousands of applications? See Box 5.4.

Clearly Box 5.4 shows a tongue-in-cheek perspective, but it's one with a very serious message. Advertisements or instructions to third

---

Box 5.4 Parkinson's Law

Parkinson (1957) comments on the problem of filtering application forms:

'We draw . . . the useful conclusion that the failure of [selection] methods is mainly due to there being too many candidates. There are, admittedly, some initial steps by which the total may be reduced. The formula 'Reject everyone over 50 or under 20 plus everyone who is Irish' is now universally used, and its application will somewhat reduce the list. The names remaining will still, however, be too numerous. To choose between three hundred people, all well qualified and highly recommended, is not really possible. We are driven therefore to conclude that the mistake lies in the original advertisement. It has attracted too many applications. The disadvantage of this is little realized . . . that people devise advertisements in terms which will inevitably attract thousands. A post of responsibility is announced as vacant, the previous occupant being now in the House of Lords. The salary is large, the pension generous, the duties nominal, the privileges immense, the perquisites valuable, free residence provided with official car and unlimited facilities for travel. Candidates should apply, promptly but carefully, enclosing copies (not originals) of not more than three recent testimonials. What is the result? A deluge of applications, many from lunatics and as many again from retired army majors with a gift (as they always claim) for handling men. There is nothing to do except burn the lot and start thinking all over again. It would have saved time and trouble to do some thinking in the first place.'

parties should be accurate and realistic, with the aim of producing a small number of suitably qualified applicants. In the current economic climate it is common for posts advertised nationally to attract thousands of applications; some graduate trainee schemes receive in excess of 25,000 applications every year. The task of filtering these to a manageable number is horrendous: if it takes ten minutes to read and determine the strength of each application, 25,000 applications would take 4167 hours or 2 years, working 8 hours a day, 5 days a week, without a break, for one person to produce a shortlist. Clearly, variations on the 'Reject everyone over 50 or under 20 plus everyone who is Irish' rule are very attractive (with apologies to my mother and father and everyone from Ireland!).

Biodata

We know that the filtering of applications is usually carried out with very little science, and has very low validity; researchers therefore have tried to develop techniques to help. One approach is known as biographical inventory or biodata. This is a technique for designing and scoring application forms by analysing the biographical details of successful and unsuccessful people in the organization. The biographical details are correlated to success and, where a significant correlation is found, the biographical detail is included on the application form. So there might be questions about parents, interests, schooling, place of birth and so on. Technology is sufficiently advanced for the forms to be fed into one end of the computer and a series of acceptance or rejection letters emerge from the other end.

The perfect solution? Unfortunately not. Biodata is both expensive and highly specific. For the system to have any validity a full biographical survey must be done on the people doing, or those who have done, the job that applicants are applying for. The survey very quickly loses its validity and it needs a lot of people to study. But research has shown that the technique has moderate validity, perhaps because biodata partly assesses how well applicants will adapt to the organization's culture. There are, however, considerable doubts about the fairness or wisdom of this technique, which, at best, produces clones of existing members and therefore discriminates against people not representative of the *status quo*.

The problems surrounding biodata mean that it has really only one practical application: for large volume graduate or school-leaver entry. In any other circumstance it is almost certain to be based on insignificant findings and therefore to be indisputably discriminatory. So how does one filter applications to produce a shortlist?

First of all you carry out a job analysis and produce a job description and job specification. You use these to write advertisements or to give instructions to third parties that only encourage suitably qualified people to apply. You use these documents again to produce a scoring system. It may help to identify the key skills or experience necessary to do the job well, and you compare each application to the criteria. Those applications that most closely match the job specification are short-listed, and polite letters sent to those that you have not selected thanking them for their interest. This is the fairest way to filter applications.

Graphology and astrology

Believe it or not, graphology – the analysis of handwriting – and astrology are used to select people. In France graphology is widely used. Surprisingly, it is also used in several large UK organizations, e.g. SG Warburg and Sons. Astrology is not widely used in Europe, but it is very popular in the Far East. Unfortunately for their advocates, there is no evidence to suggest that either technique has any validity at all for selecting staff.

Selection as a social process

The title of this chapter is 'Making fair selection decisions'. But so far we have only considered one of the parties having to make a choice – the selector. Applicants also have a series of decisions to make: whether to apply, whether to fill out the application form, whether to turn up for each round of testing, what attitude to take during the tests, whether to accept any job offer and whether to turn up on the first day of work. It is to the organization's advantage if the better candidates at each stage choose to continue with their application. It is to no one's benefit – applicant nor organization – if the process is completed and the best person selected only for that person to reject the offer of a job. Moreover, it is even more disastrous if the best person is recruited only to leave after a month or so. Organizations have therefore a duty to portray themselves accurately so that candidates can make informed decisions. Many organizations now try to incorporate realistic job previews into their selection procedures. See Box 5.5

Box 5.5   Realistic job previews at McDonalds

McDonalds ask each potential trainee manager to spend two days as a crew member between the first and second interviews. Each shift lasts between eight and twelve hours and the applicant gets treated in the same way as a normal crew member – apart from a short break to complete some analogous tests such as writing replies to complaint letters. The applicant gets only a very short break and remains standing most of the day. At the end of a late shift, about 1 am, the applicant might be asked to count stock in the −20°C freezer. In this way applicants get a realistic picture of what the job will be like and whether or not it is for them.

Realistic job previews are becoming increasingly widespread. They are similar to analogous tests, and there is some evidence to suggest that they increase new employees' motivation. There are many different forms of realistic job preview, and the most effective appear to be ones similar to the McDonalds example, with applicants actually getting the chance to do the job. Realistic job previews based on glossy brochures, films, etc., seem to have little impact.

Selection though is more than just the choices that selectors and applicants make; it is also concerned with the relation between the organization and the employee. Herriot (1989) sums this up well,

> recruitment and selection procedures constitute the initial episodes in the developing relationship between individual and organization. Selection is not the gate through which applicants must pass before they can relate to the organization; it is itself part of the relationship.

This is important, because, if you agree with Herriot, it means that the organization cannot simply pick what it regards as the selection method with the highest validity without regard to the impact on the applicant. It is just as important to use appropriate methods and procedures. The use of inappropriate techniques risks candidates dropping out of the process because of dissatisfaction with the way in which they have been treated. The candidates transfer the atmosphere of the selection process, perhaps correctly, to the culture of the organization. The argument of appropriateness gives the unstructured interview an extended life, and perhaps also explains why the unstructured interview has retained its popularity.

Self-development activity

Think about your relationship with your current (or last) employer. What events can you recall that shaped that relationship? Ask others in your organization how well they recall their selection experience.

Why does it not surprise us that the unstructured interview remains popular, given what we know about its predictive validity? Why do effective business people choose to ignore the advice of researchers and psychologists and persist in using it? Part of the answer lies in its perceived necessity. Very few would feel confident about offering full-time permanent jobs without first meeting the applicants, and, similarly, few who can choose would accept a job without first meeting representatives of the organization.

Researchers, after finding the unstructured interview only a moderate selection tool, respond by suggesting that the interview needs to become more structured, that trained psychologists conduct the interviews, and that interviews should not be used for selection. But this misses the key point about the interview: it is a vital social process, acting to help individuals make decisions that will noticeably affect the rest of their lives. Researchers try to make the interview more like other forms of selection rather than realizing that it, and indeed all recruitment procedures, have another purpose – to help individuals and organizations shape their future.

For a moment let us turn the tables and consider what the applicant expects from the selection and recruitment processes. Research has shown that most applicants have similar expectations; they want to be interviewed. Applicants have a further subset of expectations about the interview. They expect the interviewer to give them information on the job and the organization and expect that they will have to talk about themselves, their experience and suitability. Generally they believe that not enough is said by the interviewer, but they expect, and think it's a good sign, if they do the majority of the talking. In short, applicants want their *day in court*. Despite what we know about the relative validity and fairness of the unstructured interview, it remains popular with candidates.

Box 5.6   The popularity of interviews

The vast majority (95%) of the interviewers and almost as many candidates (85%) felt interviews were a fair method of selecting people, despite all the adverse publicity they have had over the years. When asked whether panel interviews were more fair than one-to-one interviews, 52% of the interviewers said yes, 35% were unsure, and just 13% said no. However, nearly two-thirds of the candidates stated a preference for one-to-one interviews, with only 13% positively preferring the panel approach (Fletcher, 1992).

The popularity of the one-to-one unstructured interview is due, most likely, to the fact that it is usually the most comfortable selection experience. This is especially the case if a warm atmosphere develops during the session. The candidate feels less like a laboratory specimen and more like a human being.

Earlier we noted that the interview is good at assessing the social skills of candidates. This links to the need to assess whether the candidate is going to be able to operate and thrive in the organization's culture. There is a large body of research demonstrating the power of cultures to impact upon the individual's success or failure, and employers are aware of the need to recruit only those who will adapt favourably to their culture. This can only be assessed by a face-to-face encounter such as an interview with realistic job previews. Research also suggests that organizations recruit and retain those in their image, the implication being that those recruited are either similar in their beliefs, attitudes, etc., to the organization, or they rapidly become so. If they are or cannot, they leave and are replaced.

Developing a selection strategy

So how can we pull all this together? Part of the answer lies in the recognition of different stages and different requirements within the selection process. Selection is more than simply trying to identify the 'best' candidate; it is also concerned with the integration of the new employee into the organization and with treating applicants fairly. During this chapter we have seen that different selection techniques have different strengths and weaknesses. The unstructured interview, for example, is fairly poor at discovering the 'best' candidate, but it is good for negotiating with candidates, answering candidates' questions, giving the selection process a 'human face' and managers the opportunity to participate in the selection decision. It seems sensible therefore to divide the selection process into separate stages, with each stage having a specific purpose. Below we set out how this might work.

Begin by conducting a thorough job analysis, one that results in an understanding of the job and the skills, experience, etc. required to do it. The job analysis is used to produce a job description and a job specification, which can be used to establish job-related criteria. The job description should also be examined to see if the job is well designed by referring to a well respected model of job design.

Care is taken to design a recruitment strategy that will produce a manageable number of suitably qualified applicants. Application forms, if they are to be used, should be designed to incorporate the job-related criteria in a manner that can be rated for quick and accurate filtering.

Tests are used to discover how well each applicant can do the job. Here the selector uses appropriate selection technique(s) with the highest validity, probably structured interviews or analogous tests. A small number, those who correspond best to the job-related criteria, are shortlisted to progress further. Only a small number of candidates, say two or three for each vacancy, should progress to the next stage. In this way the selection process preserves as much predictive validity as possible, while recognizing the realities of the 'real world', i.e. that line managers want to make the decision about who joins their team and will probably opt to do so by using an unstructured interview.

Applicants are made fully aware of the realities of the job, if possible, by using a realistic job preview that allows each applicant to actually do the job for a period of time.

Unstructured interviews are used to answer candidates' questions and to give them the chance to meet people from the organization. It is also an opportunity for members of the organization, especially line managers, to meet the candidates and play a part in the decision. The interviewers select the candidate who seems most able to adapt to and thrive in the organization's culture.

Finally, the performance of the successful candidate is monitored to see if any changes are needed to the selection process to make better decisions in future and to check for bias.

Summary

As has already been said, there is no ideal way to select staff; every method has its strengths and weaknesses and every method will be more or less appropriate to each situation. The best way to ensure that you have designed a fair and appropriate system is to carry out a thorough job analysis first and write it up as a job description. From the job description you should be able to produce a job specification, which is a description of the skills, experience, qualifications, etc. needed to do the job; this will help you pinpoint suitable selection methods for that job. Table 5.3 summarizes the strengths and weaknesses of the main selection techniques.

Table 5.3 A summary of the strengths and weaknesses of the main selection techniques

Technique	*Validity*	*Cost*	*Applicability*	*Fairness*
Unstructured interviews	Moderate	Medium	High	Untested
Structured interviews	High	High	High	No problems
References	Poor	Low	High	A few doubts
Biodata	Moderate	High	Moderate	Some doubts
Mental ability tests	Hign	Low/medium	High	Major doubts
Aptitude tests	Poor	Low	High	Some doubts
Personality tests	Poor	Low/medium	High	Untested
Assessment centres	High	Very High	Fairly high	No problems
Analogous tests	High	High	Blue collar	No problems
Graphology	None	Low	High	Untested
.Astrology	None	Low	High	Untested

Adapted from Muchinsky (1986) and from Cook (1993).

References

Blinkhorn, S. and Johnson, C. (1990) The insignificance of personality testing. *Nature*, 348, pp. 671–2, 20–27 December.

Carlson, R. E. (1967) Selection interview decisions: the effect of interviewer experience, relative quota situation, and applicant sample on interviewer decisions. *Personnel Psychology*, 20, pp. 259–80.

Cascio, W. F. (1982) *Costing human resources: the financial impact of behaviour in organizations*. Kent, Boston, Massachusetts.

Cook, M. (1993) *Personnel Selection and Productivity*. (2nd edition). John Wiley and Sons, Chichester.

Coussey, M. and Jackson, H. (1991) *Making Equal Opportunities Work*. Pitman Publishing, London.

Dipboye, R. L., Arvey, R. D. and Terpstra, D. E. (1977) Sex and physical attractiveness of raters and applicants as determinánts of resume evaluation. *Journal of Applied Psychology*, 62, pp. 288–94.

Fletcher, C. (1981) Candidates' beliefs and self-presentation strategies in selection interviews. *Personnel Review*, 10, pp. 14–17.

Fletcher, C. (1992) Ethics and the job interview. *Personnel Management*, March, pp. 36–9.

Gaugler, B. B., Rosenthal, D. B., Thornton, G. C. and Bentson, C. (1979) Meta-analysis of assessment center validity. *Journal of Applied Psychology*, 72, pp. 493–511.

Gifford, R., Ng, C. F. and Wilkinson, M. (1985) Nonverbal cues in the employment interview: links between applicant qualities and interviewer judgements. *Journal of Applied Psychology*, 70, pp. 729–36.

Gordon , M. E. and Kleiman , L. S. (1976) The prediction of trainability using a work sample and an aptitude test: a direct comparison. *Personnel Psychology*, 29, pp. 243–53.

Hackman, J. R. and Oldham, G. R. (1976) Motivation through the design of work: Test of a theory. *Organizational Behaviour and Human Performance*, 16, pp. 250–79.

Herriot, P. (1989) Selection as a social process, in Smith, M. and Robertson, I. T. (eds) *Advances in Selection and Assessment*. John Wiley and Sons, Chichester.

Herriot, P. (1990) *Recruitment in the 90s*. Institute of Personnel Management, London.

Herriot, P. and Rothwell, C. (1983) Expectations and impressions in the graduate selection interview. *Journal of Occupational Psychology*, 56, pp. 303–14.

Hunter, J. E. and Hunter, R. F. (1984) Validity and utility of alternative predictors of job performance. *Psychological Bulletin*, 96, 72–98.

Industrial Relations Services (1991) The State of Selection – Current practices and main results, Recruitment and Development Report 16, page 2, April 1991.

Keenan, A. and Wedderburn, A. A. I. (1980) Putting the boot on the other foot: Candidates' descriptions of interviewers. *Journal of Occupational Psychology*, 53, pp. 81–89.

Kinicki, A. J. and Lockwood, C. A. (1985) The interview process: an examination of factors recruiters use in evaluation job applicants. *Journal of Vocational Behaviour*, 26, pp. 117–25.

Latham, G. P., Saari, L. M., Pursell, E. D. and Campion, M. A., (1980) The Situational Interview. *Journal of Applied Psychology*, 65, pp. 422–7.

McDaniel, M. A., Whetzel, D. L., Schmidt, F. L., Hunter, J. E., Maurer, S. and Russell, J. (1987) *The validity of employment interviews: a review and meta-analysis*. Unpublished.

Martin, H. J. (1985) Managing Specialized Corporate Cultures, in Kilmann, R. H., Saxton, M. J., Serpa, R. and Associates (eds) *Gaining Control of the Corporate Culture*. Jossey-Bass, San Francisco.

Mintzberg, H. (1973) *The Nature of Managerial Work*. Harper and Row, New York.

Muchinsky, P. M. (1986) Personnel Selection Methods, in Cooper, C. L. and Robertson, I. T. (eds) *International Review of Industrial and Organizational Psychology*. John Wiley and Sons, Chichester.

Parkinson, C. N. (1957) *Parkinson's Law*, Penguin, London.

Peters, L. J. and Hull, R. (1970) *The Peter Principle*, Pan Books, London.

Reilly, R. R. and Chao, G. T. (1982) Validity and fairness of some alternative employee selection procedures. *Personnel Psychology*, 35, pp. 1–62.

Robertson, I.T. and Makin, P.J. (1986) Management selection in Britain: a survey and critique. *Journal of Occupational Psychology*, 59, pp. 45–57.

Rundquist, E. A. (1947) Development of an interview for selection purposes, in Kelly, G. A. (ed.) *New methods in applied psychology*, University of Maryland Press, College Park, MD.

Rynes, S. and Gerhart, B. (1990) Interview assessments of applicant 'fit': an exploratory investigation. *Personnel Psychology*, 43, pp. 13–35.

Schmitt, , N., Gooding, R. Z., Noe, R. A. and Kirsch, M. (1984) Meta-analysis of validity studies published between 1964 and 1982 and the investigation of study characteristics. *Personnel Psychology*, 37, pp. 407–22.

Schneider, B. (1987) The people make the place. *Personnel Psychology*, 40, pp. 437–53.

Shackleton, V. (1989) *How to pick people for jobs*, Fontana, London.

Shackleton, V. and Newell, S. (1991) Management selection: a comparative survey of methods used in top British and French companies. *Journal of Occupational Psychology*, 64, pp. 23–36.

Smith, J. M. (1989) *The paradox of talent, occasional research paper*, Coutts Career Consultants, London.

Springbett , B. M. (1958) Factors affecting the final decision in the employment interview. *Canadian Journal of Psychology*, 12, pp. 13–22.

Tett, R. P., Jackson, D. N. and Rothstein, M. (1991) Personality measures as predictors of job performance – a meta-analytic review. *Personnel Psychology*, 44, pp. 703–42.

Tucker, D. H. and Rowe, P. M. (1977) Consulting the application form prior to interview: an essential step in the selection process. *Journal of Applied Psychology*, 62, pp. 283–7.

Ulrich, L. and Trumbo, D. (1965) The selection interview since 1949. *Psychological Bulletin*, 63, pp. 174–200.

Vineburg, R. and Joyner, J. N. (1982) *Prediction of job performance: a review of military studies*. Human Resources Research Organization, Alexandria, Virginia.

Wanous, J. P. (1978) Realistic job previews: can a procedure to reduce turnover also influence the relationship between abilities and performance? *Personnel Psychology*, 31, pp. 249–58.

Wiesner, W. H. and Cronshaw, S. F., (1988) A meta-analytic investigation of the impact of interview format and degree of structure on the validity of the employment interview. *Journal of Occupational Psychology, 1988*, 61, pp. 275–90.

6 Managing career development

Introduction

In many ways career development and management succession planning are at the core of human resource development. If an organization is taking training and development of its staff seriously, then it will be encouraging employees to take part in planning their own career development in relation to organizational and personal career goals. Both career development and succession planning require the integration of human resource planning, assessment, selection and

---

Box 6.1 Some comments on organizational practice

It has become fashionable recently to take the approach that because of the changing nature of organizations, and because people expect to have several different employers in the course of their career, it is pointless to invest effort in career management . . . But an organization has a vested interest in promoting the careers of its staff. They are its prime asset yet probably most have less than one third of their available potential utilized; this wastage needs to be added to the cost of losing people whose careers have been frustrated (Andrew Mayo, Director of Personnel, ICL (Europe), 1992, p. 37)

In many organizations, succession planning has simply meant executives or their peers secretly meeting to hand-pick successors, often without even their would-be replacements knowing their selection until the last minute (Mabey and Iles, 1993, p. 17)

. . . it has been suggested that despite some recent improvements to the process such as the use of the term development centre to replace the rather clinical sounding assessment centre, the improved effectiveness of assessor training and the use of rigorously developed performance criteria, a substantial determinant of actual performance is genuinely unaccounted for – the candidates' views of themselves and their situation (Burgoyne, 1989). We would contend that without this vital information, the quality of decisions taken about an individual's future development and career in the organization must be seriously reduced (Jacobs and Bolton, 1993, p. 55).

placement, appraisal, training and development, performance and reward management within organizational structure and culture. As such, they should be of central importance, yet are often neglected.

Comments such as those in Box 6.1 imply that career and succession planning have largely been neglected by organizations. But how serious is this? To what extent should organizations take responsibility for the careers of their employees and how much should individuals accept responsibility for planning their own careers? And should human resource development concentrate on employee development in the interests of achieving organizational objectives, or on career development; and are these concepts mutually exclusive? These are issues we explore in this chapter.

The term 'career' can mean a number of things. It can imply advancement – persons move 'up' in their career rather than 'down', although we refer to 'career moves', which may also be lateral. We also refer to people 'having a career in' some form of profession, such as medicine, banking or management, and there is an implication, if now largely out-of-date, that a career is likely to be stable over time. In fact it is becoming more common for people to think in terms of 'career portfolios', interrelated sets of work experiences that may be combined to provide career evidence for a range of jobs. Because of this, we shall define career as 'the pattern of work-related experiences that span the course of a person's life'. This definition not only broadens the concept of 'career' but makes it as relevant to unskilled and manual operators as to engineers and professors.

While it is becoming recognized that the concept of the lifelong career is disappearing, there is also an awareness that perspectives and career aspirations change, depending on the stage of an individual's life and career development. Thus you would expect to find significant

---

Box 6.2 Career planning at Sainsburys

Sainsburys launched a scheme at ten London stores in 1992 that was designed to provide better career advice to non-managerial staff. Called 'Choices', the scheme is now to be extended throughout the supermarket chain. The programme is available to both full-time and part-time weekly paid staff and aims to help them develop personal skills and achieve their full potential.

Staff are invited to attend a short seminar before being asked to complete a questionnaire that assesses their individual strengths and weaknesses. Later, they can attend a one-to-one careers guidance discussion with their branch personnel manager before deciding what further action they can take.

This scheme is particularly interesting in that if focuses on staff below the level of manager and includes part-time workers, who form a large part of the retail food industry's workforce.

differences in perspectives on careers in a twenty-year-old and someone approaching retirement.

Career planning and development

Before tackling the issues of career and succession planning, we need to consider the different categories of people employed in organizations and the range of ways in which they may, or may not, achieve their potential in career terms. Figure 6.1 offers one way of differentiating between individuals in terms of their performance and potential.

In Figure 6.1 the high flyers are those with both high performance and high potential, the people on the fast track who will either rise quickly through the organization or, if frustrated and dissatisfied, will leave and go elsewhere. The high performers should be the organization's key workers, as they consistently perform well in the job they are doing. Some may already have reached the peak of their performance abilities but the danger is that they can be lodged in jobs that they have outgrown and that no longer challenge them. Often it is assumed that high flyers can look after themselves in career terms and that 'fast-track' programmes will provide them with all the necessary development opportunities. But such programmes are often designed from an organizational perspective, and take little account of individual career planning or career aspirations.

In the top left hand quadrant in Figure 6.1 are those employees who have been identified as 'high performers' in that they consistently perform well but are considered to have reached the peak of their potential. This should not mean that they do not have a future, a career, in the organization, nor that they do not need training and development opportunities. Indeed their high performance may drop

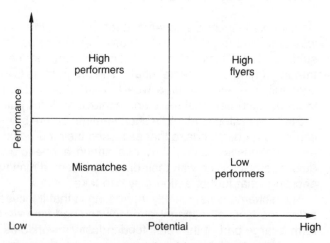

Figure 6.1 *The career matrix (adapted from Armstrong, 1991)*

if they are not offered variety and the chance to develop in their chosen career.

The low performers with high potential form one of the problematic areas, necessitating investigation into why these people are not achieving their potential and moving into one of the upper quadrants of the matrix. There may be any number of reasons, including dissatisfaction with one or more aspects of the organization, leading to lack of motivation to perform well (see Chapter 7). Or the reasons may be related to lack of training in certain aspects of the job, leading to below average performance. In either case organizational opportunities such as appraisal should be designed not only to measure performance but to identify what can be done by the organization to help individuals achieve their potential in both performance and career terms.

The bottom left-hand quadrant holds the most problematic employees of all – those with low performance and low potential. They are referred to in this model as 'mismatches', since they are obviously not closely matched to organizational requirements and objectives. It could be argued that they should never have been recruited in the first place but, realistically, all organizations have their share of 'mismatches'. In some cases these are individuals who failed to change with the organization; in others they were employed for a role that has disappeared; yet a third reason may lie in the organization's recruitment and selection processes. There is little hope of improving the performance of 'mismatches' in their current job or role, since low potential has already been identified. They might, however, benefit from moving to a different job, within their potential – but often this means a downward move, which is seldom received well by the individual.

The career matrix suggests that there can be movement between each of its quadrants, usually (and preferably) in an upward direction, whereby those in the lower quadrants can attain the upper ones. There may be sideways movement as well, although this is less common and less desirable; you don't want a company composed entirely of high flyers any more than one in which the bulk of the workforce can be classified as 'mismatches'. Downward movement, the least desirable, would usually only result where an individual became seriously demotivated as a result of organizational policies or practice.

Self-development activity

You might like to classify your own staff on the career matrix and see what kind of balance you have between the four categories. You could also consider what kinds of training and development opportunities are available to them and whether these are appropriate in relation to their position on the career matrix.

Organizational versus individual responsibility for career planning

One aspect of career planning that creates problems for human resource managers is the extent to which the individual and the organization take responsibility for careers. There appears to be agreement that career management usually receives little support when it is wholly centralized and the sole province of the organization; there needs to be a balance between central management and individual development. There are, too, a number of drawbacks in organizational planning for career development. It is often difficult to foresee staff turnover accurately, particularly today as people move between organizations more quickly; and if organizations take responsibility for career development, individuals can cease to seek opportunities for self-development. There is also the danger of dependence on the opinions and influence of superiors in the assessment of the individual, and an evaluation of a person's potential is often judged on past performance and present experience rather than on potential.

Charles Handy (1985), Visiting Professor at London Business School, has described organizational planning for career development as a human hurdle race. In highly structured organizations particularly there are too many hurdles to be overcome, with no short cuts available even for high flyers. There is also usually no retrieval mechanism available whereby individuals who have failed at one hurdle in the early stages of their career have an opportunity to try again – and again. Finally, in the career hurdle race, 'the faster you move, the more successful' ethos tends to prevail, which means shorter and shorter time horizons at each stage. Managers are concentrating so much on the next hurdle and how to overcome it that, in their current role, they neglect anything that is not seen as directly relevant to promotion.

However, if the organization has no interest in career and succession planning, individuals will find it difficult to make their own career plans; as with highly structured, centralized organizational planning, the lack of any planning is likely to result in a high turnover of staff. In Box 6.3 we offer one view of a compromise between organizational and individual career planning.

Andrew Mayo has provided a useful framework for managing careers, in which both the organization and the individual take certain responsibilities, separately and jointly. In his opinion organizational responsibilities within a career management framework should include clearly communicated career and grading structures; policies, for example, for high flyers or expatriates; human resource and succession planning; and person specifications for jobs and appointment processes. The individual should take responsibility for his or her choice of career and for undertaking relevant self-development activities, but will need career counselling, either from within the organization via a mentor or from a specialist consultant. The

---

Box 6.3 Individual versus organizational perspective

From an organizational or managerial standpoint, career development involves tracking career paths and developing career ladders. Management seeks information to direct and to monitor the progress of special groups of employees, and to ensure that capable managerial and technical talent will be available to meet the organization's needs. Career development from the organization's perspective is also called organizational career planning.

In contrast, individual career development, or career planning, focuses on assisting individuals to identify their major goals and to determine what they need to do to achieve these goals. Note that in the latter case, the focus is entirely on the individual and includes his or her life outside the organization, as well as inside. So while organizational career development looks at individuals filling the needs of the organization, individual career development addresses each individual's personal work career and other lifestyle issues (De Cenzo and Robbins, 1994, p. 290).

---

organization also needs to use appraisal and development reviews, and provide assessment and development centre opportunities, career breaks and alternative methods of employment.

In order to create a career management framework, Mayo (1992) suggests that a number of analyses and reviews need to take place. These would include:

- an assessment of the human resource needs of the organization and of the knowledge and skills required in the future;
- a review of the culture and processes of the organization in terms of senior management;
- commitment to the process of career management, clear policies and systematic processes that ensure fairness and efficiency, the extent to which individuals have freedom of choice in promotion and job movement and the resources available to support the career planning process;
- an analysis of the structure of the organization and how it encourages, or impedes, career progress upwards and across functions;
- a plan for managing and using data relating to individual and organizational career;
- planning and how this is reviewed and evaluated.

Table 6.1 attempts to bring together the views of Mayo, De Cenzo and Robbins, and others on the relative responsibilities of organizations and individuals in respect of career planning and management. It

Table 6.1 Organizational and individual responsibilities in relation to career planning and management.

Organizational responsibilities	*Individual responsibilities*
Recruitment, selection, appointment, and downsizing	Choice of education and training (within limits)
Internal promotion and career structures	Choice of job/organization (within limits)
Grading and pay structures	Undertaking self-development plans and activities
Appraisal scheme as opportunity for discussion of individual career aspirations	Willingness to discuss career plans and to take/follow advice
Provision of training and development opportunities	Choice of training and development
Provision of career counselling and mentoring	Taking opportunities provided by the organization
Provision of career resource centres, career seminars, career planning workshops, career breaks and alternative work experiences	

lays emphasis on the organization's responsibility for providing career development opportunities in such a way that the individual can make an informed choice. But the individual must take responsibility not only for making the choice but for maximizing the benefit to be gained from training and development opportunities. Ideally the career planning process should be jointly undertaken, with both the organization and the individual recognizing and accepting their distinct areas of responsibility.

Career planning programmes

Iles and Mabey (1993) make a useful differentiation between career planning and career management programmes. In their view it is generally expected, and preferred, that career planning is the prerogative of the individual, calling for self-assessment, assessment of career opportunities and action planning in relation to career goals. The organization's role is to provide materials for self-study and assessment, career workshops, counselling and information.

Self-study materials that can precede self-assessment have many advantages in that they are designed to be studied at the individual's preferred pace and are not seen as competitive. They can lead to completion of a career preference form, as the basis for career discusions or for a self-assessment of strengths and weaknesses in relation to career options. Similarly, structured group workshops, with a strong emphasis on experiential activities, can provide a basis for self-assessment with support from peers and others in the organization.

Career counselling may be formal or informal, provided by staff within the organization or by consultants who are brought in, or with external agencies. The latter is most common where outplacement is concerned, and Iles and Mabey suggest that it is ironic that 'often employees about to leave got – or get – better career counselling from their organization than those to be retained'.

Although such career planning activities may be provided by the organization, their effectiveness is rarely evaluated. There has been some evidence that such activities increase participants' awareness of the career choices and constraints within which they can operate within their current organization and that they experience increased control over their careers. However, their interest in their jobs does not appear to improve. This is not surprising in the light of research into employee commitment (see Chapter 7) and the identification of commitment to work itself, the job, the individual's career and the organization, any of which may be mutually exclusive.

In general, there seems to be little evidence that career planning workshops, workbooks or counselling help advance participants' careers by such criteria as salary progression, job level or job satisfaction, or help participants perform better or have fewer work/non-work conflicts. Such career planning programmes may be of greatest benefit to 'internals', as all career planning programmes assume that individuals can influence the direction of their careers and take an active role in fostering career growth. Work and career success itself seems to enhance the expectancy of 'internal control, raise motivation to succeed and to enhance tendencies towards internal control.

Career management programmes

Career planning programmes are seen as serving the interests of individual career development. Career management programmes, however, are considered to be organization-centred initiatives in which the organization provides work experience opportunities for employees in relation to their career plans and preferences. These opportunities often include job assignments, job rotations, evaluations of potential or selection, appraisal, and training and development activities. Career management programmes may be generally available or contain within them specific elements that can be targeted to the career development of, for example, high flyers, women or minority groups. Most of them incorporate the provision of career information about job vacancies, training programmes and career paths within the organization.

Not all organizations are as forward looking as Cathay Pacific (see Box 6.4) and, too often, the appraisal system may identify training

---

Box 6.4   Making your career with Cathay Pacific

Cathay Pacific has designed a career management system, building on the final stage of its appraisal form, which is concerned with personal development. Around 300 managers and future leaders have their career managed by a staff conference, while the career development for other staff is supported by a range of resources and programmes. These include development discussions with appraisers, internal advertisements, personal development programmes, limited psychometric assessment and a job bidding system. In particular, career planning is facilitated by a career-point counselling and resource centre, a career-building interactive programme, career counselling from managers and peers, open learning packages and a human job library.

---

needs that cannot be met or for which there has been no provision. Alternatively, staff development opportunities may be out of date and no longer meet organizational or individual needs. If the appraisal system has not been appropriately designed, there may be a tension between performance-related training needs and career-related development opportunities.

Career planning and development techniques

Methods of career planning and development that can be encouraged or provided by the organization include career reviews and career counselling, formal or informal mentoring schemes, the provision of information about career paths within the organization, fast-track programmes, psychometric tests, self-assessment materials, development centres and career planning workshops.

Performance review as part of a performance management system is discussed in Chapter 9. Essentially any performance review related to an individual's career development needs must be separated from performance measurement for purposes of pay or promotion. Counselling sessions, as part of performance review, provide opportunities for individuals to discuss their career aspirations with a line manager and to receive comment on these and suggestions for career development activities.

Mentoring, which is also discussed in Chapter 3, has been established in many organizations, such as the UK National Health Service, with varying degrees of success. Although Iles and Mabey found that organizational assignment of mentors was considered to be the fairest development process in their survey (see Box 6.5), they appeared to have little impact on career development. This may be

Box 6.5 Reactions to career development techniques

A sample of 120 managers participating in a part-time MBA programme and representing private, public and voluntary sector organizations, were asked to evaluate a range of career development techniques that they had personally experienced, either with their existing or previous employers. Though absolute numbers were small for some techniques, some interesting findings have emerged. The extent of use of individual techniques is summarized in the table below:

Technique	Used in present organization (%)	Personally experienced in present or previous organization (%)
Career reviews	77	70
Informal mentoring	43	30
Career path information	35	27
Fast-track programmes	34	12
Assigned mentors	26	11
Psychometric tests with feedback	22	20
Self-assessment materials	19	18
Development centres	18	6
Career planning workshops	16	6

The table represents a relatively small sample but accords with results in similar surveys undertaken in America. It would appear that the most popular forms of development are those that do not require particular investment outside day-to-day organizational working practice.

Having **mentors** assigned to them was seen as the *fairest* process of those listed, but with a relatively low impact on career development. In contrast, informal mentors were not only more widespread but also seen as more *useful and influential* in career terms; however, probably because of its 'hit or miss', 'who you know' nature, these were perceived as considerably less fair than assigned mentoring.

Fast-track programmes appeared to suffer from a similar concern, even by those on them!

Career reviews with superiors were highly rated across all dimensions. Tapping into the power nexus of the enterprise may be the crucial factor here: not only is the technique seen to be just and useful but it is also anchored in organizational reality. It is perhaps for this reason that the more passive techniques of **career path information** and **self-assessment materials** met with a more muted, though still favourable, response.

> **Psychometric tests with feedback** were also highly rated by participants. They were perceived as assisting personal and career development, as well as enhancing the organization's effectiveness. This represents a remarkable difference from the relatively low ratings of psychometric tests when used in a selection context; and the opportunity for feedback appears to account for this favourable reaction to similar techniques. Only a small sample had experienced **developmental assessment centres**, all of whom saw them as useful in helping personal development. While not all felt it a fair process, of all techniques it engendered the most positive feelings about the organization, as against **career planning workshops**, which engendered the least, and were surprisingly rated as helping least in career development. This could well be the result of the individual focus of development centres and the collaborative nature of ensuing feedback sessions. By contrast, career planning workshops may be viewed as providing useful tools for personal development, but not organizationally specific enough to assist career planning.
>
> Overall, there seems to be a disparity between the low usage of some techniques and their favourable reception as career development tools. This applies particularly to psychometric tests with feedback and development centres, which on the basis of these data, represent unexploited potential in terms of human resource management. (Iles and Mabey, 1993, pp. 112–14).

because mentoring is often seen as a peripheral activity for, and by, middle managers who have too little time to expend on it and are unclear about what it means. Informal mentoring, particularly where the individual has freedom to choose a mentor or mentors, is more likely to reflect the individual's needs rather than organizational objectives. Thus, finding a mentor in one's chosen career field is likely to have a greater impact on an individual's career development – if one who is willing to give time to the mentoring activity can be found. Without organizational support, mentoring has little chance of formal recognition in terms of time and training.

It is surprising how many large organizations fail to provide employees with substantive **information about career options**, particularly when the organization is multinational or consists of a number of relatively autonomous business units. This is a major area where managers could provide, for example, information on common career paths, and on those less common, for their subordinates, to which can be linked relevant training and development opportunities, as well as information about internal job vacancies, movements and work assignments.

Fast-track programmes cater for the high flyers, offering job experiences, accelerated promotion and training and development specifically designed for the employee who has been identified as having high potential, while **self-assessment materials** may include workbooks, video or computer programs on career planning and development. **Psychometric tests** can include tests of ability, personality, values, interests or preferences, with feedback from trained personnel (see Chapter 5 for a discussion of psychometric techniques).

The use of assessment centres for development – and hence their description as **development centres** – has been gaining ground. As described in Chapters 4 and 5, candidates in assessment centres are assessed against criteria derived from job analysis, either for selection or performance measurement. When used as a development centre, assessment is designed to identify long-term potential through the generation of a profile of strengths and weaknesses. These are discussed by a trained specialist with the individual and appropriate development activities planned. In general, development centres are highly regarded by those who have participated in them, perceived as fair and of help in making career decisions. It has also been found that they can tend to disturb preconceived career plans and expectations, which may have been too complacent or narrow in the first place. Like any form of assessment centre, development centres require a relatively high investment of resources, including trained personnel to design and interpret the form of assessment and give individual feedback. Unlike assessment centres – and this has been a criticism of their design – development centres do not have a 'pass – fail' image, nor do they appear to participants as a career hurdle that, if not cleared, cannot be attempted again.

Career planning or development workshops bring together groups of employees with their line managers to work on common problems and misconceptions and to share their separate expectations. These may be provided for employees on entry to the organization and at mid- and late-career. Such workshops may include self-diagnostic activities, diagnosis of individual–organizational mismatches, discussion of career alternatives and career development opportunities.

There are a number of commercially available career planning and development tools, most of which require trained administration and interpretation. Box 6.6 gives an example of a diagnostic career development questionnaire, which lacks a psychometric pedigree but which can, nevertheless, provide information about an individual's hopes, aspirations and attitudes to work.

The results of questionnaires such as the career values inventory can provide a 'snapshot' of an individual's preferred work, but there are three things to remember about work preferences in relation to careers. First, they take time to stabilize. As school-leavers or newly qualified graduates, we are unlikely to have a firm idea of what our work priorities are because it takes a few years to test out our expectations and taste the reality of different work experiences. Second, they are not static: even when established, priorities change. Early in our careers we

---

Box 6.6　Career values inventory

Sort the values listed below into five columns with regard to your *ideal* job. The five column headings are:

- ALWAYS VALUED
- OFTEN VALUED
- SOMETIMES VALUED
- SELDOM VALUED
- NEVER VALUED

The ALWAYS VALUED column should have eight or less values in it.

When you have sorted the values into the five columns, prioritize the values in the ALWAYS VALUED column from 1 (highest value) to the lowest value. Finally, circle each of the values in all the columns that you believe you already have in your present job.

Creativity	Security	High earnings
Independence	Promotion	anticipated
Time freedom	Help society	Profit, gain
Exercise competence	Moral fulfilment	Affiliation
Influence others	Knowledge	Community
Help others	Challenging problems	Artistic creativity
Recognition	Make decisions	Aesthetics
Power and authority	Creative expression	Change and variety
Supervision	Intellectual status	Excitement
Work on frontiers of knowledge	Location	Job tranquillity
Competition	Status	Work with others
Adventure	Work alone	Work under pressure
Fast pace	Public contact	Stability
Precision work	Friendship	Physical challenge

---

may place more value on creativity, initiative and risk-taking, but later we may sacrifice this for security of tenure. Third, priorities do not exist in a vacuum. Naturally our career choices and decisions at work can be strongly influenced by our commitment to leisure and/or social activities, by the buoyancy of the labour market or by family attachments.

A more graphic and less cerebral way of getting at the same sort of information is to ask an individual or group to plot their experiences chronologically along a horizontal line from the beginning of their career, or the start of their career with a particular organization, to the present day. This is known as a *time line,* and may be illustrated with significant developments in the individual's career in the form of pictures. An alternative is to ask someone to create a career map instead of a straight line; this may be in the form of a river, a road, a railway line, a flow chart or whatever graphic representation the individual chooses.

> ### Self-development activity
>
> Rate your own work preferences in the Career Values Inventory or create your own illustrated time line or career map. What does the experience tell you about your own career development and work preferences?

We have used many of the career planning and development techniques outlined above with a range of individuals from different organizations and educational backgrounds. There is usually initial suspicion, particularly when people are asked to create something like a career map, but the experience inevitably generates discussion and stimulates shared experience.

Career development versus employee development

Given earlier discussions in Chapter 3, you may be wondering what differences there are, or should be, between career development and employee development. Both employ similar developmental techniques, and there is an argument that they should run in tandem. But not all organizations can make provision for career development that will fulfil the career aspirations of all, or even of the majority, of their employees.

The main difference is in timescale. Employee development is aimed at improving performance in the current job or in relation to medium-term promotion; it has a sense of immediacy that is not manifest in career development. The organization and its managers that are looking beyond the next few years are intent on developing people who will improve organizational effectiveness in the longer term. Even the smaller organization can take this futuristic stance and link employee development to career development, providing managers are clear about their long-term human resource needs and use these to inform decisions about selection, training and development (see Box 6.7).

Management succession planning

Essentially succession planning comprises defining managerial and other human resource requirements over a period of, say, three to five years, in terms of the skills and characteristics required for successful performance; and identifying managerial potential and ensuring managers' development in order to meet forecast requirements. In

---

Box 6.7 The importance of effective career development to the organization

Assuming that an organization already provides extensive employee development programmes, why should it need to consider a career development programme as well? A long-term career focus should increase the organization's effectiveness in managing its human resources. More specifically, we can identify several positive results that can accrue from a well-designed career development programme:

1 Career development is consistent with, and a natural extension of, human resource planning. Involving employees in the planning and management of their careers in line with organizational objectives will increase the probability that the right people will be available to meet the organization's changing staffing requirements.
2 High quality employees are more likely to give preference to employers who demonstrate a concern for their employees' future. If already employed by an organization which makes provision for career development, these people may exhibit greater loyalty and commitment to the organization.
3 Career development programmes can ensure that the needs of minority groups and women do not get overlooked and can make a positive contribution to their growth and development in the organization.
4 Restructuring and downsizing often destroy existing career paths and career levels. Career planning and counselling can help to reduce frustration in employees in this kind of situation.
5 If employees think their employing organizations are concerned about their long-term well-being, they are likely to project positive images of their organization outside their work environment; this promotes organizational goodwill to the organization's advantage (De Cenzo and Robbins, 1994, pp. 291–3).

---

practice, given the highly volatile working environment of today, increasingly flexible succession planning is taking over from formal programmes. Succession planning is not merely replacement planning; it is differentiated by its strategic focus on the active development of potential successors.

Organizations have developed a variety of means to ensure succession planning. Some attempt to identify management potential at recruitment, while others provide a range of training and development activities for updating valued existing staff. High flyer

---

Box 6.8 Planning the advancement of staff with high potential

Rank Xerox managers have long-term objectives aligned with company strategy and clear corporate vision. There is a strong succession planning process and 80 per cent of jobs are filled from the succession plan. Planned successors are not told in advance specifically which jobs it is planned that they fill but they are briefed on a range of career options.

Rank Xerox tries to plan the advancement of those with high potential and is increasing the focus on moving them more quickly through the organization. However, people identified as having high potential are not informed of their status.

Succession planning has also become part of the culture at Royal Insurance. For example, all director-level jobs are backed up with possible successors, bearing in mind the need for cross-functional and general management skills. Top functional jobs, such as finance director, are treated somewhat differently as they require specific qualifications. Below director level, the process involves considering a far wider population and allows for changes in the organization or in managerial roles. The objective is to identify pools of high-potential candidates who could be promoted to a range of jobs. Managers are well aware of the management development philosophy at Royal Insurance and every effort is made to meet individual preferences for career development (Wallum, 1993).

---

and fast-track programmes are another common way of preparing people for career advancement in line with their potential. In some organizations succession planning is widely disseminated and linked to performance appraisals and development planning; a 'pool' of immediate replacements and successors who could take over key positions within a specified time frame may be available. In contrast, other organizations rely strongly on internal politics and the power of senior management; yet others follow a policy of recruiting successors for senior posts from outside the organization altogether. In today's rapidly changing world external recruitment is becoming more common as new and different skills are required, and potential successors have not acquired them.

This lack of appropriate skills in the existing management cadre indicates a concomitant lack of forward planning and analysis of the kinds of skills necessary for top management. Information for management succession planning should come from organization reviews and demand-and-supply forecasts, as well as from performance and potential assessments. But, as we have indicated, management succession planning is a somewhat random exercise and, even where it exists, implementation of succession planning can be problematic. See Box 6.9.

Box 6.9   Problems with implementing succession planning

Barriers to effective succession planning may include the following factors:

● A lack of perceived strong candidates at middle and senior levels. For example, in one construction and property company based in the South of England we have worked with, the new chief executive wanted to fill a number of senior positions but found no one inside the company to be suitable. The existing management development and succession planning systems were excellent at running sites and projects but deficient in commercial and business skills.
● A reluctance of managers to give up high potential people for developmental job moves.
● Uneven implementation of formal systems, perhaps due to business unit autonomy and diversity.
● Dilemmas over how to evaluate and integrate management potential in acquired or in merged companies.
● A 'pragmatic' and 'professional' rather than a 'strategic' orientation. Again, the southern construction company discussed earlier tended to have a 'professional' culture oriented towards professional excellence rather than strategic positioning in a changing market place.
● Under-resourced human resource functions.
● A task-oriented management style – again characteristic of the southern property and construction company referred to earlier.
● Barriers to planned lateral or cross-functional movements within a company. These seem more characteristic of Japanese companies than British ones.
● A turbulent operating environment, which may create fast moving markets with shorter product life cycles and rapid technological change (Mabey and Iles, 1993, p. 20).

Linking career development and succession planning

In 1993 a survey of nineteen major international UK and US organizations was carried out in order to develop and test a checklist of those aspects of succession planning and related activities that might reasonably be expected of progressive organizations. The researchers found that whereas, in the past, career planning and succession planning had been separate activities in most organizations, the two were becoming closely linked. Organizations were discovering that successful succession planning had to take full account of individual career aspirations.

Many of the organizations surveyed were planning major changes to their succession planning processes, recognizing that they needed to plan for new roles emerging from their business plan and strategic vision rather than identifying specific people as possible successors to specific posts. There was a recognition also that the earlier focus on jobs was no longer valid since jobs tended to change as organizations restructured and evolved; instead there was a need to focus on knowledge of people. Several organizations had experimented with a competency-based approach to succession planning but had encountered a dilemma in that autonomy was also encouraged. However, the definition of management competencies to meet future rather than current requirements was generally seen as the key to effective succession planning. Where these had been developed, they could be used within the organization for a number of purposes, including internal and external selection, assessment, analysing training and development needs and performance management.

Despite the major conclusion regarding the strong links being forged between career development and succession planning, only a small minority of the organizations in the survey encouraged widespread recognition of these links. There were reservations about letting individuals know they had been identified as high flyers or that they had reached their career potential. Consider the following extract from Wallum:

> Our survey therefore confirmed that, while leading organizations are seeking to improve their succession planning practices, the major advances over the next few years will be by those organizations which seek to undertake succession planning within a very broadly defined framework, embracing both succession and career management. We envisage a fusion of work from succession planners and those concerned with career development to provide an ingtegrated solution to succession and career management issues (Wallum, 1993, p. 45).

This, then, is the challenge for managers in the next decade. To bring career planning and management higher up on the human resource agenda and to link it with employee development and succession planning. In order to do this, senior management will need to be clear in articulating the kinds of skill and competency that will be required to meet the competitive demands of the future, and communicate these to line managers responsible for employee and career development. They, in turn, will need to foster collaborative diagnosis of training and development needs, and appropriate activities that will direct the development of individuals in line with their career aspirations and the competency needs of the organization.

Summary

Before launching into any discussion of career planning and management, it is useful to be aware of the different categories of staff, in terms of performance potential, whose career needs may have to be met. The career development needs of low performers and those who, apparently, have achieved their full potential require consideration in the same way as high flyers.

There are a number of dichotomies surrounding the concept of career development, one being the question of responsibility; does the organization or the individual take responsibility for his or her career development? Ideally it should be a collaborative process, with both taking responsibility for certain elements, and it is argued that career planning should be an individual responsibility, with support from the organization in, for example, the provision of relevant information about organizational career paths. The management of the individual's career should be an organization-centered initiative, based on full knowledge of the individual's career aspirations and the career opportunities available. A full range of career planning and development techniques was discussed, including an evaluation of their effectiveness in terms of career progression.

A second dichotomy besetting this topic is that of an apparent tension between employee development and career development. Are they the same thing? The difference lies in the timescale over which the development is planned, but the two should be indivisible in practice if they are to be effective and meet all the development needs of the individual.

The final section of this chapter has been concerned with management succession planning and the problems surrounding this in today's turbulent working environment. However, this environment itself is seen as making succession planning even more essential, particularly where it is clearly linked to career planning and development.

References

Armstrong, M. (1991) *A Handbook of Personnel Management Practice* (4th edition). Kogan Page.

Andrisani, P. J. and Nestel G. (1976) Internal-external Control as a Contributor to and Outcome of Work Experiences. *Journal of Applied Psychology*, pp. 61.

De Cenzo, D. A. and Robbins, S. P. (1994) *Human Resource management; concepts and practices.* John Wiley and Sons Inc., New York.

Hanson, M. E. (1982) Career Development: Maximising Options. *Personnel Administrator*, 23 (5), pp. 58–61.

Jacobs, R. and Bolton, R. (1993) Career Analysis: The Missing Link in Managerial Assessment and Development. *Human Resource Management Journal*, Vol 3, No 2, pp. 55–62.

Handy, C. (1985) *Understanding Organizations* (3rd edition). Penguin Business Books, Harmondsworth.

Iles, P. and Mabey, C. (1993) Managerial Career Development Programmes: Effectiveness, Availability and Acceptability. *British Journal of Management*, Vol 4, No. 2, June, pp. 103–18.

Mabey, C. and Iles, P. (1993) The Strategic Integration of Assessment and Development Practices: Succession Planning and New Manager Development. *Human Resource Management Journal*, Vol 3, No. 4, pp. 16–34.

Mayo, A. (1992) A Framework for career management. *Personnel Management*, February, pp. 36–9.

Wallum, P. (1993) A broader view of succession planning. *Personnel Management*, September. pp. 42–5.

7 Developing motivation and commitment

Introduction

In his work on 'scientific management' Frederick Winslow Taylor stated that the principal object of management should be to secure the maximum prosperity for the employer, coupled with the maximum prosperity of each employee. For the employer, in Taylor's terms, this meant not only short-term profit, but long-term prosperity; for the employees it meant not just higher wages but achieving their full potential. Employers and management researchers have long sought for the secret of consistent high productivity through the effort of the workforce – and failed to find a definitive solution. Although research uncovered a wide range of factors that increased, or decreased, the will to work, none was universal.

This 'will to work', or motivation, seemed to be an elusive concept, sometimes apparently related to reward systems but, at other times and in other situations, independent of rewards. The term 'rewards' has largely been replaced with 'outcomes', since these appear to relate more closely to the process of motivation; a reward has financial overtones whereas it has been shown that there is a range of social, status and achievement outcomes valued by individuals in the work situation. And, since behaviour can also result in punishment and sanctions, the word 'reward' becomes inappropriate. In recent years the idea of motivation itself, while still valid, has been superseded by the concept of 'employee commitment'.

Commitment is a broader concept than motivation, with different levels (career, job and organizational) at which individuals may demonstrate their belief in, and acceptance of, factors related to the organization in which they work and the extent to which they are willing to exert additional effort. Obviously the concept of 'a committed workforce' is desirable, with its connotations of loyalty, conscientiousness, responsibility and reliability. But, in order to create this ideal, it has been argued that management needs to engender a sense of identification with the organization, a feeling of 'ownership' among its employees, a sense of excitement in the job and confidence in its managers. These, then are the challenges for managers of human resources.

In this chapter we shall be reviewing some of the major theories of motivation in the work context, with an emphasis on the recognition that what acts as a motivating factor for one person will not necessarily motivate someone else. This leads us to consider how motivation and job satisfaction are linked – how the design of jobs, for example, can be improved to increase employee satisfaction – and the link between job satisfaction and performance. Finally, we look at the whole area of commitment and the ways in which the principles and practice of human resource management and development can impact upon it.

Motivation as a process

Much of the early research into motivation concentrated on unsatisfied and satisfied needs, in particular the work of Maslow and Alderfer. Maslow (1943) constructed a 'hierarchy of needs', beginning with the most basic human physiological needs of food, drink and shelter and suggesting that, once lower-level needs were satisfied, the individual moved on to the satisfaction of higher-level needs such as security, acceptance, esteem and 'self-actualization', which included the recognition of achievement.

Alderfer (1972) disputed the idea of a strict hierarchy and proposed that individuals all had needs of 'existence' (physiological and security needs), 'relatedness' (relationships with others) and 'growth' (progression), and that they might have needs in all three categories at the one time.

A third researcher of importance in this area was McClelland (1961), who identified three basic motivating needs; like Alderfer, he suggested that the existence of one of these needs did not preclude the existence of the other two. If all three needs are present, an individual

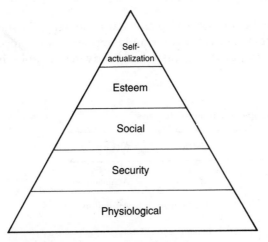

Figure 7.1 *Maslow's hierarchy of needs*

is likely to be strongly motivated. The three basic needs identified and measured by McClelland were:

- *the need for affiliation* – similar to Maslow's 'social' needs and Alderfer's needs of relatedness, this relates to an individual's desire to be part of a group and the need to maintain good working relationships;
- *the need for power* – a desire to be the leader and to be dominant in working relationships, seeking to exercise influence and control;
- *the need for achievement* – related to a strong need for success and recognition of achievement, combined with an equally strong fear of failure

McClelland found that, in general, managers had strong needs for achievement and power but lower needs for affiliation. He saw this as a disadvantage, since managers have to work through other people and gain their co-operation. People with a strong need for achievement often have the following personality and behavioural characteristics:

1 They have good memories, particularly in relation to unfinished projects, and dislike leaving things uncompleted.
2 If they feel people or events are hindering their performance, they can be antagonistic, unfriendly and unsociable.
3 They tend to be workaholics, always in a hurry, working to deadlines and finding it difficult to relax.
4 They prefer tasks that are challenging and in which they have to achieve a standard of excellence to routine activities.
5 They value feedback on how well they are doing so that they can improve their performance.
6 They are unhappy with activities carrying a high risk of failure; equally, they dislike low-risk activities, since these are not challenging enough.
7 They tend to prefer darker or muted colours in what they wear.

The three theories are complementary and Table 7.1 shows the links between them. However, they only represent one approach in the search for explanations of what motivates people in the work situation.

Table 7.1 A comparison of needs theories

Maslow	Alderfer	McClelland
Self-actualization Esteem }	Growth	Achievement
Social	Relatedness	Affiliation
Security Physiological }	Existence	

De Cenzo and Robbins (1994) argue that, if an individual is experiencing deprivation because a particular need is unsatisfied, this can lead to either *functional* or *dysfunctional* tension. Functional tension is necessary to affect motivation – it is the positive desire to satisfy a particular need and to expend effort in doing so. The effort expended is exhibited through outward behaviour, although this behaviour may not always be immediately visible. If the effort results in satisfying the need, the functional tension built up in relation to that particular need will be reduced and there will be a temporary calming effect. We could therefore define motivation as a state of functional tension: the greater the tension, the greater the need to bring about its relief. However, encouraging functional tension through the provision of deprivation is not concomitant with the ideas and principles of human resource management.

Deprivation can also lead to what is described as 'dysfunctional tension' and apathy. Dysfunctional tension occurs when the effort does not, or is not expected to, relieve the dissatisfaction. For example, if a woman employee realizes that, no matter how hard she works, she cannot achieve a target that will reduce her dissatisfaction, she is likely to settle for the bare minimum that will enable her to keep her job. The employer cannot understand why this particular employee, who has considerable potential, does not improve her productivity – and probably doesn't ask her. The answer may lie in the organization's reward systems or in the particular individual's specific unsatisfied needs.

One process model of motivation, known as 'expectancy theory' or 'path–goal theory', shows the relation between effort and outcome. The emphasis here is on the expected outcome of a particular behaviour. If an outcome is to be effective in affecting an individual's decision to behave in a certain way, e.g. to exert additional effort, the individual must believe that this effort will increase the probability of obtaining the desired outcome. The assumption underlying expectancy theory is that all human behaviour is directed by the expectations people have about the relation between their behaviour and the achievement of desired goals.

At its simplest, expectancy theory can be demonstrated by the example of the salesperson who increases his or her effort in making sales in order to win a holiday abroad or a new car. The salesperson 'expects' that, by improving performance, the outcome will be achieved. However, as you will see later in this chapter, the outcome has to be achievable and has to be desired by the individual. If targets are set too high, people will become frustrated, and the effort put into performance will probably decrease (dysfunctional behaviour). Equally, if the individual has no interest in holidays abroad, or has a fear of flying, the expected outcome is not likely to motivate that person to improve performance. Additionally, the outcome itself may not be what was intended; given a high need for achievement, a person may put in extra effort to win the prize not for its value but for what

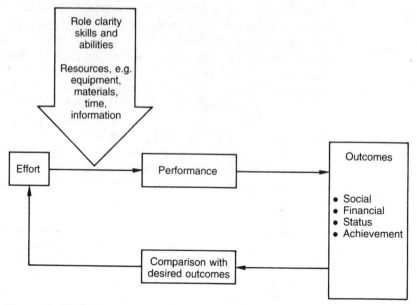

Figure 7.2 *The link between effort, performance and outcomes*

it represents – recognition of achievement and a tangible proof of excellence. Figure 7.2 gives an outline of the expectancy model of motivation.

When an outcome is expected, it is usually for the *results of effort* – i.e. performance, not the effort itself. In Figure 7.2 therefore we have shown this link. If the process of motivation is to be effective, however, it is the strength of the links between effort, performance and outcomes that determine the result. If there are no links present, or if one or more of the links is weak, the outcome will not motivate effort.

Certain factors will have an effect on the strength of the link between effort and performance, including the extent to which it is clear to the individual just what constitutes good performance (role clarity), that person's particular skill abilities and the availability of the necessary equipment, materials, time and information, etc. If we continue to use the example of the salesperson, he or she will need to be capable of undertaking the task. There is no point in expecting someone who is not competent in selling, or who is unable, for example, to demonstrate the technical properties of a product to a potential customer, to be able to meet performance requirements, much less exceed them.

Second, the salesperson will need to be quite clear about the objectives of the activity, know exactly what is required and feel able to meet these requirements. If he or she has had no product training, or is uncertain of the properties of what is to be sold, there is little chance of that person meeting, or exceeding, sales requirements. Finally, adequate resources need to be available. If, for example, the organization cannot meet the delivery dates promised by the salesperson, or the instruction manual is not ready, this will reflect on performance. Equally, if the time period in which the salesperson is expected to achieve sales is unrealistically short, performance will be affected.

The link between performance and outcomes depends on what the individual knows or believes about this link. There is no point in offering outcomes if these are not understood, e.g. many bonus systems are extremely complicated and difficult for potential recipients to understand. No improvement in performance is likely if a person is unaware that there is any desirable outcome.

The importance and value of outcomes

Outcomes can be classified into those that are intrinsic and those that are extrinsic. Intrinsic outcomes are those that result directly from the performance of the work without the intervention of an intermediary. They include feelings of satisfaction and achievement that are independent of any other person, although sometimes praise from a respected colleague or superior may trigger this type of outcome. The praise itself is, however, an extrinsic outcome, since it originates from someone else. The most common extrinsic outcome is usually financial, represented in increased pay through bonuses or awards or through other tangible rewards such as a new car. Intrinsic outcomes are particularly important if you think back to the needs theories outlined earlier. A sense of achievement or satisfaction that a job has been completed fulfils the higher-level needs identified by Maslow, Alderfer and McClelland. But, like the links between effort, performance and outcome, this intrinsic outcome has to be strongly present if it is to affect future performance; it also has to meet the individual's particular needs.

Table 7.2 illustrates some possible intrinsic and extrinsic outcomes at work.

Table 7.2 Possible outcomes at work

Intrinsic outcomes	*Extrinsic outcomes*
Self respect	Pay
Sense of achievement	Status within company
Feeling of having learned something	Status outside company
Feeling of having done something worthwhile	Fringe benefits
Feeling of having completed a job well	Pleasant working conditions
Feeling of having contributed something to an enterprise	Variety
	Praise
	Promotion
	Move to different work
	Free time/flexitime
	Training and development

Of course there are negative outcomes as well. Negative extrinsic outcomes might include loss of pay, privileges or benefits; loss of status; and forms of social punishment, such as removal from a favoured workgroup. In intrinsic terms negative outcomes might include fatigue, increased stress, loss of valued leisure time or the failure to achieve personal targets.

The lists given in Table 7.2 are not exhaustive and one of the problems managers encounter in this area is that many of the extrinsic outcomes are outside their control, dependent on organizational or industrial standards and payment schemes. Praise (or criticism) as an outcome, for example, although within the manager's discretion, will lose its value if applied indiscriminately or too frequently and in the absence of other outcomes.

Earlier we noted McClelland's research into the needs of managers and his profile of the characteristics of individuals with high achievement needs. Not all managers and certainly not all individuals, however, value a sense of achievement as an intrinsic outcome in the same way. Some people have stronger needs for affiliation or for power; others have more basic needs to fulfil and they can only be satisfied by extrinsic financial outcomes. Furthermore, needs will vary not only between individuals but in the same person at different times in his or her life cycle.

In Chapter 6, looking at career development, we identified individuals we classified as low performers with high potential; these are people who for some reason are not performing to the standard expected of them. Although there may be a number of reason for this low performance, factors that should be considered are whether their belief in the outcomes resulting from high performance is misconceived or that the outcomes themselves do not fulfil their individual needs. There is no point, for example, in offering an employee more responsibility when what that person desires is better working conditions or increased leisure time.

Victor Vroom (1964) attempted to measure individual motivation through the construction of an expectancy equation:

$$M = E \times V$$

where M = motivation to behave
             E = the expectation that the behaviour will be followed by a particular outcome
             V = the *valence* of the outcome

Valence is the preference that the individual has for a particular outcome, ranging from +1 (highly valued) to –1 (of low value) with 0 representing neutral value. The equation also needs to reflect that, usually, a number of different outcomes can result from a particular behaviour. As the complete equation below shows, motivation to behave in a particular way depends on the sum of all the possible outcomes multiplied by the individual's valence:

$$M = \Sigma (E \times V)$$

To return to our hypothetical salesperson, let us suppose that there are a number of outcomes an individual might expect will result from achieving more than target sales. These outcomes might be:

- increased commission on sales over target;
- respect from colleagues and superiors;
- promotion to senior salesperson;
- a two-week holiday in Benidorm;
- less leisure time;
- high stress levels;
- increased fatigue;
- disrupted/minimal social life.

To each of these possible outcomes the individual could assign a value between +1 and –1 to represent how important each outcome was to them personally; these would be 'V' values. They could then assign a value between 1 (highly probable) to 0 (no probability) that represented the likelihood of attaining each individual outcome – these would be 'E' values. By putting these values into the expectancy equation, the individual could calculate his or her personal 'M' score. As you might imagine, a salesperson with strong needs for achievement and power would be likely to have a different 'M' score from someone whose strongest need was for affiliation, providing the targets were realistically achievable and both individuals had similar abilities.

Self-development activity

Although we have only given a brief outline of Vroom's expectancy equation, you might like to carry out an assessment of your own motivation score and ask some of your colleagues to do the same. A comparison of the scores could be very revealing.

It is highly unlikely that, as a manager, you could estimate the motivation scores for all your staff on the basis of what we have been able to outline in this chapter. There are some commercial 'motivation questionnaires' available, but these should be treated with caution unless they are designed to be carried out by trained experts. However, what expectancy theory and other process theories of motivation reveal is the need to have a range of outcomes, some of which can meet the needs of most individuals; alternatively, you recruit staff with more or less identical needs – in the knowledge that these may change in individuals over time.

Content theories of motivation

The two most robust, and linked, theories about what motivates employees to perform well are those of Herzberg and of Hackman and Oldham. Herzberg (1968) carried out an in-depth study of engineers and accountants, examining what events occurred in their working lives and, through self-report, what aspects of their jobs they valued most. His investigations have been replicated many times, using different groups of working people in a variety of different cultures. All this research has shown that there are two distinct sets of factors behind job satisfaction (and motivation) or job dissatisfaction. Herzberg states that the opposite of job satisfaction is not job dissatisfaction but *no*, or decreased, job satisfaction. He believed that the growth or *motivator* factors that are intrinsic to the job are those related to achievement, recognition for achievement, the work itself, responsibility and growth or advancement. The dissatisfaction-avoidance or *hygiene* factors, which are extrinsic to the job, include company policy and administration, supervision, interpersonal relationships, working conditions, salary, status and security.

You will recognize strong echoes of Maslow, Alderfer and McClelland in Herzberg's ideas. Indeed many management texts cluster these theories together, but we prefer to see them differentiated in that the earlier three saw motivation as a process whereby the individual was motivated to perform in order to fulfil a need.

Herzberg considered that the motivator factors could be manipulated to motivate employees, particularly through job enrichment or what he called 'vertical job loading'. Table 7.3 outlines Herzberg's starting points for vertical job loading.

Table 7.3 Principles of vertical job loading

Principle	*Motivators*
A Removing some controls while retaining accountability	Responsibility and personal achievement
B Increasing the accountability of individuals for their own work	Responsibility and recognition
C Giving a person a complete natural unit of work	Responsibility, achievement and recognition
D Granting additional authority to an employee in his/her job	Responsibility, achievement and recognition
E Making periodic reports directly available to the individual rather than to the supervisor	Internal recognition
F Introducing new and more difficult tasks, not previously handled	Growth and learning
G Assigning individuals specific or specialized tasks, enabling them to become experts	Responsibility, growth and advancement

---

Box 7.1 When will internal motivation occur on the job?

Our theory suggests that there are three key conditions. First, the person must have *knowledge of the results* of his or her work. If things are arranged so that the person who does the work never finds out whether it is being performed well or poorly, then that person has no basis for feeling good about having done well or unhappy about doing poorly.

Secondly, the person must *experience responsibility* for the results of the work, believing that he or she is personally accountable for the work outcomes. If one views the quality of work done as depending more on external factors (such as the procedure manual, the boss, or people in another work section) than on one's own initiatives or efforts, then there is no reason to feel personally proud when one does well or sad when one doesn't.

And finally, the person must *experience the work as meaningful*, as something that 'counts' in one's own system of values. If the work being done is seen as trivial (as might be the case for a job putting paper clips in boxes, for example), then internal work motivation is unlikely to develop – even when the person has sole responsibility for the work and receives ample information about how well he or she is performing.

It appears necessary for *all three* of these factors, labelled 'critical psychological states', to be present for strong internal work motivation to develop and persist (Hackman and Oldham, 1980).

For managers of human resources there are a number of lessons to be learned from Herzberg's research, and they can be put into practice in order to increase the motivator factors in the jobs of their employees. Most of these are related to ways in which an individual's job could be enriched. In Herzberg's view job enrichment should be aimed at bringing the job up to the level of challenge commensurate with an employee's skill level; if the individual's skill level is higher than the job requires, either there has been a mismatch in the selection process or that person will move upwards fairly quickly (or out of the organization altogether if there are no promotion opportunities).

If you are considering job enrichment, there are a number of ground rules that should be followed:

- Make changes to jobs where you are sure that a problem related to low motivation or low job satisfaction actually exists.
- Ensure that you are increasing motivating factors, not hygiene factors.

- Ensure that your ideas for job enrichment are feasible.
- Be prepared for performance to drop initially as changes in job content may lead to a temporary reduction in efficiency.

Hackman and Oldham (1980) were the original proponents of increasing motivation through the design of work, expanding on Herzberg's ideas on job enrichment. They used the term 'internal motivation' as roughly similar to Vroom's 'M' in his expectancy equation.

You can see the strong relation between Herzberg's work and the theory developed by Hackman and Oldham, particularly when we look at their 'core job characteristics'. Hackman and Oldham proposed that, in order to foster the desired critical psychological states in individuals – which were internal to the individuals concerned and therefore not directly manipulable – there were five core job characteristics. Figure 7.3 shows the relationships between these characteristics, the critical psychological states and the outcome of high internal work motivation.

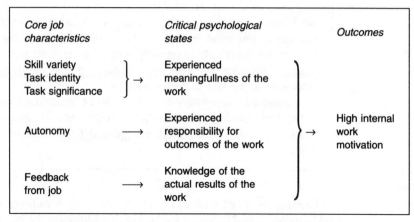

Figure 7.3 *Job characteristics that foster the three psychological states (from Hackman and Oldham, 1980)*

The first three job characteristics combine to influence the experienced meaningfulness of work:

- *Skill variety* – the degree to which a job requires a variety of different activities, requiring a number of different skills and talents; the more skills required, the more meaningful the job is likely to be
- *Task identity* – the degree to which a job can be seen as a 'whole' and identifiable piece of work, done from beginning to end with a visible outcome; jobs covering only a small part of a larger task are seen as less meaningful
- *Task significance* – the degree to which a job impacts significantly on the lives of other people, inside or outside the organization.

If all three characteristics are present in any job, the person performing that job is likely to experience meaningfulness; this can also be the case even if one or two of the characteristics are reduced.

- *Autonomy* – the degree to which a job provides freedom and discretion to the individual in scheduling the work and determining how it should be carried out appears to have an influence on the extent to which the person carrying out the job experiences a sense of responsibility.
- *Feedback from job* – the provision of direct and accurate feedback on performance provides knowledge of results, the third of Hackman and Oldham's critical psychological states.

The work context is also considered to be important as it was in Herzberg's theory, where he saw such factors as pay and company policies affecting the level of an individual's job satisfaction. Hackman and Oldham also believe that if an individual is experiencing job satisfaction, he or she will respond more positively to jobs which also contain the core job characteristics.

The relation between job satisfaction and performance

Let us return to the statement by Taylor (1947) at the beginning of this chapter: 'the maximum prosperity' of both employer and employee is usually seen in relation to performance and productivity. For the employer increased productivity means increased profits, leading to maximum prosperity; for the employee increased productivity may lead to valued outcomes that also lead towards maximum prosperity (if not always in financial terms). It is not surprising therefore that so much research has been undertaken – and is still continuing – into ways in which human productivity can be increased. The relation between job or employee satisfaction and performance can be looked at in two ways: the effect of satisfaction on performance and, conversely, the effect of performance on satisfaction.

Herzberg adopted the first of these viewpoints as a result of his original study on accountants and engineers, showing a high correlation between increased job satisfaction and increased performance. Subsequent studies failed to support this finding, however, although Herzberg argues that this is because replications of his research confounded the issue by trying to establish causal links between both motivators and hygiene factors in relation to performance. He has always maintained that reducing job dissatisfaction is not the same as increasing job satisfaction, and therefore should not be seen as related to changes in performance. Instead later research has relied on expectancy theory, suggesting that high job satisfaction and increased productivity occur when high productivity is seen as leading to a valued outcome and this outcome is achieved.

Porter and Lawler suggest that this causal link is in fact the main factor in improved performance – that variations in effort and performance cause variations in levels of job satisfaction. This relation is dependent on both intrinsic and extrinsic rewards and the perceived equity of those rewards. Extrinsic rewards not closely tied to performance are likely to result in both low performance and low job satisfaction.

Implications for managers

The reality is that many people are dissatisfied with their jobs. It is interesting to note that, in surveys of job satisfaction, supervisors and managers frequently report a high level of satisfaction in their staff, which is refuted by the employees themselves. The following lists show just how different these perceptions can be:

● *What employees say they want from their jobs*
   1 Challenging work.
   2 Recognition for good work.
   3 Being part of what is going on.
   4 Job security.
   5 Good wages.
   7 Promotion and growth opportunities.
   8 Loyalty to employee by management.
   9 Appropriate discipline.
   10 Employee assistance programmes

When managers were asked to rank the same ten outcomes on behalf of their employees, their list was quite different:

● *What managers think employees want from their jobs*
   1 Good wages.
   2 Job security.
   3 Promotion and growth opportunities.
   4 Good work environment.
   5 Challenging work.
   6 Employee assistance programmes.
   7 Loyalty to employees by management.
   8 recognition for good work.
   9 Appropriate discipline.
   10 Being part of what's going on.

The differences between these two lists should give you cause for concern. If organizations and their managers are designing jobs and reward systems based on this degree of mismatch between their own perceptions and those of their employees, job satisfaction is unlikely to be very high. The belief (by management) that financial reward is the most important factor in an employee's hierarchy of needs has been out of date for a long time – and yet it continues to prevail.

A review of financial incentive schemes also shows that many of them are not related to any understanding of expectancy theory. Some of these are outlined below.

- *Time rate systems* (payment by the hour, week or month) – no links between effort and performance or performance and outcome
- *Individual payment by results (PBR)* – strong links between effort and performance and between performance and outcomes (although the outcome is extrinsic); however, the strength of these links is often dependent on the management of work flow, which may be outside the individual's control.
- *Group PBR* – difficult to establish direct, strong links in large groups between effort, performance and outcomes and the links are subject to external factors such as the performance of other members of the team and management of work flow.
- *Measured day work* (pay based on a specific level of performance, usually at a higher rate than that for time rate employees) – does not provide any motivation to exceed the specified level of performance.
- *Profit-sharing schemes* – weak links between performance and outcome since the results of improved performance take a long time to come through.
- *Merit rating/performance related pay* (bonuses linked to systematic assessment of an individual's performance) – should have strong links between effort, performance and outcomes but, too often, merit-rating schemes have unclear objectives and a wide range of criteria; also the level of reward is determined by subjective assessment rather than by more objective criteria.

Thus, an understanding of motivation theory exposes the weaknesses in many financial incentive schemes. But what about other incentives?

The examples in Box 7.2 highlight the fact that the key to incentives appears to lie in flexibility: only then is it possible to strengthen the links between effort, performance and outcomes in individual cases. Flexible incentive schemes allow individuals to select from a 'menu' of rewards those that most closely meet their needs. Such schemes should not be confused with employee benefit schemes whereby a 'benefit package' is offered to attract staff into the organization, including, for example, health care, parental leave, child care arrangements, low-interest mortgages or discounts on products. These benefits do not increase motivation as they are not linked to performance, although they may on occasions be linked to promotion and status.

There is also a need to consider the different abilities of the workforce. Highly skilled people are more likely to value the intrinsic rewards that come from challenging, varied work, such as recognition

---

Box 7.2   Alternatives to financial incentives

After informal research, a project team at ICL discovered that the traditional symbolic awards of bronze, silver and gold medals for excellence had little value for employees. They have replaced the medals with a choice of gifts from which successful employees can make a selection.

Abbey Life offer luggage bearing the corporate logo to high-performing sales staff; top performers are given the opportunity to attend conventions at exotic locations. However, 'I once worked for a firm that rewarded its top people with a cruise. I can't imagine anything worse than being trapped on a yacht with a lot of other life assurance salespeople'.

---

and increased autonomy. Less skilled workers with limited potential are more problematic. In too many cases their job satisfaction is not considered to be important, since they can be replaced relatively easily and cheaply. However, jobs that do not require a high level of skills can often be made more satisfying by increasing individual responsibility.

In his study Herzberg (1968) identified 'responsibility' as having the strongest long-term effect on job satisfaction. In many organizations, however, work practice is well defined and supervised and employees are expected to refer any problems to supervisors or technical experts. This practice effectively reduces any sense of responsibility or autonomy, leading to job *dis*satisfaction. From the supervisor's or manager's viewpoint, giving employees more responsibility over their work increases the risk of failure, and, as you saw, people with a high need for achievement dislike this level of risk.

The concept of job satisfaction is one that concerns managers, as they see it as the key to high performance in their staff; they may call it 'motivation', but conceive of it in terms of the attributes of the job. The research appears to be of the 'motherhood and apple pie' category; we all *know* that employees value recognition, autonomy and a chance to practice and develop their skills, but we are unsure about how to practise what the researchers preach. Below is a summary of the main findings of research in this area.

Job satisfaction is affected by:

- the content and design of the job itself;
- the individual's values and expectations.

It is positively related to educational achievement, age, income and occupational level and tends to decrease the longer a person is in the same job. There are no observable effects of gender or race on levels of

Box 7.3 Making the transition from traditional middle management to facilitator

In the United States, there is currently a move towards 'self-management' for both individual employees and teams. One of the barriers to increasing self-management is the attitude of managers, particularly those in middle management, who find it difficult to make the transition from the traditional view of a 'manager' to that of becoming a facilitator. In their book *Business without Bosses* Manz and Sims identified several stages through which managers had to go before making this transition.

(*a*) Initial suspicion, uncertainty and resistance: managers felt threatened by and resented the change to self-managed teams. They were not only uncertain about the proposed change but feared that their own authority would be challenged; ultimately, they feared for the security of their jobs.

(*b*) Gradual realization of the positive possibilities in the new system: if the initial suspicion and uncertainty have been handled sensitively with the recognition that these feelings are a natural reaction to changing to self-managed teams, managers began to realize that their staff were competent and responsible; they started to see possibilities in the new role of facilitator, and positive advantages to it. This role would become increasingly advisory, increasing their expert power. With less time spent on direct supervision and monitoring, there would be time to identify and develop staff, particularly those in key positions.

(*c*) Wrestling with the new role: the role of facilitator is not easily defined, nor was it easy for managers to accept wholeheartedly the idea of self-management. 'Managing the self-managed' was a new concept, requiring different skills and changes in attitudes.

(*d*) Learning a new language: there had to be changes in the way managers communicated with their staff – changes in the way they went about the communication process and changes in the words they used. There was a need to respect the self-management of the individual but, even more difficult for many managers, there was a need to learn how to communicate with teams when you are no longer the 'leader' of that group of employees. You may be dealing with an individual's problem but there is a team audience to be considered as well (Manz and Sims, 1993).

job satisfaction, although of course sexual or racial harassment will engender job dissatisfaction. Financial reward systems appear to have some effect on satisfaction, but less on motivation, since they are rarely directly linked to effort and performance. Organizational structure and job satisfaction do not appear to be clearly linked, but there is evidence that organizational cultures that encourage participative decision making can have a positive effect on an individual's perceptions of satisfaction. Job *dis*satisfaction is often manifested in increased absenteeism and employee turnover.

> ### Self-development activity
>
> From your knowledge of motivation and job satisfaction, what steps might you take to increase the motivation of those for whom you are responsible.

There are a number of strategies you might adopt in order to increase motivation, including:

- creating expectations, you can fulfil, i.e. certain efforts will result in desirable outcomes;
- providing appropriate rewards, which individuals desire as outcomes;
- providing feedback on performance; designing/redesigning jobs that fulfil the core job characteristics identified by Hackman and Oldham;
- strengthening the links between effort and performance and between performance and outcomes.

Employee commitment

One of the factors linked to employee turnover, and thus to job satisfaction/dissatisfaction, is that of commitment. The Employment in Britain study (1992) surveyed 5000 employees with the aim of profiling their priorities, motivations and general commitment to work. As might be expected from other research in this area, money and job security, while important, were not valued as highly as control over the way that work was carried out; participation in organizational decision-making also featured highly. Box 7.4 outlines some of the findings of the survey.

In fact the survey contained no great surprises to people familiar with motivation theory and the principles of job design. Employees

---

Box 7.4   A survey of commitment

'The most powerful influence over a worker's perception of the general quality of management/employee relations was the degree of participation allowed to employees over decisions involving changes in work organization . . . The most striking feature of our data is just how rare it is for employees to be involved in this kind of decision.'

This survey was undertaken during the recession and found that attitudes towards job security had changed, with 'continuity of employment' becoming more significant over the previous five years. Training was also considered to be important, following job security, satisfying work content and good relations with one's manager in that order. However, only 20 per cent of those who wanted training felt they were likely to get it. It was clear that employee expectations about training and development were being raised, too often unrealistically.

Targets were considered to be more important than pay in influencing the amount of effort people put into their work and their individual quality standards.

'This analysis reinforces the importance of developing "responsible workers", especially where raising quality standards is a central aim.'

A significant proportion of those surveyed valued increased contact with clients and customers and their social relations with colleagues; the latter were considered to be very important to job satisfaction (Gallie and White, 1993).

---

were committed to organizations demonstrating that they valued their participation in organizational decision-making and providing opportunities for training and development. This kind of commitment-based approach is one that is gradually finding favour with enlightened managers and employers.

'Commitment', however is a general term that needs to be unpacked or there is a likelihood that an individual's commitment may be misunderstood. For example, employees may be committed to the value of work or paid employment as a general construct but not to their particular job or to the organization in which they work. Other employees may be very committed to their chosen career in, for example, accountancy, medicine or management, but not to their present job or organization. There is a need to distinguish between these forms of commitment in order to understand them fully. Figure 7.4 identifies the antecedents and consequences of commitment to a particular job and to a career.

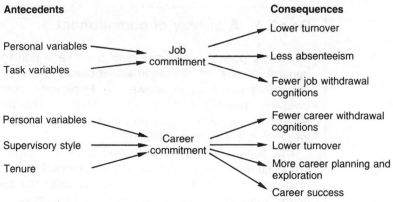

Figure 7.4 *Antecedents and consequences of job and career commitment (from Iles et al., 1990, p. 149)*

The consequences identified in Figure 7.4 would appear to be beneficial to organizations, although there appears to be only a weak relation between commitment to the job and high job performance. Of the antecedents, there are areas in which managers can consider improvement in individual cases. For example, in relation to job commitment the 'task variables' are clearly linked to the work of Hackman and Oldham; and in relation to personal variables the importance of the right-person/right-job match is likely to impact on commitment.

Career commitment, while distinguishable from commitment to a specific job, is likely to be broader and stronger. It relates to a career field rather than to a set of work activities, and it is the extent to which the requirements of a particular job fulfil an individual's career aspirations, which is crucial. Obviously where the match between job requirements and career aspirations is high, the consequences are likely to benefit the organization as well as the individual, and factors such as performance management, review and career planning should be designed to optimize commitment. However, there is always the chance that people who are highly committed to their careers may leave the organization in order to further their advancement.

In terms of organizational commitment the policies and practices of the organization can have a positive or adverse effect on employees. Some of the antecedents and consequences of organizational commitment are shown in Table 7.4.

The complex and relatively numerous antecedents that affect organizational commitment present a challenge for managers. There is evidence that employee perceptions of human resource management and development in areas such as fairness of promotion practices and the accuracy of merit systems have a stronger influence than task, role or supervisory behaviour variables. Other individual perceptions, such as fairness in selection and assessment procedures, are also highly important in relation to organizational commitment.

Table 7.4 Antecedents and consequences of organizational commitment

Antecedents		Consequences
Personal variables Task variables Role variables		Longer tenure
Supervisory variables Freedom of choice	→ Organizational → commitment	Less absenteeism
Match of expectations to assessment decisions		Less lateness
Experience of training and placement processes Recruitment and entry practices		Higher performance?

From Iles *et al.*, 1990, p. 152.

Self-development activity

In relation to yourself and to those for whom you are responsible, can you identify different forms of commitment – to work in general, to a particular job or career, to the organization? In what ways as a manager could you increase commitment – and would you necessarily want to do so?

As Box 7.5 demonstrates, the way in which human resource policies and practice are carried out and perceived can have a profound effect on an individual's commitment, particularly on how he or she feels about the organization. But there should not be complacency that HRM is the answer to everything, since employee commitment is so obviously multi-faceted and idiosyncratic. There is a consideration, for example, that highly committed employees may not in fact be what the organization needs; commitment is not necessarily synonymous with innovation or flexibility. And organizational commitment may stem from a fear of changing jobs or career rather than from a shared vision, loyalty or a desire to achieve organizational objectives. There is still no strong evidence that high organizational commitment results in high job performance.

Richard Walton described what he termed a 'commitment strategy' he observed at General Motors (GM) in the United States in the 1980s, with local managers and union officials agreeing to sponsor quality-of-life or employee involvement activities. A commitment strategy has high performance expectations and, instead of defining minimum standards, emphasizes continuous improvement through 'stretch objectives'. Rewards reflect group achievement, the expanded content of individual jobs and 'equity' (gainsharing, stock-ownership or profit-sharing). Some assurance of job security is important, often through a

---

Box 7.5 The impact of selection and assessment on organizational commitment

A study carried out in a large British based financial services organization studied the impacts of assessment and selection procedures on the commitment of employees. At the time the organization employed a management development and tiering programme in which staff were assessed at various points in their early and mid career. As a result of this assessment, staff maintained or failed to maintain a place on the organization's fast-track programme.

Those people who failed the assessment, when compared with those who had passed, showed, in general, significantly lower organizational commitment and more frequent thoughts about leaving their jobs and careers, especially if they were in the early stages of their career. While this finding may not be surprising, it does indicate that organizations which install fast-track pro-grammes very early (e.g. from 18 years of age) may well suffer from the lower commitment and higher turnover displayed by employees who feel rejected at such an early career stage. This would seem to support the concern expressed in Chapter 6 at the 'career hurdle race', in which there is no second chance if an individual falls at an early hurdle. For people at an early stage in their career, the selection *decision* and its perceived impact on their career future seemed overwhelmingly important in determin-ing their feelings about the organization and their thoughts about leaving their current jobs and careers. For people in mid-career, who have invested in their career and fear the costs and difficulties of leaving the organization or abandoning their career, it is the way that the decision is arrived at rather than the decision itself which has most impact.

The negative effects of assessment can be reduced if the decision itself is not seen as an absolute 'pass' or 'fail' and if it is accompanied by feedback or counselling provision with opportun-ities for retrying if this is considered to be in the individual's best interests (Robertson *et al.*, 1990).

---

policy of retraining programmes, as is the opportunity for employees to contribute to decisions on issues concerning methods of production and human resource policies and practices. A commitment strategy is based on the belief that increased employee commitment will result in enhanced employment.

Walton also identified the 'costs of commitment', particularly as these affected managers who worked in organizations that adopted this approach:' managers have had to invest extra effort, develop new skills and relationships, cope with higher levels of ambiguity and uncertainty, and experience the pain and discomfort associated with changing habits and attitudes. Some of their skills have become obsolete, and some of their careers have become casualties of change ... For their part, workers have inherited more responsibility and, along with it, greater uncertainty and a more open-ended possibility of failure'.

Summary

The concept of motivation – the will to work – has been considered in relation to both the process and content of motivation. Process theories, such as those of Maslow, Alderfer and McClelland, were related to individual needs and the concept of desirable outcomes. The links between effort, performance and desirable outcomes is central to expectancy theory wherein the individual 'expects' to achieve a particular outcome as a result of effort; this effort is translated into performance. The stronger these links, the more likely it is that an individual will be motivated to expend effort in order to achieve particular outcomes.

Content theories, such as those proposed by Herzberg, and Hackman and Oldham, concentrate on the particular aspects of an individual's relationship with his or her work that motivate him or her to improve performance. Herzberg's theory of job satisfaction is closely linked to Hackman and Oldham's identification of core job characteristics and critical psychological states. The five core job characteristics – skill variety, task identity, task significance, autonomy and feedback – are seen as essential to job satisfaction and high internal work motivation. However, links between increased job satisfaction and improved performance are tenuous, although the reduction of job *dissatisfaction* is obviously appealing.

In relation to employee commitment, research has identified that this is a multi-faceted concept, embracing (and distinguishing between) commitment to work or paid employment as a construct, commitment to a specific job or to a chosen career, and commitment to the organization. The factors that contribute to these different types of commitment have been identified, along with a range of consequences and implications for the way in which managers can encourage and increase the level of commitment of their employees. 'Commitment', however, is not necessarily always to the benefit of either the organization or to managers, nor has it been shown to correlate with high job performance. However, perception of fairness in assessment decisions has been shown to have a strong impact on organizational commitment.

References

Alderfer, C. P. (1972) *Existence, Relatedness and Growth: Human Needs in Organizational Settings.* The Free Press, New York.

De Cenzo, D. A. and Robbins, S. P. (1994) *Human Resource Management.* John Wiley and Sons Inc., New York.

Gallie, D. and White, M. (1993) *Employment commitment and the skills revolution; first findings from the Employment in Britain survey.* Policy Studies Institute, London.

Hackman, J. R. and Oldham, G. R. (1980) *Work Redesign,* Chapter 4, Addison–Wesley, Reading, Mass.

Herzberg, F. (1968) One more time: How do you motivate employees?. *Harvard Business Review,* Vol. 46, pp. 53–62.

Iles, P., Mabey, C. and Robertson, I. (1990) HRM Practices and Employee Commitment: Possibilities, Pitfalls and Paradoxes. *British Journal of Management,* Vol. 1, pp. 147–57.

Kovach, K. A. (1987) What Motivates Employees? Workers and Supervisors give Different Answers. *Business Horizons,* September–October, p. 61.

McClelland, D. C. (1961) *The Achieving Society.* The Free Press, New York.

Manz, C. C. and Sims, H. P. Jr. (1993) *Business without Bosses.* John Wiley and Sons, New York.

Martin, P. and Nicholls, J. (1987) *Creating a Committed Workforce,* Institute of Personnel Management.

Maslow, A. H. (1943) A theory of human motivation. *Psychological Review,* p. 50.

Ogilvie, J. R. (1986) The role of human resource management practices in predicting organizational commitment. *Group and Organization Studies,* 11, 4, pp. 335–359.

Porter, L. W. and Lawler, E. E. (1968) *Managerial Attitudes and performance.* Irwin-Dorsey, Homewood, Illinois.

Robertson, I. T., Iles, P. A., Gratton, L. and Sharpley, D. (1990) The psychological impact of selection procedures on candidates, quoted in Iles *et al.* (1990).

Taylor, F. W. (1947) *Scientific Management,* Harper and Row.

Open University (1990) *The Effective Manager.* Open Business School.

Vroom, V. (1964), *Work and Motivation,* John Wiley, New York.

Walton, R. E. (1985) From control to commitment in the workplace. *Harvard Business Review,* Vol. 63 (2), pp. 77–84.

8 Building effective teams

Introduction

If you were asked to define a team, you would describe it as a group of some kind. However, a team is more than a group. When you think of all the groups that you belong to, you will probably find that very few of them are actual teams. For instance, some of these groups will be family or friendship groups, which are formed to meet a diverse range of needs such as affection, security, support, esteem, belonging or identity. Some may be committees, where members usually represent different interest groups who come together to discuss their differing perspectives on issues of interest. Perhaps you can think of an occasion when you were part of a true team that was particularly effective. Sometimes a team of people – none of whom is particularly outstanding – can achieve the extraordinary; for some reason a deep loyalty to fellow members develops, there is an excitement about the task in hand and a sense of pride attached to membership. Too often, however, our experience of teamworking is quite the opposite. What makes the difference, and what part can teams play in the outworking of HRD plans and strategies? In this chapter we attempt to pinpoint the factors that characterize effective teamworking and give some practical team-building suggestions.

The contribution of teams

Katzenbach and Smith (1993) have developed a single framework for team performance (Figure 8.1). They distinguish a working group which is 'a collection of individuals for whom there is no significant incremental performance need or opportunity' from a real team, which is defined as: 'a small number of people with complementary skills who are committed to a common purpose performance, goals and an approach for which they hold themselves mutually accountable'.

In between there is the 'psuedo team', so called because no joint benefit accrues and individual performance is actually hindered by confusion over purpose and inability to handle personality difficulties. The 'potential team' describes the situation where individuals are all too aware of a given performance need and are seriously seeking to improve their impact upon it, but they still lack clarity about their aims as well as the discipline (or 'norms') needed for a common working

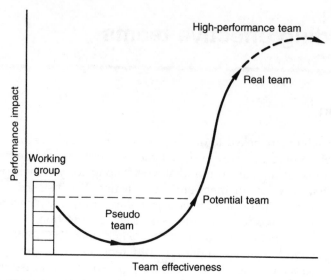

Figure 8.1 *The team performance curve (from Katzenbach and Smith, 1993, p.84)*

approach, and mutual accountability is still missing. In contrast, high performance teams have all these ingredients in place, engendering deep commitment to the personal growth and success of their members.

When is a group a team?

Teamwork is usually appropriate in circumstances where the following rate medium or high:

- work demand;
- task/project uncertainty;
- requirement of diverse expertise from members;
- need for commitment to outcomes;
- rewards are given for team efforts rather than individual efforts;
- team goal achievement is significant for the organization;

If the work demand is low then it may be a waste of time to set up a team when the work could be more easily achieved by one individual. If work demand is high though, it may be better if one person does it all, because teamwork is time consuming. It depends on the deadlines, the amount of work and the breadth of expertise required. When there is a low requirement of expertise from members, then perhaps not all members can make a valid contribution to the team, which would be wasteful of human resources. However, the experience of working within a team may also offer excellent opportunities for staff to develop their skills and knowledge by learning from others about their work and organization.

Self-development activity

When do you think team work is appropriate? Mark points on each continuum below to reflect your ideas.

work demand	low	medium	high
task/project uncertainty	low	medium	high
need for a fast decision	low	medium	high
need for an innovative solution	low	medium	high
requirement of diverse expertise	low	medium	high
need for commitment to a course of action	low	medium	high
shared objectives	low	medium	high
reward for individual efforts	low	medium	high
significance for the organization	low	medium	high

When shared objectives between members are low, then it may be difficult to secure group commitment and cohesiveness. This could have a disruptive influence on the team as the team members and leader attempt to manage the intrusiveness of hidden agendas and the connection between team and individuals' goals. Unless members of a team can begin to establish shared goals and objectives, the team is unlikely to form and perform. It is also important that teams are rewarded as teams. When rewards are primarily for team not individual efforts, this can help to establish the team's identity, cohesiveness, team spirit and commitment to shared goals, at the possible risk of alienating star performers.

Team management is a sensitive and demanding process. If the team's work is not significant for the organization's strategy and the team has no management support, the team may encounter more difficulties. For example, an office waste paper recycling project was set up by a group of secretaries during working hours without any initial management support. Despite teamwork, the project failed (in this case), because although it was innovative it was perceived (rightly or wrongly) as irrelevant to the organization and wasteful of organizational resources.

Teamwork may be appropriate irrespective of whether task/project certainty is high, medium or low. However, the greater the task uncertainty, then the more important teamwork is, especially if it is important to represent the differing perspectives of concerned parties. This is evident in government decision-making in areas such as technology and innovation policies, where scientific facts may be collated to support opposing arguments for new policy developments. In such situations scientific facts do not always point to an obvious policy or strategy for innovation support and development, so that decisions are partially based on opinions and visions. When expertise does not point to obvious solutions for problems, then teamwork can come up with a compromise between the varying perspectives and vested interests of concerned parties. This can be hard work, as Box 8.1 shows.

On the negative side, teams may produce more conventional rather than more innovative responses to problems. The reason for this is that team decisions may regress towards the average, with group communications cancelling out the more innovative decision options. It depends on how innovative the team is in terms of its membership, its norms and its values. A team that is anchored to creative values, and prides itself on its originality, may work to an innovative behavioural average.

Teamwork may be also inappropriate when you want a fast decision made. For instance, team decision making is usually slower than individual decision making because of the need for communication and consensus about the decision taken. Despite the business successes of the Japanese companies, it is now recognized that promoting a collective organizational identity and responsibility for decisions may significantly slow operations down.

Box 8.1   Teamwork can be hard work

Most functional executives, brought up in the turbulence of politics and interfunctional warfare, find the transition from functional to strategic mode very difficult to make; they do not always see the difference – and if they do, they are reluctant to leave their mountain top, the summit of knowledge, experience and hence power, for the equality and shared uncertainty of strategic decision-making. And yet this is one area where real teamwork is not only necessary but vital . . .

Strategic planners are often guilty of pushing management groups towards handling uncertainty without the concomitant abilities to share and work with feelings. Team-builders are often guilty of the converse sin – pushing management groups to be open and share their feelings when the group has no intention whatever of getting into work where the level of uncertainty is high. Neither will succeed. It is no coincidence that both strategic planning and team-building can fall quickly into disrepute; it may be too late to save strategic planning from the management scrapheap – it is not too late to save team-building. (Critchley and Casey, 1986, pp. 427, 436).

In this section, we see that there are many factors, internal and external, that will influence the choice of working in groups or teams. These are summarized below:

When to work alone or use groups	When to build teams
For simple tasks or 'puzzles'.	For highly complex tasks or problems.
When co-operation is sufficient.	When consensus decisions are essential.
When minimum discretion is required.	When there is high level of choice and uncertainty.
When fast decisions are needed.	When high committment is needed.
When few competences are required.	When a broad range of competences is required.
Where member interests are inherently conflicting.	Where member objectives can be galvanized.
Where the organization credits individuals for operational outputs.	Where the organization rewards team results for strategy and vision building.
When innovative responses are sought.	When balanced views sought (but see section on group think, p. 181).

The place of teams in HRD

So what part do the building and developing of effective teams play in an organization's HRD strategy? Teambuilding is not a panacea for all organizational ills. Indeed some, like Elliot Jaques, argue for *individual* accountability within an effective (or 'requisite') hierarchy rather than a woolly clamouring after team consensus and problem-solving in fluid, networked organizations. Neither is team-building universally appropriate for all modes of work, as we have seen above. However, there are aspects of HRD that are uniquely well served by teams and team-building techniques. These can be categorized into three areas:

1 the building of interpersonal skills;
2 the learning of effective group skills through team introduction;
3 the enhancing of task performance through teamworking.

Obviously such elements overlap: e.g. interpersonal skills will be derived not only from achievement of the tasks but also from the quality of team relationships and the more social aspects of teamwork. For instance, self-employed business owner/managers, who work almost entirely on their own, miss the opportunity to bounce ideas off colleagues in team situations and the experience of solitude in their work can, over time, impair their performance.

In the rest of the chapter we shall take each of these three team areas and discuss two or three specific team-building techniques that can be used to enhance team effectiveness. The costs of a team working acrimoniously and inefficiently are high, both in human and financial terms. On the other hand, when a team operates effectively, it becomes a dynamic working unit achieving superlative outputs and attracting all sorts of positive regard throughout the organization.

Building interpersonal skills

It is difficult to build our people-handling skills without a group of people! Yet just because we are working in a team context does not automatically mean that we develop interpersonal proficiency. The first and most painful step is discovering what we are good at and what we are poor at.

Raising self-awareness

It is a feature of organizations that constructive and critical feedback is hard to come by (see Box 8.2).

Feedback is communication to a person or group that gives the receiver information on how he or she affects others. The giving and receiving of feedback is a skill that can be acquired. When conducted effectively, it can have a significant galvanizing effect on the team, deepening levels of trust and mutual respect. The following guidelines may help in giving feedback:

- Be descriptive by describing one's own reaction. This leaves the receivers free to accept or reject the feedback, whereas evaluating or interpreting their behaviour will lead them to react defensively.
- Be specific, not general. Being told that one is 'dominating' is less useful than being told that 'just now when you were deciding the issue, you didn't listen to what others said, and I felt forced to accept your arguments or face attack from you'.
- Direct it towards behaviour the receiver is in a position to do something about. People can change how close they stand to their listener(s), but they can do little about their height and stature.
- Ensure that it is being given for the receiver's benefit rather than to serve your own needs. 'Speak the truth in love' is a good, scriptural principle.
- Be timely in giving feedback, preferably straight after the given behaviour, when the effects are still apparent.
- It is most effective when requested rather than imposed. For instance, colleagues working together may at the outset agree on a 'contract' of giving and receiving feedback to one another after each team session.

Box 8.2 The case of the shrinking repertoire of skills

One of the most important areas to explore in the assessment and development of top managers is their own capacity for self-insight. It is also one of the most difficult.

Few people get to the top of an organization without sacrifice. Most have to be psychologically driven to accept the rigours of the journey. Successful senior managers are rarely perfectly balanced individuals – to achieve their pre-eminence they have had to give up many of life's satisfactions to reap those offered by a rapid career climb. As they reach the top, their choice of behaviour narrows. They repeat the thoughts, decisions and actions that worked for them and abandon those that did not deliver quick results.

Tough, decisive and relentless managers become even tougher, more decisive and more relentless leaders. Such people tend not to get enough feedback. They do not seek it for fear of appearing indecisive and subordinates are reluctant to offer it for fear of incurring the boss's anger and risking their jobs.

Sooner or later though, something catches up with the driven executive. His (or, less often, her) superiors begin to think and then to say: 'He delivers, and he delivers exceptionally well, but we can no longer excuse his shortcomings. We can't do without him, but unless there is a substantial change in the way he behaves, we will soon have to learn how'.

How can these people be saved from themselves? It is never easy. First they need to take a completely fresh look at themselves as people, in the round. They must examine what they perceive as weaknesses and try to accept them as being human. They have to think about what drives them, and assess whether it still should. They must reconsider the lessons of their lives. This is hard enough: it risks loss and tests self-esteem, a condition they rely on to function.

The second step is harder. They must recast their ambitions, values, expectations and self-image in a way that permits them to be all of themselves and not just the small part they have become used to exhibiting.

Third, they have to work through this, exploring the newness of it all, looking for feedback from any who can offer it. There is no point in learning how to be a better listener if you have not first accepted that what people have to say is important (Thorne, 1992).

Receiving feedback is just as much an art. Some criteria for making most of feedback might be:

- Listen, without interrupting.
- Only respond by asking for greater clarity. Avoid the temptation to defend, explain or in any way excuse the behaviour being referred to.
- Take on board only what you choose to. Perceptions of our behaviour are real, but not necessarily true. However, if impressions are shared by several team members, it usually means there is a gap between our intended and our actual behaviour.
- Thank the giver of the feedback. It can be a difficult thing to do, and acknowledgement encourages future use of this valuable behaviour.

Another way of raising our self-awareness is to complete a self-diagnostic or psychometric test. Such instruments can provide valuable insights into our strengths and weaknesses, at an individual level, but they are especially powerful when interpreted in a team setting. An example is Belbin's questionnaire, which identifies a person's preferred team roles.

For instance, Belbin concluded from his research that it was crucial that at least one member of a team had analytical abilities. However, teams filled with exceptionally clever members tended to perform poorly. He suggested that an example of this type of team are NHS hospital surgeons. Such teams have problems because the members have similar aspirations. In other words, they seek to apply their brains to the most intellectually difficult part of the team project. More seriously, they tend to regard the leader as the most intellectually able of them all, which leads members to refuse all attempts by others to organize the team. Belbin called this the Apollo syndrome. It can lead to unsuccessful teamwork, poor team spirit and difficulties in decision-making. Belbin's typology is interesting because it identifies the strengths of certain team roles, which represent useful people to have in your team.

The roles that people take in a team, however, are seldom evident at all from their features or general appearance. A person making a creative suggestion may look very much like one supplying information. A readiness to engage in dialogue is barely distinguishable from someone trying to take charge. With so much visual noise about, the correct signals cannot be read with any confidence. That is why when a group of strangers meet for a purpose, so much time is spent in probing, weighing up each other and avoiding getting down to real business. It may even be argued that such 'wasted time' is well spent, for in the course of these personal interactions, preliminary manoeuvres allow perceptions to be formed. From these, basic relationships can be established. Such a seemingly profligate use of time may in reality serve to increase the prospects of success.

Table 8.1 The nine team roles

Roles and descriptions – team-role contribution	*Allowable weaknesses*
Plant: creative, imaginative, unorthodox. Solves difficult problems.	Ignores details. Too preoccupied to communicate effectively.
Resource investigator: extrovert, enthusiastic, communicative. Explores opportunities. Develops contacts.	Overoptimistic. Loses interst once initial enthusiasm has passed.
Co-ordinator: mature, confident, a good chairperson. Clarifies goals, promotes decision-making, delegates well.	Can be seen as manipulative. Delegates personal work.
Shaper: challenging, dynamic, thrives on pressure. Has the drive and courage to overcome obstacles.	Can provoke others. Hurts people's feelings.
Monitor evaluator: sober, strategic and discerning. Sees all options. Judges accurately.	Lacks drive and ability to inspire others. Overly critical.
Teamworker: co-operative, mild, perceptive and diplomatic. Listens, builds, averts friction, calms the waters.	Indecisive in crunch situations. Can be easily influenced.
Implementer: disciplined, reliable, conservative and efficient. Turns ideas into practical actions.	Somewhat inflexible. Slow to respond to new possibilities.
Completer: painstaking, conscientious, anxious. Searches out errors and omissions. Delivers on time.	Inclined to worry unduly. Reluctant to delegate. Can be a nitpicker.
Specialist: single-minded, self-starting, dedicated. Provides knowledge and skills in rare supply.	Contributes on only a narrow front. Dwells on technicalities. Overlooks the 'big picture'.

Strength of contribution in any one of the roles is commonly associated with particular weaknesses. These are called allowable weaknesses. Executives are seldom strong in all nine team roles.

From Belbin, 1993, p. 23

Table 8.1 lists the nine team roles uncovered by Belbin, giving a brief description of their contribution to teamwork, along with the allowable weaknesses that accompany these strengths. Belbin recommends that we *perfect* those team-role styles that are high on our profile so that they can be enacted with skill and professionalism; that we *improve* those that are not naturally part of our repertoire but need to be held in reserve; and that we *outlaw* those that are foreign to the self.

Understanding and appreciating difference

Part of the value of an inventory like that devised by Belbin is the way it vividly depicts our differences. As we use this common 'language' to identify the behaviour of team members around us, we can begin to appreciate the contributions of others rather than simply be irritated by them because they are different from the way we would operate. This apparently simple shift of perspective is in fact a powerful and vital foundation to team-building. One situation where this appreciation of difference is especially crucial is where team members are of different national or cultural background, as Box 8.3 illustrates.

Managing conflict

For many managers conflict is threatening, and the traditional view of conflict in organizations is that it is unnecessary and harmful. However, a pluralist or radical view of organizations would argue that conflict is inevitable and that a moderate level of it actually enhances performance (Morgan, 1986). Conflicts are nearly always caused by people having differing points of view, or by people trying to achieve their personal or group goals at the expense of others. Clearly the manager should identify the true source of conflict before dealing with it or helping teams to resolve it. In their book on management skills, Hannaway and Hunt (1992) list the following possible sources:

- *Conflict regarding roles* – usually takes the form of deciding who is responsible for what activities.
- *Interpersonal* – differences between individuals.
- *Task independence* – the reliance of one group on another for information, people, support, materials, maintenance, finance, etc.
- *Shared resources* – when two or more groups share the same resources, e.g. equipment, offices, staff, etc.
- *Different perceptions* – these may occur as a result of different beliefs and values, e.g. trade union and management.
- *Goal differences* – unresolved goal differences may result in conflict. The goals for quality control may conflict with production goals.
- *Differentiation* – different groups may need to operate in different ways. The approach of a credit department to a customer may be very different from that of a sales team. The timescales of a research unit may differ from those of a production department.

Box 8.3 Multinational team-building

Another example is teams working together face to face consisting of different nationals, where we often find problems that relate to the cultural and national 'baggage' that we all carry with us. Different inclusion rituals can trip multinational team members up. The formal handshakes that feel like a comfortable fit for UK and German nationals feel cold and aloof to Italian nationals.

Language issues create wonderful barriers to trust building. Communicating through the veil of non-mother tongue brings its own challenges, of which a key is not to be taken in by appropriate smiles and nods. International managers, operating outside of their mother tongue, are often exceptionally well skilled in smiling and nodding in apparent agreement at the appropriate points in the conversation. When you go back and check for clarity of understanding it becomes very clear, very quickly, that the correct message has not been picked up.

Language can be both an inclusion issue and a control issue. We recently met a UK manager working in Spain with a Spanish team. He was explicit about not seeing the need to learn Spanish. He went on to reveal that he had a major fear of 'no longer being in control' when using an unfamiliar language and for him, being in 'apparent' control was very significant.

A climate should be fostered that encourages the giving and receiving of feedback between all members. This open, trusting climate is the antidote to misunderstandings and misinterpretation. Multinational differences melt into the background because we respect each other as people and have the means and confidence to address interpersonal issues as they arise. Conflict is not something to avoid; surfacing conflict and seeking to understand the reasons for it can help performance. This open climate will enable team members to feel free to challenge one another's ideas, express their views and work through issues, and disagreements in a constructive way (Davies, *et al.*, 1992).

Self-development activity

Take a few moments to consider the positive and negative aspects of conflict when working in teams.

Conflict can be positive in and between teams when it opens up discussion of an issue, results in problems being solved, increases individual interest in an issue, improves communication between individuals, helps to release latent emotion, and when it helps people to develop their abilities. On the other hand, conflict can hinder progress when it diverts people from dealing with the really important issues, and creates feelings of dissatisfaction and unresolved tension, which may in turn lead to individuals and groups becoming insular and should be prevented, and in other cases surfaced and resolved.

Successful conflict resolution has to be based on an accurate and thorough understanding of the actual conflict itself. There are five broad approaches that can be taken for successful conflict resolution. The approach adopted should match the particular characteristics of the conflict situation.

1 *Denial or withdrawal.* A person tries to solve the conflict by denying its existence. This can be satisfactory if the conflict is relatively unimportant, or if there is a need for a cooling-off period before the conflict is tackled head on.
2 *Suppression or smoothing-over.* Differences are played down, and a harmonious façade is constructed. Again, this approach can be satisfactory for relatively unimportant conflicts, or where the relation between the two parties in conflict must be preserved at all costs.
3 *Domination.* The conflict is resolved by one party using its authority or position. A third party with such authority may also resolve a conflict in this way. This approach can be satisfactory where the domination is based on clear authority or where the approach has been agreed upon by the parties concerned.
4 *Compromise.* The conflict is resolved by each party giving up something in order to meet halfway. This approach can be satisfactory if both parties have sufficient room to alter their positions, although commitment to the 'agreed upon' solution may be in doubt.
5 *Collaboration.* While differences between individuals are recognized, the conflict is resolved by focusing on a group consensus solution, where all participants in the conflict feel that they have won. This approach can be satisfactory if the time is available, and the individuals believe in the approach and have the necessary skills.

Building effective group skills

Just as teams afford excellent opportunities for developing individuals' understanding of their own, and other's, strengths, weaknesses, preferences and priorities, so too teams provide the perfect incubator for the growth and cultivation of group skills. Again, much depends on the level of maturity of the team as to whether these learning opportunities are taken. Think about a particularly successful team in which you have participated. Do you recall the group going through various stages prior to its success? Observation of many groups and teams in organizations has led researchers to discern five typical 'episodes' within the development of a group.

Each 'episode' is associated with typical behaviours related to the task, on the one hand, and group processes, on the other. The Counselling and Career Development Unit at the University of Leeds has summarized these, and suggested ways that a team leader or facilitator might help the group move through the stages (see Table 8.2).

Table 8.2 Leading a group through the stages of group development

	Task Orientation	*Group Processes*	*Possible ways of Assisting Goups through Process*
Stage 1 **Forming**	What is task? Grumbling about the setting Intellectualizing irrelevant issues Attempts at defining the situation Mutual exchange of information Suspicion/little work	Considerable anxiety Testing relationships Dependancy on the leader Hesitant participation Will they let me join?	Clear introductions, 'safe' starters Visibility of the leader Opportunity for group members to contribute
Stage 2 **Storming**	Resisting the validity of the task People react emotionally towards the demand of the task Hostility where high personal commitment is required	Conflict emerges between sub-groups Ambivalence to leader Fighting–flighting Defensiveness, competition, jealousy	Open recognition of conflict/anger Opportunity to express ideas that are valued by leader if not by whole group Allow members to challenge in a constructive, not a destructive way
Stage 3 **Norming**	Asking and giving opinions Ability to express feelings to help the task Plans are made and work	Group cohesion develops Norms emerge Authority problems resolved Members identify with group	Allow time for members to begin to work, talk, draw up plans, make preliminary decisions
Stage 4 **Performing**	Strong goal orientation Insight and understanding	Clear but flexible roles Pragmatism in support of task Satisfaction in achievement	Let them do it and join in if appropriate
Stage 5 **Mourning**	Seeking extra things to do, looking for further tasks Evaluating the effectiveness of the group	Wanting to meet again Not recognizing the group's life may be over Members may show extra energy or enthusiasm for the group Members may want to make a rapid exit	Recognize that group is coming to an end Summarize what has been achieved, agreed and where to go from here Allow time to 'say goodbye'

Here we deal briefly with three related areas of group behaviour where a team leader can help its members become more productive: improving communication, challenging unhelpful norms and building cohesion rather than conformity.

Improving communication

Table 8.2 above refers to task orientation and group processes. What sorts of behaviour typify these two orientations? The task orientated behaviours are geared towards helping the group towards the achievement of its goals, whereas group processes comprise relationship-orientated behaviours that are concerned with maintaining the team members and their interpersonal relationships, so that the team will work effectively towards the team goals (see Table 8.3).

You may feel that, as a team leader, fulfilling all these functions is a tall order! Some of us are goal-driven and will naturally focus on the task, others of us are inclined to emphasize team relationships. Few people get a good balance between the two. But the key is to ensure the functions are fulfilled without necessarily doing it all yourself. In terms of team roles it is down to *someone* (usually, but not always you as the leader) to act as 'co-ordinator', giving freedom to the

Table 8.3 Examples of important team behaviours

1. *Task orientated behaviours*	
Proposing	Initiating ideas, suggestions, courses of action relevant to the task
Seeking information	Asking for facts, opinions or clarification from other members of the team
Giving information	Offering facts, opinions or clarification concerning the task
Testing understanding	Seeking to establish whether or not an earlier contibution has been understood
Summarizing/building	Restating succinctly the content of the previous discussion, and extending a proposal made by someone else
2. *Maintenance orientated behaviour*	
Encouraging	Being warm, friendly or supportive of others by verbal or non-verbal means
Gatekeeping	Opening (positively attempting to bring others into the discussion) or closing (excluding, cutting off or interrupting others)
Harmonizing	Being prepared to compromise and actively accommodate others in order to preserve group harmony
Giving feedback	Giving positive feedback on feelings and opinions contributed by others

Table 8.4 Examples of self-orientated behaviours

Attacking/defending	Attacking or rejecting others, or defensively strengthening one's own position
Blocking/stating difficulties	Placing blocks or difficulties in the path of others' proposals or ideas without offering alternative proposals or giving reasoned arguments
Diverting	Moving the discussion away from areas in which you feel your position is threatened or weak
Seeking sympathy/recognition	Attempting to make others sorry for you, and therefore willing to support you; or actively attempting to gain positive feedback on the value of your contribution to the group process
Withdrawing	Refusing to make a contribution
Point-scoring	Seeking to score points off other members to enhance your status
Over-contributing	Monopolizing discussion in the group, using the group process to satisfy individual power and control needs
Trivializing/diluting	Picking on minor points of discrepancy in others' proposals or contributions in order to undermine their positions

(Kakabadse *et al.*, 1987, p. 168)

'teamworker' to attend maintenance-orientated behaviours, and the 'shaper', 'implementor' and 'completer finisher' to regulate the task-orientated behaviours.

Even if all these functions are carefully catered for it is still possible for teams to struggle. This is because individuals frequently bring personal motivations and agendas to the group situation, which, if unchecked, will sabotage teamworking (Table 8.4).

However, as the authors point out, it is sometimes difficult to see the difference between maintenence-orientated behaviour and self-orientated behaviour; the same behaviour may be displayed, but the motive for this behaviour, e.g. gate-opening or closing, may be either to maintain group harmony or to satisfy personal needs. One of the characteristics of a team that has 'stormed' is that it monitors and analyses these processes, using this observational data and confronting dysfunctional behaviour when it occurs.

Challenging unhelpful norms

The norms of the team refer to the rules and procedures for action, often unwritten, which have been accepted by the group. They clarify what is expected of team members, and this can help one to avoid embarrassing or inefficient interpersonal relations. Ideally these norms should be conducive to both task achievement and good relations between members. Throughout the development of the team it is important that work methods and team procedures relevant to the team goals and objectives are established. Team norms will usually reflect group values, goals and identity, and when this happens, group stability and satisfaction are enhanced. It is easier for groups to agree on norms when the values, attitudes and interests among members are compatible, otherwise there may be conflict while the group works out what set of norms it should subscribe to. The group is unlikely to perform unless some clear norms and contracts are established, e.g.

- How does the group deal with problems such as people feeling left out, people feeling unsure of themselves, people feeling angry or hurt, and so on? Do any particular individuals take on an obvious socio-emotional support role?
- Is the atmosphere open and trusting, or closed and defensive? Are team members responding to each other, energetic, enjoying themselves, or is the atmosphere somewhat tense and uncomfortable?
- How does the group react to non-verbal signals of irritation or boredom? For example, a person leaning back apparently to opt out of the group; a person tapping on the table, yawning, reading the noticeboards, looking out of the window; or a general atmosphere that is sluggish and tired, etc.

Some teams, especially those involved in humanitarian, innovative or alutruistic areas, can set very demanding norms. In these cases the established ethos requires members to centre their lives entirely on the team goals, working evenings and weekends as well as weekdays on the project. Financial rewards are played down and members may feel bad if they draw the team's attention to their employment and salary conditions. Pay is almost a dirty word, because it focuses on the individual's needs, which seem petty by contrast with the wider importance of the team's project. Members who cannot feel enthusiastic about these demanding norms or whose enthusiasm has waned have few choices. They can leave the team, they can conform, they can try to change the norms or they can play a deviant role in the team.

So how would you go about trying to change unproductive norms? Team leaders may be expected to establish norms or change unproductive norms in teams. The key to understanding and changing team norms is to consider what is currently reinforcing the team. In the case above the power of social reinforcements could easily be underestimated. You may be able to think of ways to harness this more constructively, to establish more productive norms. In the current climate of rapid and economic, social, technological and political changes, it is highly likely that team norms that are not flexible enough to external changes will quickly become more unproductive, even if they were productive to start with.

Teams norms represent the group's learning contract and provide guidance on how to cope with tasks, goals, roles and responsibilities. If the resultant productivity is less than required in an organization, then team norms become a problem for the organization. On the other hand, if productivity is excessive, then there may be other problems, such as ill-health or stress among the members and problems in the interface between home and work. In both cases team norms are inappropriate, and it is time for the team to be confronted with the negative consequences of the way they it is operating. This re-evaluation of initial assumptions and entrenched patterns of behaviour is in fact a painful but necessary stage in team formation.

Building cohesion

There is a fine line between cohesiveness and conformity. The more similar the team members are in terms of their backgrounds, values and attitudes, the more satisfaction and cohesiveness its members will experience. However, this can lead to undue conformity among its members and a process called 'groupthink' can result. This was identified by Janis and Mann (1979) as a group phenomenon that emphasizes consensus and harmony to the extent that unwelcome ideas, evidence or information are deliberately ignored. Janis and Mann studied high level government policy teams and found that some of them were particularly prone to 'groupthink'.

This leads to defective decision-making, because the objectives, alternatives and risks attached to decisions are not properly surveyed and appraised. There is an under-utilization of the competences of a team if all members are conforming to a dominant member or ideology. So how do you promote cohesion and minimize the undesirable aspect of conformity? Simple counters to groupthink are:

- giving open and supportive feedback to team members;
- avoiding backbiting and malicious gossip;
- confronting interpersonal problems;
- tolerating criticism that is constructive;
- tolerating differences of opinion;
- allowing disaffected members to withdraw;
- showing an awareness that individual objectives may be distinct from group objectives;
- discouraging scapegoating, i.e. blaming particular team members on particular problems.

Although homogeneous groups may be more stable, mixed groups may be more exciting and volatile, offering more innovative and challenging responses to team problems.

Enhancing performance through teamwork

The third area in which HRD can benefit from building and developing teams is that of the superior output and performances achievable by certain teams. Although the idea of giving degrees of autonomy to a team is not new, there has been a resurgence of interest in this approach in recent years. In many ways, a production environment lends itself most readily to teamworking, and an increasing number of employers are allowing teams to allocate responsibilities and tasks among themselves (see Box 8.4).

Box 8.4 Self managed workgroups at Rank Xerox

Rank Xerox (UK) Ltd has converted its entire customer service division of 2,200 people into 205 self-managed work groups (SMWGs). John Prevost, a field supervisor who is 'coach' to a team of 11 engineers servicing photocopying machines, says that the collective approach leads to greater efficiency. 'Some engineers are very fast, others are slow but very thorough. In the past, the slow engineers might have been penalized for not keeping up with productivity targets but in a team you've got room for both types of people, provided everyone recognizes their individual role. You need a blend, but it is important to point out the strengths and weaknesses so that everyone feels comfortable with what's happening'.

To achieve this high degree of awareness, Mr Prevost is planning to introduce a system to allow members of the group to appraise each other's work. He has found that the members of his work group take a more responsible attitude towards performing their jobs. Problems with servicing customers' machines that used to be 'swept under the carpet' are now discussed openly.

Vernon Zelmer, Rank Xerox's UK managing director, says: 'We have basically told the teams to run the business'. However, authority to take important decisions is only gradually being devolved to the Rank Xerox work groups. At present, they are responsible for fairly low-level decisions, such as setting their own holiday schedules and working out how best to achieve the corporate goal of 100 per cent customer satisfaction.

But Shaun Pantling, the company's director of customer service, sees practically no limit to the amount of authority that can ultimately be invested in the SMWGs. 'We are looking at ways that teams could eventually carve up their own salary increases, for example', he says.

But Rank Xerox is cautious about the contentious issue of whether teams should be leaderless. 'This is one of the hot questions around the whole work group philosophy at the moment – do you have a team leader or not?' admits Mr Pantling. 'We think that you do, but we think that he or she should come out of the team rather than be appointed by management' (Oates, 1993).

There are three ways in particular in which group processes can be harnessed to improve the quality of output: improved decision-making, better problem-solving and by cultivating higher levels of creativity.

Improving decision-making

The way decisions are made can have a considerable effect on team members' commitment.

Self-development activity

How many ways of arriving at decisions can you think of? In what order of importance would you rank them?

According to Makin *et al.* (1989) the most common indications of organizational quality in ascending order of effectiveness are:

- *Apathy.* No one contributes to the group discussion, not because they are in agreement, but because they are totally disillusioned.
- *Plops.* A suggestion is made, but totally ignored.
- *Dominance.* One particular individual dominates the meeting. This is often accompanied by apathy from the other members.
- *Pairing.* This is the simplest form of groups within a group. The psychological support offered by pairing is considerable.
- *Voting.* Voting is sometimes the only way to resolve disagreements. There are some times, however, when it is appropriate and others when it is inappropriate.
- *False consensus.* If agreement cannot be reached, one way out of the impasse is to couch the decision in such broad terms that a number of interpretations are possible. A false consensus becomes apparent when the time comes for the decision to be implemented. Each side has a different understanding of what was agreed.
- *Consensus.* This is the most desirable conclusion. Genuine agreement leads to genuine commitment.

The problem is that most work teams have been assembled to address given tasks, will comprise technical specialists, and will be expected to focus their expertise on *what* is to be achieved rather than *how* it is done. In these circumstances decisions get carried through without checking with other team members, minority groupings (or pairings), or discussion drifts inconclusively from topic to topic. Someone, perhaps the leader or chairperson needs to regulate the process. Among other things they might:

1 Issue an agenda ahead of time and ensure balance of time and discussion for given items.

2 Point out to the team if new proposals and ideas are getting 'lost', either by default or deliberate inattention.
3 Occasionally test to see how the team feels about the decisions being made (rather than what they *think* about them, which would lead back into the task).
4 Summarize the team's progress, especially when an important and/or complex dialogue has taken place.
5 Facilitate a consensus decision by allowing broad team contribution. If this is not possible, acknowledge the feelings of minority groupings when they are outvoted.
6 Avoid taking sides, or if such neutrality is inappropriate or untenable, pass the 'chair' to someone else. In extreme circumstances call in an external facilitator or arbitrator.

Deciding on appropriate decision-making procedures is one of the process norms that a 'storming' group will arrive at. If this is done ahead of time, it can provide a useful ground rule to refer back to in the heat of a decision debate.

Better problem-solving

Teams can run aground at one of a number of stages of problem-solving, whether it be diagnosis, solution generation, evaluation or final choice. Based on the common process problems associated with each stage, a number of guidelines can be offered. Again the team may look to its leader to carry out these corrective measures, or if the team is more mature (i.e. a 'high performance team'), each member will bear some responsibility for ensuring their collective effectiveness. The following steps are important:

● At the problem diagnosis stage it is important to distinguish facts from opinions, separate symptoms from root causes, avoid scapegoating, prevent biasing of the diagnosis to favour a preferred option, and avoid premature solutions before the real problem is understood
● When generating solutions, it is necessary to check the relevance of each proposed solution to the problem, focus on present possibilities rather than past 'if onlys', facilitate discussion of pros and cons for each solution and avoid the unthinking use of past solutions.
● At the stage where solutions are being evaluated a good leader will push the team to forecast the multiple outcomes of solutions, avoid bias when estimating consequences, encourage critical comments on solutions rather than on the solution-givers, and ensure adequate evaluation before seizing on one solution.
● Finally, having made a solution choice, the leader should not confuse silence with consent. He or she should solicit minority views, and test the feelings of each team member.

Cultivating creativity

Alongside the ability to cope with and solve problems, teams provide a unique opportunity to develop innovative ideas and creative solutions. Yet too often these capacities are undervalued or underused. The majority of meetings are 'filter meetings', where proposals are blocked and objections to new ideas dominate, and invariably it is the weakest, least potent idea that gets through. Consequently team members become demotivated and uncommitted to the actions agreed.

Self-development activity

Read Box 8.5 and apply the 'team innovation checklist' to a team you belong to. Where are the principal blocks to creativity coming from and how might you set about releasing this creative energy?

Box 8.5   The team innovation checklist

Vision

Does the team have a clearly articulated vision, mission, or set of objectives?
Is this vision (set of objectives) shared by all team members?
Is the vision or set of objectives clearly stated?
Was the vision (set of objectives) originally developed and negotiated by the whole team?
Is this vision (set of objectives) attainable?

Climate for excellence

Is excellent task performance of central importance to the team?
What procedures and methods are used to monitor and improve performance levels?
Are all team members committed to excellent standards?
Are team members prepared to discuss opposing ideas fully?

Participative safety

Do team members share information fully with each other?
Do all team members participate in decision-making?
Are team members ready to propose new ideas which challenge existing ways of doing things?

Do team members discuss one another's work related anxieties and successes?

Is there a climate of trust and warmth within the group?

Support for innovation

Do team members support new ideas?

Do team members give time, co-operation and resources to help each other implement new ideas?

Does the team leader support and encourage new ideas?

Does the team leader offer practical help and resources for the development of new ideas? (From Anderson *et al.*, 1992)

The critical success factors of effective teamworking

At the outset we asked what it was that differentiated a group of individuals from a cohesive, high performing team. The Counselling and Career Development Unit (University of Leeds) identifies nine such distinguishing criteria, which summarize well the ground we have covered in this chapter. An effective team:

1 Shares clear objectives and agreed goals
- clarifies roles;
- agrees on what differences are tolerable;
- discusses values, and a general consensus on the underlying philosophy of the team is reached.

2 Has a climate of support and trust
- people display the relation-building skills of conveying respect, genuineness and empathy;
- feelings are recognized and dealt with;
- strengths are built upon;
- people give and ask for support;
- people spend time together.

3 Has open lines of communication
- positive and negative feedback is given;
- each person's contribution is recognized;
- people are skilled at sending and receiving messages in face to face communication;
- people talk to one another about issues horizontally as well as vertically in the organization;
- discussions about work are the same inside and outside the organization;
- people are open to being influenced.

4 Recognizes that conflict is inevitable and can be constructive
- issues are dealt with immediately and openly;
- people are assertive;
- people are encouraged to contribute ideas;
- problems are seen as normal and dealt with constructively;
- unhelpful competition is minimized;
- people are not blamed, discussions are problem-centred;
- people use 'I' and not 'you' statements.

5 Has clear procedures
- for making decisions;
- for delegating responsibility;
- for meetings.

6 Has leadership appropriate to its membership
- the leader models the philosophy of the team;
- the leader utilizes the strengths of all its members.

7 Reviews its progress regularly
- reassesses its objectives;
- evaluates the processes the team is using;
- does not spend time dissecting the past.

8 Is concerned with the personal and career development of its members
- regular reviews are carried out with each team member;
- the leader looks for opportunities to develop each member;
- members look for opportunities to develop other members;
- members look for opportunities to develop their leader.

9 Relates positively to other groups
- clarifies and meets the expectations of its 'sponsor';
- manages the boundary between itself and other internal/external groups and teams.

Summary

In this chapter we have pointed out the unique opportunity that teams provide for building individual awareness, groupworking skills and enhanced task performance in organizations. As such, a concerted effort to make appropriate and effective use of teams should be a key plank in any organization's HRD strategy. However, teams do not just happen when a group of people gather around a table. They require members who are willing to take risks, give/receive feedback, express feelings and confront unhelpful behaviours when they arise, and leaders who are aware of the peculiar dynamics and pitfalls of teamworking, and who are willing, where necessary, to release their leadership to the team itself.

References

Anderson, N., Hardy, G. and West, M. (1992) Management team innovation. *Management Decision*, 30, 2, pp. 17–21.

Belbin, M. (1981) *Management Teams: Why they succeed or fail*. Butterworth-Heinemann, Oxford.

Critchley, B. and Casey, D. (1986) Teambuilding. In Mumford, A. (ed) *The Gower Handbook of Management Development* (3rd edn) Gower, Aldershot, pp. 423–437.

Davies, G., Smith, M. and Wood, D. (1992) Ganging up – how to build a multinational team. *Human Resources*, Spring, pp. 40–43.

Hannaway, C. and Hunt, G. (1992) *The Management Skills book*. Gower, Aldershot.

Janis, I. L. and Mann, L. (1979) *Decision-making: a psychological analysis of conflict, choice and commitment*. US Free Press, Macmillan Publishing Co. Inc.

Jaques, E. (1990) In praise of hierarchy, *Harvard Business Review*. January/February, 1, pp. 127–33.

Kakabadse, A., Ludlow, R. and Vinnicombe, S. (1987) *Working in Organizations*. University Press, Cambridge.

Katzenbach, J. and Smith, D. (1993) *The Wisdom of Teams*. Harvard Business Press, Mass.

Makin, P., Cooper, C. and Cox, C. (1989) *Managing People at Work*. The British Psychological Society, Leicester.

Morgan, G. (1986) *Images of organization*. Sage Publications, London.

Oates, D. (1993) Team players stretch ahead of the rest. *The Times*, Appointments, page 2, Thursday 27 May.

Thorne, P. (1992) Driving Forces, *International Management*. December, p. 17.

9 Assessing and appraising performance

Introduction

Earlier chapters in this book have been devoted to getting the right person with the right skills into the right job. Others have considered influences on the individual's motivation to work and the ways in which managers can develop their staff and help them in their career planning. Central to the effective management of all these processes is the development and management of performance through performance appraisal.

Most managers are familiar with the concept of performance appraisal, and there is evidence that an increasing number of large and medium-sized organizations operate formal appraisal systems. Many of these systems have been criticized for their emphasis on reviewing past performance, whereas we would argue that they are equally, if not more, essential in providing the opportunity for the development of individuals and their future performance. They are also frequently linked to remuneration and promotion possibilities, and this multiple purpose can create conflicts in their operation.

Despite these issues and others we will explore in this chapter, an effective and fair appraisal system can be the linchpin of human resource development

Performance management systems

Performance management systems (PMS), having been widely used in America, were introduced into the UK in the late 1980s. An evaluation of the operations of these systems has been carried out through surveys of public and private sector organizations in the UK, undertaken in 1991 by the Institute of Manpower Studies on behalf of the Institute of Personnel Management. The survey found 'no evidence to suggest that improved organizational performance in the private sector is associated with the operation of a formal performance management system'. This was a damning indictment of what had been hailed as the answer to the human resource specialist's prayer.

According to the literature, most of it stemming from the USA, a performance management system should include the following elements:

- the organization has a shared vision of its objectives, or a mission statement, which it communicates to all its employees;

- the organization sets individual performance management targets, which are related both to operating unit and wider organizational objectives;
- it conducts a regular, formal review of progress towards these targets;
- it uses the review process to identify training, development and reward outcomes;
- it evaluates the effectiveness of the whole process and its contribution to overall organizational performance to allow changes and improvements to be made (Bevan and Thompson, 1991).

Self-development activity

As stated above, what problems might you foresee with performance management systems?

You might have 'unpicked' most of the statements with some misgivings. First, a mission statement may be communicated to all employees, but this does not imply that they share organizational objectives. Second, it is 'the organization' that apparently is responsible for setting 'individual performance measurement targets' rather than joint objective-setting or, at least, consultation with employees as to what targets are realistically achievable. In fact, of the organizations surveyed, 38 per cent said that performance objectives were set by the manager. Third, the 'review process' has the tripartite outcome of 'training, development and reward', which can be problematic to achieve and whose constituents can counteract each other; too often, reward systems can frustrate the training and development objectives of the process. You may also have felt that the last statement sounded too good to be true!

Probably one of the most problematic areas in performance management is that concerning outcomes and whether these are reward-driven or development-driven. It seems difficult, if not impossible, to reconcile these, and the prevalent model in the UK is currently reward-driven, linking appraisal with performance-related pay.

However, Fletcher (1993) argues that PMS can deal with this multiplicity of outcomes where performance appraisal alone cannot. An effective performance management system can be used to separate out objective setting and review, and performance-related rewards, from the other functions of appraisal, most notably those concerned with individual development. The example in Box 9.1 has attempted to do this, although development needs are closely linked to achievement of objectives, where, it may be argued, they should also be related to personal and career development; this model of PMS does not appear to consider these factors.

Box 9.1   Performance management in British Airways: a case of good practice

This file of guidelines and working papers is for your use – as either manager or subordinate – to help you manage performance throughout the year.

WHAT IS PERFORMANCE MANAGEMENT?

Performance Management in British Airways is about getting the important things done well. It is the way you keep track of:

- what is expected of you – the results you are to achieve, the priorities and the link with the company's business goals
- how you are doing – you regularly discuss progress and feedback with your manager
- your development needs – you develop an understanding of your strengths and how to build on them, you discover areas where you need to develop existing or new skills and plan accordingly

The Performance Management System also forms the basis of recommendations for the distribution of performance related pay to managers.

   Clearly these aims can only be effectively achieved when there are regular meetings between you and your manager and thus Performance Management is a continuous process not just an annual event. You share a joint interest and responsibility with your manager in making reviews happen on a regular basis, that is at least quarterly.

   While companies such as British Airways (Box 9.1) and Adcol (Box 9.2) appear to have implemented a performance management system with some success, others have failed or abandoned the attempt part way through implementation. From such failures, there are lessons to be learned, and some of the more common mistakes are outlined below:

- *Introducing PMS too quickly* – like any other organizational change, time needs to be allowed for communication and acceptance of the proposals. Employees need to be fully informed of how changes, e.g. in reward systems, are going to affect them personally;

Box 9.2 Making the system work

Adcol is part of a large multinational company with a comprehensive and sophisticated performance management system. Strategic objectives are set by the senior management team and communicated to all members of the workforce in the company's mission statement; the mission statement is written in 'user-friendly' terms and incorporated into individual job descriptions. In this way, every employee can see clearly how their efforts will contribute to the objectives of Adcol.

At departmental level these objectives are translated into measurable targets, which are agreed between managers and the staff for which they have line responsibility. In many cases team targets are set, since this is the prevalent working practice. These targets, whether for individuals or for teams, are reviewed quarterly, and there is also an annual review, which centres on target achievement and which is used to inform the company's system of merit pay. At the quarterly reviews, when targets may, if necessary, be renegotiated, the individual's development needs are considered in relation to achieving the agreed targets. Meeting these development needs is a line responsibility but the company has invested resources in self-study materials and there are a number of staff in the personnel department who have experience and can give assistance and advice in this area.

The company operates a performance-related merit pay system, which is determined at departmental level and subject to peer review so that comparison across individuals can be made. Adcol is trying to avoid the pitfall of divisiveness that performance-related pay can create by ensuring it is perceived as fair and clearly related to target achievement (adapted from *Performance Measurement and Evaluation*).

---

managers may need to be trained in objective-setting and performance measurement as well as in some of the more formal appraisal techniques and record-keeping; there needs to be an operational system for human resource development as a result of appraisal. Overall, PMS may represent a desire to change organizational culture that can be expected to generate widespread suspicion and resistance if not communicated clearly.

● *Not fully costing the scheme* – partly as a result of lack of time given to implementation, full costs in real terms are not accurately forecast. These do not only include direct financial costs such as those that may be incurred in setting up a performance-related pay system, but indirect costs in terms of time needed for operating the system, e.g. in departmental target-setting and quarterly review sessions.

- *Targets are unrealistic* – if the company has little experience of joint target-setting in line with organizational objectives, the targets set may be unachievable for the majority of the workforce – or even for a minority – although they may have a motivating effect on high flyers.
- *No clear mechanisms for feedback* – although individual feedback at the review sessions seems relatively straightforward, managers and team leaders often find that there is no clearly-defined system for giving feedback upwards from departmental level, nor sharing the experience between departments.
- *Confusing language* – performance management systems have developed a set of terms and acronyms which may be meaningful to those familiar with the system, or who work in personnel, but which serve to confuse nearly everyone else. The 'language' of PMS includes terms such as 'job profiles', 'core accountabilities, 'competences', 'work control management systems', 'key result areas' etc., most of which require definition to the lay person and with which they find it difficult to associate.
- *Confusion between quality and quantity in performance measurement* – care needs to be taken over what is being measured and what constitutes 'improved performance'. If targets are based on increased productivity, an increase in the quantity of work will qualify the individual or team for merit pay based on target achievement; however, an *increase in quality* may in fact result in a *decrease in quantity*, since improved quality usually takes longer to achieve.
- *Confidentiality of review reports* – although the system is designed to be open and to provide for comparison of individuals in relation to the reward system, this can cause resentment and concern about who has access to review and appraisal records.
- *Incomplete integration of the human resource management function* – central to the successful operation of PMS is an integrated system of human resource management and development that can set up and monitor performance management and ensure that training and development activities and opportunities are both available and relevant to individual/departmental/organizational needs (adapted from *Performance Measurement and Evaluation*).

In 1992 the second stage of the Institute of Personnel Management survey on PMS was undertaken and found that:

The approaches and practices adopted are extremely diverse, and the indications are that they achieve differing results. Reassuringly, the organizations that were taking performance management most seriously and which were closest to the notion of an integrated and strategic approach did seem to be those that produced the best results . . . in terms of employee attitudes and commitment rather than the hard indices of organizational performance and output . . . However, where employees report high commitment, job satisfaction, clarity of goals, good feedback and so on, it is difficult to imagine that this has no effect at all on performance at the individual level (Fletcher and Williams, 1992, p. 42).

Fletcher and Williams found that there were four main issues which emerged from the survey and which, they argued, had implications for the survival and success of performance management as a concept. These were:

- ownership and commitment;
- the role of the human resource specialist;
- the nature of implementation;
- rewards.

Ownership and commitment

One of the main requirements of performance management systems is that they are line-driven, yet the survey revealed that the majority of organizations had not devolved responsibility successfully to line managers. The initiatives had been the brainchild of chief executives, senior human resource specialists or external bodies such as elected councils. As a result, line managers did not feel a sense of ownership of the scheme, nor committed to its success.

The role of human resource specialists

Because of this lack of ownership and commitment by line managers, the system tended to devolve on to the HR department, which found it difficult to tread the tightrope between acting as a resource for guidance and support while ensuring that control and ownership was vested in line managers. Too often HR departments in the survey found themselves acting as arbiters over issues of rewards and inequities.

The nature of implementation

Unfortunately many organizations searching for a solution to employee retention and economic survival adopt new methods because they are current 'management fads', without consideration of whether the new ideas are suitable for their organizational structure and culture. An organization that has a strong emphasis on the 'bottom line' may see performance management and performance-related pay as supporting their business objectives without consideration of the developmental aspects. In such cases the system is nearly always doomed to failure, since employees resent its one-sided approach.

Performance-related rewards

The fourth issue identified by Fletcher and Williams was that of reward systems, usually those incorporating wholly or mainly some form of performance-related pay. Although this has become popular, largely because of the introduction of performance-management systems, it is not a new concept. See Box 9.3.

Box 9.3   Performance-related pay; an old idea in a new guise

In 1862, after a review of the education system, the Newcastle Committee drew up a Revised Code of Regulations which suggested that 'the junior classes in the schools, comprehending the great majority of children, do not learn, or learn imperfectly, the most necessary part of what they come to learn – reading, writing and arithmetic'. In response to this state of affairs, performance-related pay was introduced into schools.

'The managers of schools may claim 1d per scholar for every attendance after the first 100, at the morning or afternoon meeting. One third of this sum thus claimable is forfeited if the scholar fails to satisfy the inspector in reading, one third in writing, and one third in arithmetic respectively.'

The scheme was apparently successful in that it resulted in a 16 per cent reduction in the annual grant provided by the government, but not so successful that it survived; performance-related pay in education was abandoned by the end of the nineteenth century (Hopkins, 1979).

As you know from Chapter 7, 'Developing motivation and commitment', most research concludes that pay is not a strong factor in job satisfaction or improved performance, and organizations in the survey were generally unclear about the motivating effect of performance-related pay. Although there were efforts to relate pay to performance, it was not always possible to operate the system, because of external constraints. For example, changes in legislation or in the quality of raw materials could affect productivity and thus make targets unattainable. There were uncertainty and disagreement about the proportion of pay that should be performance-related: too great a proportion made pay too dependent on external constraints while a minimal proportion would not act as a motivating force. See Box 9.4.

One company in the survey had been more imaginative, and related theory to practice by offering a wide range of non-financial rewards managers could use instead of, or in conjunction with, performance-related pay. This type of approach, while unfortunately atypical and

---

Box 9.4   Pay not related to performance

An independent evaluation of the introduction of performance-related pay into the top three tiers of management in a London borough found that there had been no increase in management productivity. The scheme had failed for two reasons. The total proportion of an employee's pay that could be offered as performance-related was only 10 per cent; many organizations in the private sector can offer up to 30 per cent, which is considered to be more meaningful in financial terms! Managers also resented being assessed on their performance and given a 'score' – they saw this as degrading and demotivating. If their score was average, they tended to perform at an average level, seeing no reason, financial or otherwise, to increase productivity.

---

possibly quite complex to administer, relates the reward system firmly to individual needs.

The performance management systems in the survey stressed the integration of a performance-related pay or reward system, but not all performance management embraces this element. Unfortunately it is performance-related pay that appears to generate most resentment and creates most problems, on the surface at least, particularly if performance rating for reward purposes is not clearly separated from performance appraisal for the determination of development needs.

Kessler and Purcell (1992) have shown that organizations have two different categories of objective in introducing a system of performance related pay and some or all of these objectives tend to operate in all cases. The first category is related to the traditional functions of any payment system, which are the recruitment, retention and motivation of employees. Within this category it should be recognized that, for managerial level staff, performance-related pay is more successful for recruitment and retention, whereas it is more likely to act as a motivator for staff below this level. Obviously the London borough in Box 9.4 was not aware of this categorization!

The second category of objectives is related to organizational change and the devolution of greater managerial control to line managers, since they will have direct responsibility for agreeing departmental objectives and assessing individual performance. Such devolution is likely to be related to a change in organizational culture that restructures the relation between an organization and its managers, in the first place, and between line managers and their staff, in the second.

In order to introduce an effective performance-related pay system, three identifiable steps must be taken – establishing performance criteria, designing performance assessment and making the link between performance and pay.

Performance measurement

One of the key issues in relation to performance management is the accurate and fair measurement of performance based on suitable performance criteria. This is a particularly problematic area as far as higher-level or professional employees are concerned, for the nature of their jobs means that criteria are likely to be more qualitative than quantitative. There is also the question of equity in performance criteria and the extent to which these can be applied throughout the organization.

Performance measurement is inherently complex, although the experience of Northelectro in Box 9.5 could have been avoided. It sounds deceptively easy, particularly in relation to measuring production outputs, for example. But output measures are not necessarily accurate if they simply relate to quantity and not quality, or if the output is not entirely under the control of the individual whose performance is being measured. The output of an assembly worker, for example, is dependent on the performance of those further up the line; and there is the danger that performance measurement is an assessment of current performance, not a predictor of potential. Yet promotion and salary decisions are often made on the basis of current performance measurement. We have to accept that, in agreeing performance criteria for human performance, no absolute standards exist. Observation 'on-the-job', self- and peer-rating, interviews and other means are the best we have available. When it comes to 'desirable' personality and behavioural traits, measurement can become increasingly subjective.

Box 9.5 Establishing performance criteria at Northelectro

Northelectro is the main manufacturing plant of Electroco, situated in the north of England, employing around 600 people. The company as a whole prides itself on its advanced production and personnel policies and Northelectro is claimed to exemplify these. Performance-related pay was introduced in 1988., The objective of introducing the system was to reflect changes in corporate and marketing strategy from a 'technology led' focus to one which was 'market driven'; it was also introduced as part of a harmonization policy in the relationship between management and workforce.

The new system was based on an annual appraisal of all staff against objectives which have been jointly agreed between the individual employee and the appraiser who has direct line responsibility for that employee. The annual appraisal is supplemented by quarterly meetings at which objectives can be discussed and reviewed. On the basis of the appraisal, each employee is awarded a grade on a scale of 1 (exceptional performance) to 6 (unacceptable performance) and this grade determines how an individual's increase in pay compares with the predetermined increase in the wage bill for the company as a whole.

Performance criteria are divided into 'objectives' and 'key criteria'. The objectives are the quantifiable goals which the individual must fulfil and include such things as output targets and quality levels. Key criteria are the characteristics and modes of behaviour which the workers must adopt in meeting these objectives and the company has identified 28 of these. They include 'tolerance for stress', integrity', 'tenacity', 'adaptability', 'decisiveness' , 'organizational sensitivity' and 'creativity'. There is provision for additional criteria to be adopted which are not in the company list. Unfortunately, since the criteria were only issued as guidelines, they were open to variance and multiple interpretation; one manager is quoted as saying, 'I set down the key criteria. There are guidelines but you can write down what criteria you want. I basically write down the type of skills that you need'. As a result, there was perceived inequity by those being appraised and graded against different criteria. The situation was compounded by the fact that, in some cases, it was difficult to isolate the contribution to overall performance made by a particular job (Proctor *et al.* (1993))

Competence-based approaches have increased in the UK in recent years, largely as a result of the Management Charter Initiative, which had the unenviable task of identifying national standards of competence for different managerial levels. This was the first major attempt, in this country, to define the manager's job in terms of competence statements, which, in general, were capable of being measured against a number of performance criteria. An example is given in Box 9.6.

The competence-based approach is not without its problems, as you saw in Chapter 2.

A number of phrases in Box 9.6 imply that subjective judgement could take place or inequity might occur. For example, (f) 'fully and correctly implemented and maintained', (g) 'appropriate measures' and (j) 'with minimum delay'. Someone, presumably the line manager, has to determine standards for these aspects of performance; and, as you saw in the Northelectro example (Box 9.5), line managers can differ in the standards they set and accept.

A further criticism of the competence-based approach is that it promotes a 'sufficiency' view and makes no allowance for excellence,

Box 9.6 An example of performance criteria from the Management Charter Initiative's management standards for first-line managers

Key purpose: to achieve the organization's objectives and continuously improve its performance

Key Role: Manage operations.

Unit 1.1   Maintain and improve service and product operations.

Element 1.1.1   Maintain operations to meet quality standard.

Performance criteria

(*a*) All supplies necessary for operations are available and meet organizational/departmental requirements.

(*b*) Operations within the manager's area of responsibility consistently meet design and delivery specifications.

(*c*) Information and advice given to customers is accurate in line with organizational policy and is within the manager's responsibility.

(*d*) All communications with customers are carried out in a manner, and at a level and pace, likely to promote understanding and optimize goodwill.

(*e*) Information about operations that may affect customers is passed to the appropriate people.

(*f*) Systems to monitor quantity, quality, cost and time specifications for service/product delivery are fully and correctly implemented and maintained.

(*g*) Factors that may cause operations to be disrupted are noted and appropriate measures taken to minimize their effects.

(*h*) Corrective actions are implemented without delay and appropriate staff and customers informed of any changes that affect them.

(*i*) Records related to the design and delivery of operations for the manager's area of responsibility are complete, accurate and comply with organizational procedures.

(*j*) Recommendations for improving the efficiency of operations are passed to the appropriate people with minimum delay.

Self-development activity

Problems with performance measurement include perceived subjectivity and inequity. In the performance criteria listed in Box 9.6 can you see any areas where subjectivity might still operate?

thus providing no motivational impact on employees. Nor is it any indicator of future potential, since it is based on current performance. It is also considered to be elitist and discriminatory, since it does not make provision for non-managerial women or people from minority groups to demonstrate managerial potential through non-traditional means.

The development of assessment centres (also discussed in Chapters 4 and 6) is now becoming widely used as part of the performance management, measurement and appraisal system, for it is considered to be more objective than most other forms of assessment. Not only are there a number of trained assessors, thus reducing assessor bias, but participants can be judged in simulated, work-related situations against the same criteria. They can also be used to measure behavioural dimensions of performance, as shown in Box 9.7

The use of assessment centres in performance measurement

Assessment and development centres have been discussed in different contexts in this book already. At this point it is sufficient to remind you that, while they are probably the best predictor of future performance and are perceived as fair (by selection candidates anyway, but also in other contexts), they are very time-consuming for managers and very costly to run. If an organization is considering investing in an assessment centre, the investment and commitment levels need to be considered carefully.

So far in this chapter we have been looking at performance management and measurement mainly in relation to reward systems. However, they have a strong developmental purpose as you saw earlier. Perhaps the most commonplace forum for diagnosing individual development needs is the appraisal interview between the manager and his/her subordinate. As we have pointed out, unless the annual appraisal is clearly separated from links to remuneration and promotion possibilities, it is unlikely to fulfil developmental objectives.

Box 9.7 Behavioural frameworks in an assessment centre

Assertiveness	*Guideline definitions*
(ability to confront others calmly but firmly, without aggression, sarcasm or discourtesy, irrespective of rank or position)	
Score	
1	Makes no effort to confront a situation or to sort it out.
2	Reacts to criticism with anger, sarcasm, or meekly accepts what is said.
3	Attempts to be assertive are clumsy, and backs off when the going gets tough.
4	Attempts to be assertive are more skilful, but withdraws if challenged directly.
5	Is assertive and is able to confront difficult situations.
6	Is assertive and remains calm even when faced with others' anger, sarcasm and discourtesy.

Resourcefulness	
(ability to find other ways of doing things and to act on initiative)	
Score	
1	Stops progress by dampening others' initiative.
2	Needs to be told what to do and how to start.
3	Initiates activity but quickly runs out of steam.
4	Initiates and maintains activity.
5	Is imaginative and is resilient under adversity.
6	Initiates imaginatively, is resilient and enables others to develop their ideas (Dale and Iles).

Performance appraisal

Randell (1984) suggests the following outcomes of appraisal:

- auditing;
- succession planning;
- identifying training needs;
- motivating staff;
- developing individuals;
- checking effectiveness;
- evaluating.

You would probably agree with his list. Not all appraisals can, nor should, attempt to result in all the outcomes suggested by Randell and the particular outcome(s) which are common in one organization may be different in another; and not only outcomes will differ, for inputs into the appraisal process can include reports on an individual's level of performance from superiors, peers and subordinates. The appraisal may not even be the traditional one-to-one interview but take the form of a peer review.

Handy suggests a slightly different set of outcomes that appraisals can fulfil:

(*a*) to provide a database for the organization's inventory of people, skills and potential;

(*b*) to provide a mechanism for the proper assessment of performance by individuals so that they may be appropriately rewarded;

(*c*) to provide individuals with feedback on their performance and personal strengths and weaknesses;

(*d*) to help individuals and their subordinates to plan personal and job objectives and ways of achieving them.

It would be fair to say that performance appraisals engender mixed reactions at different levels within organizations. Senior human resource managers and personnel departments see them as beneficial, perhaps because they contribute to the 'database for the organization's inventory of people', as Handy suggested. Line managers, in general, regard them with scepticism in the knowledge that they have often received no training in appraisal techniques, and that they rarely have sufficient time in which to carry them out or in which to provide effective feedback to individuals; in addition, many line managers dislike the need to discuss poor performance with subordinates, particularly when there appears to be no solution to the problem.

Box 9.8   Manager as god

. . .whatever the distortions that are likely to impair appraisals, one thing seems to be immune to all forms of bias: just as most people like to be the bearer of good news, so most people dislike being the messenger of doom. This is clearly apparent in the general reluctance of managers to undertake appraisals of their sub-ordinates which are less than enthusiastic and deemed likely to have a negative effect on that person's work effort. Indeed, it is the lack of interpersonal skills on the part of managers (as well as a general distrust of the validity of the system) that is often cited as their reason for avoiding the task wherever possible. McGregor (1957), for instance, suggests the underlying reason for manage-rial resistance is a dislike of 'playing god', especially when managers are constantly exhorted to be supportive of, rather than authoritarian with, their subordinates. In the words of Edwards (1988:17), 'many managers prefer dental appointments to playing 'God' in preparing appraisals' (Grint, 1993, p. 63).

Individuals' perceptions of appraisals are closely related to their own experience of being appraised. As you would expect, these perceptions are more positive if the person being appraised knows something about the appraisal process, feels able to express ideas and attitudes, and feels that the appraisal focuses on identifying and analysing problems affecting the employee's job performance and not on the appraisee's personality.

Not only do performance appraisals have multiple outcomes, but they can also have manifold benefits – for the individual, for the manager and for the organization as a whole. These benefits for the individual who is being appraised include:

● the opportunity to receive constructive feedback on performance and how it is viewed within the organization;
● a springboard for agreeing training and development plans that will help the individual to overcome identified problems and improve future performance;

- a shared appreciation of the manager's aims and priorities and a better understanding of how the individual's contribution fits into these;
- an opportunity to discuss the scope and constraints of the current job with the manager, while discussing objectives for the coming year;
- an opportunity to discuss career options;
- recognition for good performance and objectives achieved.

For the line manager who is appraising staff the benefits include:

- learning about employees' hopes, fears, plans and concerns about their present job and their future careers;
- a chance to reinforce and share important goals and priorities with employees so that they can see where their individual contribution fits in;
- mechanisms to measure changes in employee performance;
- a greater understanding of individual jobs and ways in which they overlap or where gaps exist, enabling them to make job design changes to increase organizational efficiency;
- a sound basis for transfer and promotion decisions;
- a motivational opportunity by ensuring they give recognition for good performance;
- a developmental opportunity to ensure that the needs of the department and the organization as a whole can continue to be met in the future.

Finally, there are benefits for the organization in:

- assisting with succession planning and training and development analysis;
- identifying gaps in human resource planning;
- ensuring that organizational and individual objectives are in harmony;
- improving communication;
- improving performance (from Evenden and Anderson, 1992).

Self-development activity

Which of the benefits suggested by Evenden and Anderson accrue from your own experience of an appraisal system within your organization?

But benefits always have costs attached to them. These costs include those of setting up an appraisal scheme in the first place and of providing training and development opportunities related to individual and organizational needs. These costs may already be subsumed within a human resource development plan, but they must include the 'hidden' costs in terms of time. A line manager must expect to expend several hours on the appraisal of each of his or her staff, including completing relevant forms and conducting interviews; this is not an inconsiderable amount, particularly if there is a large number of staff to appraise – and, indeed, it is suggested that one person should not appraise more than six to ten people. There is also a cost incurred (and too often omitted) in training appraisers – and appraisees – so that both can gain maximum benefit from the process. Furthermore, there may be costs associated with perceived unfairness, grievance and discrimination if the appraisal system contravenes the law in these respects. See Box 9.9.

As with performance management systems, appraisal schemes tend to founder on inadequate or too hasty implementation. A scheme that is imposed is unlikely to engender commitment if the individuals concerned have not been given an opportunity to participate in its design and do not fully understand its purpose. This latter point is important; often organizations and their managers are unclear about the purpose of an appraisal scheme, or its original purpose may have changed; and, as both Handy and Randell point out, the multiplicity of purposes only serves to confuse and dilute the effectiveness of appraisal.

If appraisal is to serve a developmental purpose, this not only has to be reflected in the design of the scheme but also be translated into some form of action. A scheme soon loses its effect if there is no follow-up and if training and development opportunities never materialize. In addition, given the extent to which organizations have been restructured over the last few years, has the appraisal scheme, if it existed, been restructured or does it reflect outdated objectives and values? Or is it still what Fletcher (1992) describes as 'a universally applied, personnel-driven, standard procedure that stays rigidly in place

---

Box 9.9 Blacklash over performance-related pay

London Underground has had to change the way in which its performance-related pay system is implemented after conceding a £60,000 racial discrimination case in 1993. The lawyer for some of the twenty black station masters claimed that the performance assessments left too much to the discretion of senior staff carrying out the appraisals. Research found black managers were being awarded lower performance pay than their white colleagues. Some managers were failing to use the appraisal system correctly, making the same remarks on all forms while awarding different levels of pay, or ignoring the assessment entirely and simply making a judgement on salary.

(perhaps kept there by the weight of its own paperwork) within the organization for years on end'.

Fletcher has also suggested some trends in appraisal that have arisen as a result of changes in organizational structures and working practice in recent years. These changes have resulted in fewer hierarchical levels and more flexible working patterns; project teams may be inter-organizational and/or international in their composition, forming for a particular task and then dispersing; initiatives such as the competence approach, TQM and Investor in People have (or should have) had an impact on the design of appraisal schemes.

In the Institute of Personnel Management's survey mentioned earlier in this chapter over 80 per cent of companies were dissatisfied with their existing appraisal systems. With the advent of performance management systems, appraisal has clearly become a line management responsibility and no longer the province of personnel specialists. But line managers need support, time and training if they are to make it work.

Alternative methods of appraisal to the traditional one-to-one interview are being introduced, particularly where the numbers of appraisees reporting to one line manager are too many for appraisal purposes. Self-appraisal is one method, still relatively unused in this

---

Box 9.10   Upward appraisal

Being assessed by peers and subordinates can be a daunting process, according to a senior manager at American Express who has seen upward appraisal slowly gain acceptance at the credit card multinational. Currently used in isolation from pay and other annual assessment methods, it is a symbol of the approval which upward appraisal has achieved that this kind of evaluation is soon to be built into the mainstream appraisal system at Amex.

Forming one part of a leadership seminar, managers are shown two questionnaires, one filled in by peers, the other by sub-ordinates, which are then discussed by the manager with a personnel specialist. The questionnaires pick out management skills such as listening and being able to deal with bad news. Peter Hall, division vice-president of American Express' European operating centre in Brighton, says that one of the surprising and potentially intimidating aspects of the process is the accuracy of subordinate opinion. 'The first time it's quite daunting. You don't know what you are going to hear. The perceptions of people around you are pretty accurate; they know your weaknesses.' All subordinate and peer opinions remain anonymous (Fletcher, 1992).

country unless it is combined with superior appraisal; it has the advantage of bringing the participant into the process but few people are likely to admit to significant deficiencies when the outcome may be linked to pay or promotion. Even if the appraisal is not, formally, linked in this way, the appraisee may perceive such a revelation as a high-risk strategy.

Multiple-source appraisal is generally perceived to be fair by appraisees although it is costly in terms of the time required to collect and collate the information. A multiple-source appraisal might consist of a self-appraisal, observation on the job and reports from other superiors (if the individual reported to more than one person) and from peers. In some cases, it might include assessment by sub-ordinates, or 'upward appraisal'. See Box 9.10.

A recent innovation in education is the upward appraisal of teachers and lecturers by their students, although this has been happening in America for some time. Like all other methods, while inherently democratic, upward appraisal has its drawbacks, not least in that the subordinate appraisers are even less likely to have received relevant training than superordinate appraisers. Criticism therefore is unlikely to be constructive and upward team appraisals are likely to be more extreme than individual ones. Not all feedback will be negative of

---

Box 9.11 Employee attitudes towards performance appraisal

An external consultant was enlisted to conduct a survey of employee attitudes towards appraisal in general and appraisal objectives in two companies which had recently merged. The main findings, which were not untypical of results of similar surveys in other organizations, were:

- most employees welcomed the idea of regular performance appraisal;
- there were mixed views on whether performance appraisal should be linked to decisions on pay and rewards, and whether it should be used to identify employee potential for promotion purposes;
- most employees sought active involvement in the scheme, and felt it should assist in communicating their views to management; their main concerns were that appraisals might not be totally fair, because of the possibility of subjective assessment being made and managers adopting inconsistent standards

> As a result of the survey, the organization's directors identified the main objectives of their appraisal scheme as:
>
> (*a*) to improve the current and future performance of employees;
> (*b*) to help employees to develop, through identifying their training and development needs;
> (*c*) to review past performance.
>
> Additionally, they felt the appraisal scheme should strengthen communications and help succession planning (Evenden and Anderson, 1992).

course, and most managers are likely to get some kind of positive feedback from their subordinates; indeed this is often a pleasant surprise since opportunities for subordinates to give managers positive feedback are fairly rare in Western culture.

Not only, then, is it likely – and preferable – that the people who act as appraisers have changed, but the content of the appraisal should reflect today's trends. As we said earlier, many organizations are using a competence-based approach, which can provide a benchmark for performance measurement. Others are redefining the purpose of their appraisal schemes as a whole. And the use of assessment and development centres (see Chapter 4) is becoming central to the appraisal process in other organizations, where they are considered to be more objective and sophisticated than traditional methods, particularly in identifying key people for the future.

The issue of objectivity and the extent to which any form of assessment can relate to 'reality' has become increasingly important from a developmental perspective. It is one of the main reasons for reviewing traditional appraisal methods whereby the individual is appraised by one person, usually his or her boss, who can only view that person's performance from one perspective. A different viewpoint may be provided by subordinates, and yet a third view by the individual of his or her own performance. How can, or should, these different views be reconciled, and is there indeed, a 'reality' between these differing perceptions? How much of an individual's level of performance is determined by his or her real abilities, and how much by the culture and structure of the organization or the manager's style of leadership? How realistic is it to strive for the ultimate in objectivity in appraisals?

The answer is that it is definitely unrealistic and probably not worth the effort, providing that the appraisal is seen for what it is and not relied upon implicitly.

Box 9.12   What's wrong with performance appraisals?

Despite the application of several generations of specialists in the field, the ineffectiveness and alleged inaccuracy of appraisal schemes have tended to lead those seeking to improve them deeper and deeper into the labyrinth that promises an objective solution to the subjective problem. It has not been argued that we should therefore abandon the existing appraisal methods. Indeed, if they coerce managers into a greater consideration of the efforts of their subordinates, then at least some useful purpose may be served by them. On the other hand, it might well be more productive to retrace our steps out of the objectivity labyrinth and accept our subjective fate. The upshot is not that we should abandon appraisal schemes but we should consider them more sceptically and more reflexively. Indeed, one way to move beyond the present impasse is to embody the subjective approach in the performance assessment schemes by developing upward appraisals. This is particularly apposite in the wake of contemporary movements to empower the workforce, to secure more participative styles of management and to promote teamwork. Upward appraisals are neither simple to adopt nor automatically popular with those being appraised, nor are they a panacea for all manner of managerial problems. But, like the search for an objective appraisal system, the search for a panacea is itself a distracting problem, not part of the solution. If upward appraisals do not solve all management problems, the tenacious grip of 'objectivity' in downward appraisals merely adds another problem to their already burdensome load (Grint, 1993).

Summary

Although assessment is discussed elsewhere in this book, its place in relation to performance management, measurement and appraisal has been the subject of this chapter. Performance management systems (PMS) are a relatively recent initiative and, ideally, should include a shared vision, individual performance measurement targets, regular performance reviews and evaluation. Their most problematic area for the management of human resources is that they have the dual outcomes of performance-related rewards and the identification of training and development needs. These can be separated only if objective-setting and review are distinguished from reward-based outcomes.

PM schemes have encountered a number of problems, usually because they have been implemented too quickly, the system has not been fully costed, targets are unrealistic, there is no clear mechanism for feedback, the jargon is unfamiliar, there is confusion between quantity and quality imperatives, concern about confidentiality and, probably most important of all, the system is not fully integrated into the human resource management function.

Performance-related rewards, usually financial, need to be integrated into a PMS and related to performance measurement if they are to be worthwhile. The measurement of performance needs to be accurate, fair and based on appropriate performance criteria. Problems arise when there is perceived subjectivity or inequity in performance measurement, either internally or in relation to external wage norms.

The performance appraisal can have a range of outcomes including, for example, auditing, succession planning, motivation and development. In a PMS, appraisal is a line management function, and many managers are sceptical about its impact; too often line managers have received no training in appraisal, particularly where an appraisal scheme has been introduced but not fully or accurately costed. However, there are clear benefits for the individual, the manager and the organization in carrying out performance appraisal and there are alternatives to the traditional superior–subordinate relation. Both peer review and upward appraisal have been shown to be effective. Traditionally, appraisals have not, nor ever can be, purely objective, but these alternative methods, together with an acceptance of a degree of subjectivity, can be a considerable improvement.

References

Anderson, G. and Barnett, J. (1987) Characteristics of Effective Appraisal Interviews. *Psychology Review,* Vol. 16, No 4.

Bevan, S. and Thompson, M. (1991) Performance management at the crossroads, *Personnel Management,* November.

Dale, M. and Iles, P. A. (1992) *Management Skills; A Guide to Competences and Evaluation Techniques.* Kogan Page, London, pp. 138 and 155.

Edwards, M. R. (1989) Making performance appraisals meaningful and fair. *Business,* July–September, 17–46.

Evenden, R. and Anderson, G. (1992) Making the Most of People. Addison-Wesley.

Fletcher, C. (1992) Appraisal: an idea whose time has gone? *Personnel Management,* September, pp. 34–7.

Fletcher, C. (1993) *Appraisal: routes to improved performance.* Institute of Personnel Management.

Fletcher, C. and Williams, R. (1992) The route to performance management. *Personnel Management,* October.

Grint, K. (1993) What's wrong with performance appraisals? *Human Resource Management Journal,* Vol. 3, No 3. pp. 61–77.

Handy, C. (1985) *Understanding Organizations* (3rd edition). Penguin Business Books, Harmondsworth.

Hopkins, E. (1979) *A Social History of the English Working Classes*. Edward Arnold, London.

Institute of Personnel Management (1992) *Performance Analysis in the UK: an analysis of the issues*. IPM, London.

Kessler, I. and Purcell, J. (1992) Performance Related Pay: objectives and application. *Human Resource Management Journal*, Vol. 2, No 3, pp. 16–33.

McGregor, D. (1957) An uneasy look at performance appraisal. *Harvard Business Review*, May–June, pp. 89–94.

Open University (1994) *Performance Measurement and Evaluation.*Open Business School.

Proctor, S. J., McArdle, L., Rowlinson, M., Forrester, P. and Hassard, J. (1993) Performance Related Pay in Operation: a case study from the electronics industry. *Human Resource Management Journal*, Vol. 3, No 4, pp. 60–74.

Randell, G. (1984) *Staff Appraisal*. Institute of Personnel Management.

10 Managing organization development and change

Introduction

Although, in earlier chapters, we have considered organizational strategies for human resource management and development, much of our discussion has centred on individual and team development. In this final chapter, we concentrate on the organization and ways in which it can develop and change. Nicholson (1992, p. 207) says:

> Organizations are systems of action for managing our environment and fulfilling our needs. They structure effort and allocate functions, to create order out of uncertainty and stability out of turbulence. At the same time, from their internal and external environments, organizations are confronted with pressures to change, which, if ignored, may lead to their downfall. Change is therefore a foremost concern of organizations, and is always problematic.

The 'problematic' reference to change is too often centred on the human response to poorly planned and managed change programmes or to 'change for the sake of change' organizational strategies. Change is part of today's working environment and, as such, needs to be integrated with human resource development.

'Organization development' (OD) is itself an approach to change, but it is also descriptive of what happens as an organization evolves and changes its purpose, its structures and its strategies. This chapter looks at the developing organization as a whole, with an emphasis on the role of human resource development in the management of change, before considering OD as one approach; other approaches include culture change programmes, total quality management (TQM) and organizational re-engineering.

Objectives of HRD

Self-development activity

If your organization has a stated policy of human resource development, what purposes or objectives does it fill? You might like to reflect on this for a few minutes before reading on.

By definition, all HRD activities and programmes imply change, whether it be at an individual, workgroup or organizational level. A number of different objectives for HRD can be identified:

HRD as a tool

First is to use it as a *tool* in pursuit of quality, cost reduction and some form of enhanced performance. Some tools are fairly blunt, used in fairly indiscriminate ways to achieve in-defined purposes. For instance, senior managers, lamenting the low morale among supervisory grades, may set up blanket leadership skill training courses in the hope that this will kindle a new decisiveness and vision among first line management. Some training activities are precision tools brought into operation to perform fixed jobs such as upgrading production operators to handle newly automated processes, or training branch managers in interviewing skills in preparation for a recruitment campaign. Others are used to shape behaviour; so, for instance, when British Telecom introduced computerized databases designed to give the public one initial point of contact with the company whatever the nature of the enquiry, the 'front office' strategy included a customer care training programme. Yet others, used less frequently, are pulled out of the toolkit to measure the completed job and assess the outcome against the original specification. This approach may sound overly mechanistic, but when preceded by careful diagnosis is entirely valid (see Chapters 3, 4 and 9).

HRD to gain competitive edge

Second is the use of HRD to gain competitive edge, both through the content of such activities and the way in which they are delivered. More and more organizations are using HRD, for example, as a way of integrating their business planning processes with wider organization development and human resource activities, from recruitment through to succession planning. This may be achieved by introducing each training event (whether technical, marketing or managerial skills) with a module linking it explicitly to the business context and strategy, or by only designing programmes containing principles and activities that demonstrably meet customer requirements. This may mean tailoring in-house packages to the specific needs of different businesses, as National and Provincial Training Services have done. This organization, along with many others, is moving away from the familiar menu of standard training products (see Box 10.1).

This account is indicative of the way many organizations are moving. Notice, too, the reference to attracting and retaining staff, for the quality of skills training and career development opportunities offered to employees is becoming a significant carrot in competitive recruitment, a trend that will be accentuated where there is a diminishing labour pool of job entrants.

Box 10.1   Tailored training at National Provincial

In 1988, anticipating the effects of the deregulation of financial services in the UK, National Provincial concluded that, if it were going to be a dynamic business capable of responding to the challenge of radical change, then it would need outstanding managers. . .In order to recruit, retain and develop people with the potential to become excellent, a well-managed, business-driven management development strategy was required. . .

Developing managers ad hoc,or because it is 'a nice thing to do' is a recipe for disaster (management development is not some self-justifying entity); it cannot succeed unless it is an integral part of the business-planning and policy-making process. Moreover, in a competitive business environment which calls for the cost-effective use of resources, the only justifiable reason for developing managers (or indeed any other member of staff) is to deliver present and future business objectives (Smith, 1990).

HRD as creator of learning climate

Third comes the use of HRD to create a general climate of *learning* in the organization. The focus here is on the learning needs of individuals, it is to be hoped in accordance with organizational goals, and the belief behind it is that within each member of staff is a vast creative potential waiting to be unleashed. Accordingly, the trend is away from structured, taught courses and towards a learner-centred approach, where methods such as on-the-job training, strategic secondments and temporary task forces are seen as the best form of development (see Chapter 2, p. 36, for a discussion of what a learning organization implies).

In this kind of environment the approach of car makers BMW is informative. Training courses are developed in response to the direct needs of individuals in their day to day work and three main factors are recognized: the workforce is generally better educated, with higher expectations than it used to be; people develop better when *they* have some control over the learning process; and learning requires a more holistic approach, whereby the activities of management and management development are interwoven rather than discrete activities.

Releasing potential in this way is equally high on the development agenda in the public sector. In part this can be attributed to the diminishing collectivist influence of trade unions in the 1980s and also to the wider and more concerted usage of systematic selection, performance appraisal and performance-related pay on an individual basis, together with a greater emphasis on accountability and leadership from line managers. While this breaking of new ground does not automatically imply the push toward facilitated self-development apparent in the more resource-rich private sector, it does indicate an important shift from the inflexibilities of bureaucratic career structures.

HRD for engineering change

Fourth is a growing recognition that HRD can be a key device in engineering organizational change and, in particular, as a way of managing change. We could cite here any number of examples, but in Box 10.2 we give some extracts from the account of change at Manchester Airport by the personnel director.

Of course it is relatively easy to change *manifestations* of culture; such things as the removal of clocking in/out, the phasing out of separate canteens for different seniority levels, the introduction of development

---

Box 10.2   Culture change at Manchester Airport

Manchester Airport became a public company on 1 April 1986. Forecasts indicated that the business would more than double in size over seven years, operating two major international terminals. The company's first business plan envisaged significant changes in business approach, range of activities, and company culture in the new operating environment.

We soon realized that the managerial style which had secured outstanding success under the previous 'local government' structure would not serve as a blueprint for the future. Significant changes were required in managerial approach: from technical expert, skilled at working within bureaucratic systems, conditioned to see the prime task as resolving short-term crises, and often working without reference to other managers, to commercially aware manager, results orientated, thinking strategically, with accountability for managing a defined business area. This brought new dimensions of delegating substantial authority to subordinates, motivating teams and working productively with other directorates to achieve company objectives.

Finally, we established eight key principles for the culture change programme:

1 The thrust of the exercise would be to *focus on what was needed*, rather than on what the individual selected as development need (in our previous experience, these rarely coincided).
2 We would firmly reinforce the policy that line managers have the responsibility for developing their subordinates. We would do this by involving their immediate manager directly at each stage so that the process would be *line management driven* (with personnel as the facilitator).

3 The programme must *stimulate and motivate* participants to take responsibility for their own learning and promote a culture of lifelong continuous learning for everyone.

4 It must be *learner not trainer centred.* Support is vital to learning; everything is focused on encouraging and enabling self-development.

5 There would be no generic solutions or mass courses; and managers would define and work to an *individually tailored* improvement plan suited to their own learning style preferences and work commitments.

6 The objective for this programme must be a *measurable improvement* in job performance for individuals, contributing to a real uplift in effectiveness for the group as a whole.

7 The new policy thrust was to make continuous improvement an *expectation and requirement* for senior management, not an optional extra, luxury or an impossible dream. It was vital for the future of the company that the new skills and behaviours were adopted across the board: nobody would be allowed to opt out of the process.

8 The principles and concepts of competences would be *integrated into all human resource practices*, providing a new 'language' for understanding job requirements and individuals' contributions.

Thus we would ensure that everyone participated in the programme with the full commitment and active participation of their bosses, and the support of their peer groups; further, that the learning and development would be consolidated and followed up. The company would measure the effects of investment in learning and development in terms of increased performance in order to ensure it actually worked. In other words we would demonstrate that people actually do make the difference.

In conclusion, we have to say that the programme has been a success. We wanted a reliable means of identifying development needs related to real business imperatives. We have enhanced managers' self-awareness, and as a reult learning has become a recognized key to improved performance. The programme provided them with the tools to develop their own effectiveness and gave them the motivation and encouragement to do so. It is clear that we are moving from a culture dominated by experts, where systems and procedures were paramount, to one that recognizes that the most effective way to raise performance is to enable managers to direct their own learning and to motivate them to develop the necessary skills and attributes for superior performance in their own jobs. The potential is there – we just need to unlock it (Jackson, 1992).

centres, the restructuring of business units, and so on. It is far more ambitious to change the ingrained attitudes and cultural norms of staff. What is significant however about HRD interventions at places like Manchester Airport in Box 10.2 is the way several 'levers' of development are pulled simultaneously, the way changes are directed at the whole organization, and the way wider human resource practices are deliberately modified to reinforce the desired cultural changes.

Table 10.1 Strategy implementation problems and the role of HRD solutions

Problem	Percentage of firms	Possible causes and HRD solutions
Implementation taking more time than allocated.	76	Employees may not have adequate training. Lack of managment expertise. Resistance to change could be managed through HRD interventions.
Major problems surfacing during implementation but not identified beforehand.	74	If people-related problems, HRD could be more involved at formulation stage. Quality of management teams may be deficient; team building could help. Mismatch between people and activities; HRD could help to achieve greater fit.
Co-ordination of implementation activities not effective enough.	66	Roles of departments and individuals not clearly defined; HRD may help. Structure and strategy may not match; advisory role for HRD/HRM. Communications; communications training; deal with line/staff problems.
Competing activities and crises distracted management from implementing the key decisions.	63	Lack of ability to prioritize and plan; management training type intervention. Lack of task groups or change committees.
Capabilities of participating employees not sufficient.	63	Recruitment and training activities not aligned; greater integration required. Insufficient analysis of employees' needs; organizational training needs analysis. Individual role ambiguity and lack of self-confidence; facilitation-type HRD intervention. HRD activities did not reach the management levels required; more emphasis on senior management development.
Training and instructions given to lower level employees not sufficient.	62	This is a direct HRD problem due perhaps to inadequate analysis of needs. Goals of functional flexibility not clarified; more systematic multiskilling. Experienced worker standard not clarified for new tasks; more systematic on-the-job training. Inadequately trained instructors; better training instructor development.
Leadership and direction provided by departmental managers was not adequate.	59	Managers may not be aware of the expectations; greater role definition required. Managers may lack the necessary management skills, systematic analysis of needs and appropriate management training intervention. Lack of team cohesion; team building interventions

Adapted from Hussey (1988).

This all represents a vast investment of effort and resources by the organizations concerned. So why this focus on HRD? The answer is that many, if not all, of the reasons why strategies falter in their implementation are associated with people problems. In Table 10.1 the top seven strategy implementation problems are listed (in order of mentions) according to a survey of ninety-three private sector firms in the US. For each of these obstacles to change, the table gives possible reasons and offers some HRD solutions.

So the range of HRD activities is extensive, and the choice of one particular training programme or development activity over another will depend on the extent of the changes sought and the capability of individuals and groups concerned with and affected by the various interventions. Garavan (1991, p. 23) says, 'It may be hypothesized that the greater the degree of strategic change the more likely it is that HRD involvement with focus on providing a basis for understanding and internalizing change and experience the results of change'. Before going on to examine the types of development that can be attempted in this context, we take a closer look at the role HRD can and does play in strategies for managing change in organizations.

The role of HRD in managing change

There are two ways in which HRD plays a central role in managing organizational change. The first is by responding to a succession of externally driven changes at an organizational level, and to subsequent shifts in strategic direction, each of which has significant effects on development-orientated practices in the workplace. Second, HRD *can* and should have an influential role internally by developing and shaping the appropriate competencies, practices and attitudes that will help the organization deliver its products and services. Hence the two-way flow of arrows in Figure 10.1 The figure oversimplifies strategies for managing change in organizations. For instance, it is rare for the mission or vision of an organization to be smoothly informing its HRD and HRM activities in the way the figure suggests. Equally it would be unusual for the 'upward thrusts' to be acting in such a concerted and sequential fashion; organizational reality is far more messy and cyclical, with strategy often evolving, rather than being deliberately planned, and culture emerging, rather than being consciously 'managed'.

However, what Figure 10.1 does depict is the key place of HRD in linking human resource systems and policies to the competitive capability of an organization. In particular it shows that:

1 The stimulus for change invariably comes from the external environment – in Chapter 2 we described this as the exposure of a business skill gap – and the implications of these identified problems/opportunities affect the whole organization rather than one sub-system within.

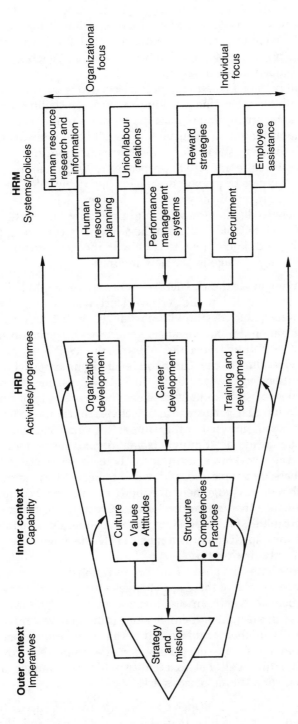

Figure 10.1 *The role of HRD in managing strategic change*

2 Change affects a complex web of interrelated elements within an organization, and trying to introduce change by addressing only one element in isolation, like structure, without taking account of its wider cultural context, and associated HRD activities within the organization, is only likely to lead to benefits that cannot be sustained in the long run.

3 The risks of alienating people associated with the proposed changes are high. Changing working practices, installing a new computer system, attempting to shift the attitudes of the workforce, and even establishing new financial targets, all have immediate impact upon the different stakeholders in an organization, and each will require slightly different HRD approaches to 'bed them in'.

4 The success of proposed changes invariably relies on goodwill and commitment of those affected by them which means giving staff access to decision-making, and providing information. Again HRD has a major role to play in the workforce, equipping them with the skills and 'know-how' to cope with the changes, and giving them a meaningful stake in the new regime.

Having made these general comments, we should look at Figure 10.1 in more detail. On the left we start with a range of factors that represent external stimuli for change, or the 'outer context' of an organization. So, for instance, government legislation in the form of the 1986 Building Societies Act and the 1987 Financial Services Act radically altered the competitive environment of financial service institutions in the late 1980s. In HRD terms this led some building societies to establish links between their corporate business objectives and individual performance objectives, and a move towards competence-based internal programmes of management development. Another external stimulus facing organizations more generally is changing workforce attitudes. There is evidence that increasing numbers of people are and will be engaged in 'knowledge work', which requires judgement, flexibility and personal commitment rather than mere adherence to procedures. Creating the structures, skills and opportunities for more staff to independently generate and act on ideas for improvement is a major HRD challenge for organizations in the twenty-first century.

Part of the purpose of an organizational mission statement is to anticipate some of these sea changes in the external environment and to articulate where an organization is going, and what it wants to achieve in the light of them. It is one thing to have a mission statement, it is quite another for this to express a future vision or set of values that is meaningful and energizing for the employees concerned. Why might individuals fail to identify with the strategic intent of their organization? Some reasons are:

● there is insufficient personal benefit from its successful outcome;
● there is dissonance between what it states and the way senior managers behave;

- there is a scepticism as to whether it can be fulfilled;
- it asks for too great a sacrifice, or too much investment, etc.;
- people are heavily committed to past history and traditions;
- it fails to inspire or secure acceptance;
- it is imposed without adequate consultation.

So the imperatives for change in an organization's outer context may be compelling, and indeed the mission statement may capture them well, but the success of any subsequent changes depends equally upon the inner context of the organization. This refers to an organization's capability to change (in the form of leadership, organization structure and culture), the values and attitudes of the workforce, the personalities of key people, the effectiveness of political processes and the adequacy of current competencies and practices to deliver the mission. Patently, HRD has a major impact on these inner capabilities for change, both in the 'softer' areas of motivation and attitude, as well as the harder areas of skill levels and management expertise.

How HRD can contribute in these areas is represented by the three boxes in the HRD column (Figure 10.1). Through the integrated use of organizational development, career development and training and development, HRD can improve the individual, group and organization effectiveness. We shall examine the practicalities of each of these in the next section.

Closely related to these three primary HRD areas are a number of HRM systems and policies. Human resource planning determines the organization's major human resource needs, strategies and philosophies, as discussed in Chapter 1; performance management systems ensure individual and organizational goals are linked through such things as appraisal and assessment procedures (Chapter 9); and selection and staffing attempts to match people and their career needs with available jobs and career paths (Chapter 5). While each of these HRM 'systems' incorporates 'development', this is not the primary orientation or process. Finally, dovetailing with these as separate but connected HR systems are, first, human resource research and information systems, which provide an HR information base to the organization; second, union and employee arrangements, which seek to ensure healthy union/organization relationships; third, reward strategies ensuring fairness and constituency in the administration of compensation and benefits; and, fourth, what might be called employee assistance, which focuses on personal problem-solving and counselling to individual employees. Each of these constitute essential underpinning to the HRD activities and programmes.

In many ways the three development areas of HRD can be viewed as a set of key leverage points in bringing about effective organizational change. The job of those responsible for HRD is to anticipate strategic changes, interpret these in HR terms, i.e. what new mindset skills and attitudes are needed, and to design and implement appropriate development activities in one, two or all three development areas to ensure that the wider HRM systems and policies of the organization support and reinforce the required behaviours in the workplace.

The integrated use of HRD

In the last section we introduced a framework for locating the place of HRD in the scenario of an organization change. Here we examine more closely the HRD options available when embarking on such strategic changes. Proposals to initiate HRD activities and programmes will usually come from the identification of particular areas for change in the organization. Building on earlier work by Pugh (1986), Table 10.2 categorizes a number of presenting problems or issues that might hinder the performance of an organization and the well-being of its workforce. For each set of 'symptoms', some examples of action are given, ranging from the remedial to the more radical. The resulting matrix represents a framework for understanding and identifying what change is necessary in an organization, and what methods to consider when initiating the change process. Notice that although all the methods have a human resource emphasis, not all are developmental in focus. The key indicates those that can be broadly classified as organization development, career development and training/development initiatives respectively.

In Table 10.2 there are two dimensions to the matrix representing the two main factors that have to be identified when preparing an HRD intervention: level of analytical focus and degree of required intervention. Where is the problem located in the organization? What level of analysis is the diagnosis going to focus on? Do the causes stem basically from behaviour at the level of the:

- individual;
- group;
- between groups or sub-units;
- organization?

These levels are represented by the rows of the matrix. For example, at the individual level, the bottom row of the matrix, the presenting symptoms might include unwillingness to consider change, feelings that the task is too easy or too difficult, a poor match of individual with job, and recognition and remuneration at variance with objectives. These sorts of problems would indicate problems at an individual level. Other problems would suggest different levels, as indicated in the matrix. Thus inappropriate working relations would suggest group level investigation, and lack of effective co-operation between departments would indicate organizational level remedies.

It is important to underline that by 'level' here we are talking about level of analytical focus, not level in the organization. Thus 'poor job definition' at the individual level may apply to any level in the

Table 10.2 Deciding on appropriate HRD initiatives

	BEHAVIOUR *What is happening now?*	STRUCTURE *What is the required system?*	CONTEXT *What is the setting or culture?*
ORGANIZATIONAL LEVEL	low morale; stress and suspicion; low response to environmental change	business strategy poorly understood; inappropriate organization structure; inadequate mechanisms for monitoring environment	poor performance due to geographic setting, market pressures, labour market, physical condition, basic technology
	e.g. *survey feedback, organizational mirroring,* **business awareness workshops**	e.g. *participative development of mission statement;* radical restructuring; redefine business processes (re-engineering)	e.g. change strategy, location, physical set-up; *change work attitudes, quality/culture; change programmes; organization-wide communication briefings*
INTER-GROUP LEVEL	lack of effective co-operation between sub-units; conflict and excessive competition; unresolved feelings and issues	lack of integrated task perspective; poor sub-unit performance	conflicting values/attitudes between departments and sub-units; physical distance
	e.g. **training in management skills** (influencing negotiation, leadership etc.); *inter-group confrontation, role analysis and negotiation*	e.g. redefine roles and responsibilities; improve co-ordination and liaison mechanisms; delayering; networking structures	e.g. reduce psychological and physical distance; exchange roles and attachments; **cross-functional group working;** *group problem-solving and goal setting*
GROUP LEVEL	inappropriate working relations; poor understanding of goals; leader not trusted, respected	task requirements poorly defined; role relations unclear; leader's role overloaded; inappropriate reporting procedures	insufficient resources; poor group cohesion; inadequate physical set-up; personality clashes
	e.g. *process consultation; team building;* **interpersonal skill development**	e.g. **multi-skilling;** redesign work; relationships (socio-technical systems); self-directed teams; competency-based appraisal and development	e.g. change technology, work layout; change group composition
INDIVIDUAL LEVEL	failure to fulfil individual needs; frustration responses; unwillingness to consider change	poor job definition; task too easy or difficult	poor match of individual with job; recognition and renumeration at variance with objectives
	e.g. counselling/career planning; **basic training (functional skills and specialist knowledge)**	e.g. job redesign; enrichment; agree on key objectives and competencies; development centre and personal development planning	e.g. personnel changes improve selection, induction and promotion procedures; **targeted education and training;** revise reward strategies

Bold italic Organizational development   Underlined Career development   **Bold** Training and development organization hierarchy, from shopfloor worker and first-line supervisor to chief executive and main board chairman. Similarly, the groups concerned with poor group relations may range from the professional social work team to the regional management board.

The second question concerns the nature of the problem. Does it fall into the area of behaviour (what is happening now?), or structure (what is the required system?), or context (what is the setting?); and, therefore, what is the degree of intervention required? This dimension is represented by the columns of the Table 10.2.

The first column is concerned with current behaviour symptoms which can be tackled directly. Since it suggests methods and changes that address the symptoms without drastically altering the required system or setting, this column comprises the least radical of the development strategies. Indeed in some cases the results may not be recognized as change at all – merely as overcoming some difficulties in the proper working of the current system (see Box 10.3).

But it may be that this degree of intervention is not sufficient to achieve the required aims. It could be that, however improved the group atmosphere and leadership style, the group will not function well because it is not clear what the organization requires of it, adequate information to carry out the group task is not available at the appropriate time, and tasks are inappropriately divided and poorly allocated to the members of the group. In these circumstances the second column in Table 10.2, concerned with organizing the required system, is the appropriate degree of intervention. This is a greater degree of intervention because it may require modifications in the structure, systems, information flows, job design, and so on, which inevitably affect a much wider range of the 'organizational environment' of the particular group.

Even this degree of intervention may be insufficient. The problems may lie in the contextual setting (changing market pressures, physical distance, poor group composition, unsupportive organization culture and so on). In these situations the degree of intervention in the third column is appropriate. This is a still greater degree of intervention, requiring strategy changes, considerable expenditure of resources (both financial and human), and carrying with it greater likelihood of disruption, with its attendant costs. It is not therefore to be undertaken

---

Box 10.3   Tinkering vs. transforming

As the result of a team-building exercise with a ward sister and her staff, the functioning of the ward, the morale of the staff, and the standard of patient care all improved. The hospital management committee regards this process not as change, but one of getting the organization to work properly.

lightly. Since going from the first column of the matrix, through the second to the third requires a greater and greater degree of intervention and commitment by the organization, it is clearly sensible to start at the first and work as far across to the third as is necessary – which may of course be right across if that is the nature of the problem.

Self-development activity

Try using the matrix in Table 10.2 for yourself in relation to a problem in your own organization. First locate the problem in one of the columns of the matrix and then decide upon the nature of the problem in the horizontal axis. Are the suggested solutions feasible?

What is organization development?

Since a number of training and career development activities have already been discussed (Chapter 3), here we shall concentrate on organization development (OD). In fact OD is more an approach to change than a list of techniques. It had been defined by French and Bell as:

> ... a top management-supported, long-range effort to improve an organization's problem-solving and collaborative diagnosis and management of organizational culture – with special emphasis on formal work-team, temporary team, and intergroup culture – with the assistance of a consultant–facilitator and the use of theory and technology of applied behavioural research, including action research (French and Bell, 1990, p. 17).

The approach is founded upon a set of values about people and groups in organizations, i.e. people have needs for personal growth, and they should be consulted and given appropriate resonsibility; workgroups are capable of major contributions to organizational effectiveness, and they should be dealt with in a trusting and collaborative manner, and so on. It is particularly appropriate where:

1 An organization is failing to accomplish its objectives (in terms of output of product or service, quality, efficiency, profitability, and so on) and the nature of the current organization is contributing to this failure by, for example, reducing the possible performance of the people who work for it. They may be trapped in inappropriate management structures, demotivated by inadequate reward systems, suffering under poor leadership styles, etc.

2 An organization wishes to improve its existing capacity to adapt more readily to environmental changes. External changes in a given market, for example, would require changes in product, which, in turn, would require changes in organizational design and/or attitudes.

3 An organization intends to adopt new technologies or new ways of working that require changes in structure, systems and attitudes for their full benefits to be realized.

4 New 'operating units' are being created (in the widest sense new factories, new regions, new departments, new tiers of management) which give the opportunity to design from scratch the new management structures and operating systems, in order to make maximum use of the input of the people in the units, and not just, as is often the case, of the machinery.

OD as a change management strategy

There has been quite an important development in the thinking of OD practitioners in the past decade. In the 1960s the emphasis (particularly in the USA) was almost entirely on improving the interpersonal relationships in the organization via training and group development, using the interventions in the behaviour column of Table 10.2. From the late 1970s, partly because of the inadequacies of working exclusively at a behavioural level when clearly structural and contextual changes were required, and partly because of the harsher economic environment, much greater emphasis has been put by most practitioners on the broader range of intervention strategies available, including those in structural and contextual columns. The open systems approach to understanding organizations lies behind the design and implementation of many change efforts, and can be seen as a particular version of OD. Other approaches having similarities with OD include:

- *Strategic planning and change*: here the emphasis is upon astute choice of long-range corporate objectives and the marshalling of information, resources and people skills to achieve these in a step by step manner. Whether change can be managed in such a rational and formalized way has been rightly questioned, e.g. by Quinn (1980) and by Johnson (1988).
- *Culture change programmes*: the importance of culture and the possibilities of culture change became very popular in the 1980s, thanks to the 'excellence literature' following Peters and Waterman. Again the notion that organization culture is first of all homogeneous, and, second, can be manipulated, has been criticized by some. Nevertheless, would be change agents have become far more aware of the need to at least address culture when implementing change programmes in organizations. In many ways culture is equivalent to the right-hand 'contextual' column in Table 10.2.

- *Total quality management* is another approach, which also became a byword in organizations during the 1980s. The TQM process is guided by seven basic principles:

the approach	: management-led
the scope	: company-wide
the scale	: everyone is responsible for quality
the philosophy	: prevention not detection
the standard	: right first time
the control	: cost of quality
the theme	: continuous improvement

  It can be seen from this list that TQM embodies many of the tenets of OD both in its objectives and in how change is implemented. Manufacturing companies were the first to experiment with such an approach – particularly targeting their production processes – but other sectors have followed suit, with often extremely positive results. Again the change technologies used overlap with many of those enumerated in Table 10.2.

- *Socio-technical approaches* attempt to optimize jointly the technical, human and organizational aspects of a given change effort. Pioneered by the Tavistock Institute of Human Relations in the 1950s and 1960s, the socio-technical approach has possibly been less popularized than those above, although some notable success stories have been reported. For instance, groupworking at Volvo made substantial contributions to quality and efficiency, as well as increasing job satisfaction and responsibility; and the design of Shell Canada's greenfield Sarnia chemical plant, where it was decided 'following considerable debate and analysis, to eliminate traditional jurisdictional boundaries and operate the whole plant virtually as a single department', staffed by six to eighteen person self-regulating teams with multiple skills, was highly successful (Pritchard, 1984).

- *Re-engineering* is the most recent change management approach to be widely acclaimed. It has been defined as 'The fundamental rethinking and radical redesign of business processes to achieve dramatic improvements in critical, contemporary measures of performance, such as cost, quality, service and speed' by Hammer and Champy (1993, p. 32). As implied by this definition, the approach requires questioning what an organization does (rather than relying on prior assumptions or givens) and then determining how to do it better by thoroughly reviewing and streamlining its internal processes, structures and technologies.

All the above change strategies are concerned with bringing about successful complex change, usually at an organizational level. Each of them incorporate some degree of HRD activity and certainly each has significant implications for the way HRD is approached by an organization. However, OD is the one change strategy that sits most comfortably under the banner of HRD.

Strategic human resource development

So far in this chapter we have noted the varying objectives of HRD – some of them tactical and limited, some more globally organizational in their intent. We have indicated the central role that HRD *can* have in the implementation of organization change, although that potential role is not always fully recognized, and we have specified a range of HRD interventions under the categories of organization development, career development, and training and development. In closing this chapter and as a way of integrating many of the themes of the book as a whole, we ask what it is that sets apart HRD from being a set of disparate training initiatives. What, to put it positively, are the characteristics of strategic HRD?

Integration with corporate objectives

Linking HRD plans and policies to the organization's strategic goals brings several benefits. It ensures the anticipation of problems and opportunities, rather than having to respond to them as they occur, with the competitive penalty that this implies. It keeps HRD 'on the map', such that questioning and exploring the human resource implications become part and parcel of strategy-setting rather than afterthoughts. It ensures that the benefits of HRD, in the form of innovative ideas, newly acquired skills and freshly identified talent, influence the formulation of strategic plans. And crucially it prevents

---

Box 10.4   HRD: integral or marginal?

Ford (Europe) expects every one of its top 2000 managers to attend its Executive Developement Centre at least once every two years for an international briefing and pooling of ideas, objectives and priorities. Nissan empowers its shopfloor teams to improve workplace layout with the help of teamleaders and inventions process training. The British Trust for Conversation Volunteers (faced with a practice and policy structure that badly lagged behind the scale and nature of its activities) equips its over-stretched staff with the skills of networking, productivity and managerial flexibility. The key in each case is the linking of the HRD provision to the strategic objectives of the organization concerned. This requires somebody or some group in the organization thinking ahead about the critical knowledge and skills required and feeding this into the human resource and management development plans, as well as allowing the outputs of HRD to guide and steer the strategic planning process.

training and development becoming an end in itself, as a well intentioned activity whose output has little or no bearing on the goals and direction of the enterprise.

This is not to say that the impact of HRD is always measurable, particularly in the case of the more experiental, open-ended approaches to development. The point is that the training activity has been conceived and set in motion with specific learning goals designed to contribute to the achievement of the business plan, whether in the form of knowledge gained or attitudes changed. The approch focuses on impact and real development rather than attendance and mere activity.

Senior management support

It goes without saying therefore that organizational leaders need to endorse HRD initiatives if only to release the resources and budget necessary to run them. But this is not enough. There needs to be consistency between the outputs that development programmes teach and cultivate and the observed actions and behaviours of the senior managers who 'sponsor' them. Unless individuals are convinced that their leaders value and practise the skills and values being taught, they are unlikely to 'buy-in' to the HRD programme themselves, except perhaps for selfish and potentially dysfunctional purposes.

Senior managers can demonstrate their commitment to the objectives of HRD in a number of ways. They can play an active role in designing and implementing formal courses, seminars and the like. If time does not permit, they can at least be present at training events, either to kick them off at the start or, perhaps more effective and less of a token gesture, to critique presentations of work done by individuals or groups by attending during the programme. Better still if the proposals being made by developers are 'real time' proposals that can be implemented as business solutions. Participation by senior managers in training events themselves not only lends immense credibility to the programme concerned but also ensures an understanding from the top of the concepts and language being used and the skills being addressed. A number of quality programmes adopted by organizations have been initiated in this way, with board members training their 'family groups' of first line reports, who then go on to train their staff and so on downwards. Providing this initial enthusiasm is seen by employees to persist, there can be few better ways of perpetuating performance models in organizations. Such visible and thorough commitment by senior managers also pays off by:

- forcing them to question and expose their own assumptions about the future and the kind of leadership it will require;
- providing dialogue across levels and functions within the organization, and increasing perceived accessibility to sources of decision-making;

- helping them stay in touch with the issues and concerns of a broad range of managers and employees in the business;
- helping to convey a sense of leadership and vision to the organization, while sending informal messages about performance requirements.

Well formulated HRD plans and policies

Garavan (1991) gives a number of strategic advantages associated with the formulation and dissemination of an HRD plan. Among the benefits are:

- It aids management in identifying and implementing appropriate HRD activities for resolving organization problems and exploiting new business opportunities.
- It helps to ensure that supervisors, line managers, and top managers are all equally aware of their HRD responsibilities and participate in HRD activities on a regular basis.
- It provides operational guidelines for management, i.e. a clear framework outlining the reason why the organization is investing in HRD and the resources that the organization is allocating for employee development.
- It acts not only as a source of information for all managers, but also sets out clearly for employees the different types of education, learning and/or development activities that they can undertake to help to develop their skills and knowledge, and therefore it complements career development activities.
- A clear policy statement helps to define the relation that exists between the organization's objectives and its commitment to the HRD function.
- It may enhance public relations in so far as new employees to the firm can see one of the key benefits on offer to them and that any skills or inadequacies that they have coming into the firm will be overcome by engaging in appropriate training and development activities.
- An HRD policy can facilitate the establishment of employee career development opportunities such that employees can identify their individual career paths. In short, an effective HRD policy continually assesses the learning needs required for releasing both the employee's and the organization's growth potential.
- It provides a guideline or framework against which HRD activities can be evaluated. Such a framework can indicate weaknesses or successes in various training or development activities and thus provides it with a strategic orientation.

Line managers' role

If senior managers can and should be instrumental in using education and training to catalyse change and achieve competitive edge, then line managers generally have a special responsibility to assess and address competence and facilitate the development of the staff they manage or supervise. The senior manager can envision the team, articulate the required standards and goals and to some extent exemplify the desired culture of the organization, but it falls to line managers to foster and sustain high performance by coaching, counselling, appraising, listening, diagnosing and motivating, on a day to day basis. As we saw from the approaches to HRD (Figure 3.1), the internalized pattern may not be the most visible, but it is nevertheless the most effective, because it is here that development activities, formal and informal training, on-the-job coaching secondments and off-the-job courses are happening naturally and effectively. In short, training becomes the bloodstream of the organization, transporting vitality, up-to-date knowledge and creativity to the parts that need it. The vital role of line managers in this process is well illustrated in relation to the issue of equal opportunities in Box 10.5.

Box 10.5 The role of line management in equal opportunities

Managers have two clear strategies open to them; they are not necessarily EO strategies, but are part of good management practice. The first is setting the targets and goals necessary for the achievement of policy objectives, and guidelines for acceptable behaviour. These must be communicated to staff with the aim of gaining commitment to the achievement of targets and goals. In terms of EO policies this means breaking down policy aims into 'bite size' pieces; it also means giving support to those individuals within departments who are actively pursuing EO policy issues. At a minimal level this means no blocking initiatives, or allowing individuals to become isolated. The second strategy is control; the day may come when individuals will be dismissed for not achieving EO targets and goals, but until that day arrives managers have to tread a fine line between encouragement and censure. 'Encouragement' must be handled sensitively; directives to female members of staff (which often come out of the blue) to go on a training programme for women, worse still one that is concerned with improving personal effectiveness, can, not surprisingly, have a negative effect upon individual women. Thus managers must also be in the business of selling EO policies to their staff. If managers themselves are unclear about what equal opportunities are, what constitutes sexist behaviours, or are ambivalent about their own feelings (initiatives that 'go against the grain'), then it is their responsibility to seek advice and guidance from those who have an exclusive brief to develop EO policies, the equal opportunities officers (Jones, 1988, p. 55).

Whether the issue be the erosion of discriminatory attitudes, as in the local government case in Box 10.5, or the development of skills, confidence or competence in other areas, the line manager has a central role. At the very least he or she needs to set and monitor performance standards that are in line with organizational objectives, and interpret such standards if they are not articulated or understood. Second, there is a need to translate these into discrete on-the-job projects or off-the-job training assignments; and, third, it is important to provide an environment of support and encouragement for newly acquired skills and attitudes.

Motivation of trainees

Not to be underestimated in this discussion of what constitutes a strategic approach to HRD, is the perception of the individual trainee. His or her experience of the training programme or development experience, and hence its longer term business impact, will be coloured by circumstances, some of which appear totally unrelated to the design and content of the training in question. Inevitably, trainees will embark on a training activity with many predispositions and perceptions about its likely benefits. This requires that all participating parties (line managers, designers of HRD programmes, tutors, trainers and trainees themselves) give as much attention to the workplace context and learning infrastructure as to the training event itself. This means being clear about the expected outcome of the training programme for the target groups concerned, being sure that the context and timing of the HRD initiative are appropriate, ensuring that the learning design matches the objectives of the programme (remembering, as we saw in Chapter 3, that trainees learn in different ways and at a different pace), and ensuring that, as far as possible, there is a readiness to learn among trainees and a willingness to support the learning transfer by their line managers.

Integration with wider HRM policy

One of the key indicators of strategic HRD is the extent to which training and development activities are linked into other aspects of the employment relationship. It will instil confidence in the trainee as well as provide a consistent flow of required competencies at an organizational level if the criteria of effectiveness instilled through HRD activities are the same as those looked for in performance reviews, and are the ones reflected at internal promotion panels and reinforced by the reward and recognition policies of the organization (see Box 10.6). A crucial aspect of linking HRD activity with wider HRM policies is the 'translation' of strategic intent into everyday behaviours that are relevant and recognizable by the organization concerned; this new language will help to differentiate the excellent performance from the average. As Box 10.6 shows, there is an encouraging trend in this direction in the UK, but it is slow.

A crucial aspect of linking HRD activity with wider HRM policies is the 'translation' of strategic intent into everyday behaviours which are relevant and recognizable by the organization concerned: this new language will help to differentiate the excellent performance from the average. As Box 10.6 shows there is an encouraging trend in this direction in the UK, but it is slow.

Box 10.6 What does strategic behaviour look like?

. . . organizations are beginning to appreciate that the process of labelling behavioural indicators into organizationally meaningful titles provides a language and a forum for capturing cultural change. Applications in this arena are fewer. A review of the literature indicates that six organizations have used the approach in this manner. British Petroleum, for instance, have made efforts to link executive competencies to a cultural competency model; Digital Equipment Europe Ltd created a business-oriented human resource strategy around competencies; Bass plc used competencies to streamline, restructure and recruit in order to build a new company culture; Rank Xerox have defined boardroom competencies for Facilitating Directors; National Westminster Bank plc accelerated change in personnel practices and business performance by defining competencies; and a medium-sized accountancy organization used competencies to articulate a changing business market (Sparrow and Rognanno, 1993, p. 52).

For too long training and development programmes have been conceived and delivered without reference to the strategic future needs of the business, in isolation from other HRM activities and without any attempt to evaluate their value and benefit to the organization. Those responsible for HRD need to have access to, or be represented among, top management, where they can make an input to strategic decision-making and interpret the HRD implications of future objectives and goals. If this avenue is closed, HRD will remain reactive and one step behind events, and training activities will not secure the full confidence of organizational leaders.

Recognition of culture

Finally, an organization may have sophisticated mechanisms for scanning its competitive environment in order to facilitate its future skills capability; this diagnostic information may be fed regularly and accurately into HRD processes that lead to timely and well tailored programmes. Yet despite all the merits of such an approach, HRD may still fail to have a strategic impact because it underestimates or misjudges the prevailing culture of the organization.

As we saw in Chapter 3 all organizations have a prevailing mindset about the place and value of HRD. This will be dependent in part on the personal experience of senior management. If senior managers do not believe training courses to have helped them in their own development – and there is evidence to suggest this is the case – then they are unlikely to be very supportive of such training for others. Even when there is 'top team' backing for HRD, it may be because they see it as an opportunity to get a certain message, and/or bundle of skills across to the workforce, which again is not necessarily conducive to effective training.

In other words, learning is as much about where the dominant cultural coalition of an organization is located as it is about the acquisition of new skills and techniques. Usually this cultural coalition is synonymous with the senior management. It is therefore essential that those designing HRD activities should ensure the support of this coalition, whoever they might be, and establish options, policies and plans that fit the strategic logic and cultural web found in the organization. A useful first step in their process of cultural recognition and alignment is the undertaking of a cultural profile/audit. Such an audit could examine both the present and desired cultural profiles. HRD activities could then, in the spirit of OD, be focused strategically on making the transition from the present to the desired future state. Of course it is possible that those responsible for HRD discern the current centre of gravity, culturally speaking, to be unhealthy for the organization, and they might therefore be reluctant to strive for this kind of alignment. Using HRD activities to *oppose* prevailing cultural norms is an uphill task, and requires the backing of at least one senior power base to succeed. One possible strategy is to establish a relatively low risk, successful HRD pilot, in one part of the organization, which can be seen to be creating positive impacts on performance.

There is evidence that more organizations are beginning to see the merits of encouraging a learning culture (see Chapter 2). These are characterized by systems for regular and positive feedback, tolerance of mistakes and their analysis for learning opportunities, the recognition and use of role models and mentors, the encouragement of intense and open communications and a management style that promotes visibility, accessibility, informality and participation.

Summary

In this chapter we have come full circle from the initial consideration of the importance of human resource management and development to a discussion of its role in managing organizational change. Human resource development can have a number of objectives, including the improvement of quality of human performance, the attraction and retention of good staff and maintenance of competitive edge, the contribution towards a learning culture in organizations and the engineering of organizational change. In short, if an organization has a strong policy of human resource development, it is likely to reduce 'people problems' in the introduction of change – and, in fact, is likely to be more innovative and successful altogether. A policy of HRD ensures that people are valued and supported and that this value and this support come from the top of the organization.

The key ways in which human resource development can contribute to the management of organizational change is through organization development, career development and training and development. The latter areas have been the subject of earlier chapters and organization development is itself only one of a number of HRD approaches to change. It does, however, embody all the developmental activities we have been discussing in this book, including the importance of effective teamworking and the motivation of people to perform well.

We hope by now that you are convinced of the importance and centrality of human resource development within a human resource management strategy. It places the development of human resources squarely on the strategic agenda, ensuring that human resource implications are addressed at an early stage in corporate planning, and that problems are foreseen and tackled in a proactive way. It focuses on the effective deployment of skills in both the short- and long-term in relation to organizational requirements and guarantees that training and development are integrated with individual, team and organizational skill needs for the twenty-first century.

References

Alexander, L. (1985) Successfully implementing strategic decisions. *Long Range Planning*, 18, 3, pp. 91–7.

French, W. L. and Bell, C. H. (1990) *Organizational Development* (4th edition). Prentice Hall, Inc., New Jersey.

Garavan, T. (1991) Strategic human resource development. *Journal of European Industrial Training*, 15, 1, pp. 17–30.

Hammer, M. and Champy, J. (1993) *Reengineering the corporation*. Nicholas Brearly, London.

Hussey, D. E. (1988) *Management training and corporate strategy: how to improve competitive performance*. Pergamon Press, London.

Jackson, L. (1992) Achieving change in business culture. *Management Decision*, 30, 6, pp. 149–155.

Johnson, G, (1988) Process of managing strategic change. *Management Research News*, 11, 4/5, pp. 43–6.

Jones, P. (1988) Policy and praxis: local government, a case for treatment, in Coyle, A. and Skinner, J. (eds) *Women and Work*, Macmillan Educational, Basingstoke.

Nicholson, N. (1992) *Organizational Change, Managing Change*, Mabey, C. and Mayon-White, B. (eds), Paul Chapman Publishing Ltd.

Peters, T. and Waterman, R. (1982) *In search of excellence*. New York, Harper and Row.

Pritchard, W. (1984) What's new organizational development. *Personnel Management*, July, pp. 30–3.

Pugh, D. (1986) B679 Planning and Managing Change, Open Business School Diploma, Open University.

Quinn, J. R. (1980) Managing Strategic Change. *Sloan Management Review*, 21, 4, pp. 3–20.

Smith, S. (1990) Developing business men and women in financial services. *CBSI Journal*, Vol.44, No.198, p. 407.

Sparrow and Rognanno (1993) *International Journal of Selection and Assessment*, Vol. 1, No. 1, p. 52.

Storey, J. (1989) *New Perspectives on Human Resource Management*. Routledge, London.

Index